Computational Methods for Integrating Vision and Language

Synthesis Lectures on Computer Vision

Editor

Gérard Medioni, *University of Southern California*
Sven Dickinson, *University of Toronto*

Synthesis Lectures on Computer Vision is edited by Gérard Medioni of the University of Southern California and Sven Dickinson of the University of Toronto. The series publishes 50- to 150 page publications on topics pertaining to computer vision and pattern recognition. The scope will largely follow the purview of premier computer science conferences, such as ICCV, CVPR, and ECCV. Potential topics include, but not are limited to:

- Applications and Case Studies for Computer Vision
- Color, Illumination, and Texture
- Computational Photography and Video
- Early and Biologically-inspired Vision
- Face and Gesture Analysis
- Illumination and Reflectance Modeling
- Image-Based Modeling
- Image and Video Retrieval
- Medical Image Analysis
- Motion and Tracking
- Object Detection, Recognition, and Categorization
- Segmentation and Grouping
- Sensors
- Shape-from-X
- Stereo and Structure from Motion
- Shape Representation and Matching

- Statistical Methods and Learning

- Performance Evaluation

- Video Analysis and Event Recognition

Computational Methods for Integrating Vision and Language

Kobus Barnard

www.morganclaypool.com

ISBN: 9781608451128   paperback
ISBN: 9781608451135   ebook

DOI 10.2200/S00705ED1V01Y201602COV007

A Publication in the Morgan & Claypool Publishers series
SYNTHESIS LECTURES ON COMPUTER VISION

Lecture #7
Series Editors: Gérard Medioni, *University of Southern California*
                    Sven Dickinson, *University of Toronto*
Series ISSN
Print 2153-1056   Electronic 2153-1064

Computational Methods for Integrating Vision and Language

Kobus Barnard
University of Arizona

SYNTHESIS LECTURES ON COMPUTER VISION #7

MORGAN & CLAYPOOL PUBLISHERS

ABSTRACT

Modeling data from visual and linguistic modalities together creates opportunities for better understanding of both, and supports many useful applications. Examples of dual visual-linguistic data includes images with keywords, video with narrative, and figures in documents. We consider two key task-driven themes: translating from one modality to another (e.g., inferring annotations for images) and understanding the data using all modalities, where one modality can help disambiguate information in another. The multiple modalities can either be essentially semantically redundant (e.g., keywords provided by a person looking at the image), or largely complementary (e.g., meta data such as the camera used). Redundancy and complementarity are two endpoints of a scale, and we observe that good performance on translation requires some redundancy, and that joint inference is most useful where some information is complementary.

Computational methods discussed are broadly organized into ones for simple keywords, ones going beyond keywords toward natural language, and ones considering sequential aspects of natural language. Methods for keywords are further organized based on localization of semantics, going from words about the scene taken as whole, to words that apply to specific parts of the scene, to relationships between parts. Methods going beyond keywords are organized by the linguistic roles that are learned, exploited, or generated. These include proper nouns, adjectives, spatial and comparative prepositions, and verbs. More recent developments in dealing with sequential structure include automated captioning of scenes and video, alignment of video and text, and automated answering of questions about scenes depicted in images.

KEYWORDS

vision, language, loosely labeled data, correspondence ambiguity, auto-annotation, region labeling, multimodal translation, cross-modal disambiguation, image captioning, video captioning, affective visual attributes, aligning visual and linguistic data, auto-illustration, visual question answering

Contents

Acknowledgments

The idea for this book was conceived by Sven Dickinson, who convinced me to undertake the task an embarrassingly long time ago. I am grateful for both Sven's and Gérard Medioni's support and patience. I also appreciate the efforts of two reviewers who provided insightful comments on the manuscript that led to numerous improvements. I am also grateful for Mihai Surdeanu's comments on Chapter 5, and Emily Butler's comments on Sections 2.2 and 7.2. Finally, I thank the editorial staff at Morgan&Claypool, including Diane Cerra, Samantha Draper, C.L. Tondo, Deb Gabriel, and Sara Kreisman and her team, for transforming the manuscript into an actual book.

Kobus Barnard
February 2016

Figure Credits

Figure 1.3c   Sub-image was derived from the Corel™ image data set as permitted within the terms of the user agreement. Copyright © Corel Corporation, all rights reserved.

Figure 1.4   From the Corel™ image data set as permitted within the user agreement. Copyright © Corel Corporation, all rights reserved.

Figure 1.6a   From the Corel™ image data set as permitted within the user agreement. Copyright © Corel Corporation, all rights reserved.

Figure 1.6b   From: K. Barnard, P. Duygulu, N. d. Freitas, D. Forsyth, D. Blei, and M. I. Jordan, "Matching Words and Pictures," *Journal of Machine Learning Research*, vol. 3, pp. 1107–1135, 2003. Used with permission.

Figure 1.6c   From: G. Kulkarni, V. Premraj, V. Ordonez, S. Dhar, S. Li, Y. Choi, A. C. Berg, and T. L. Berg, "Babytalk: Understanding and generating simple image descriptions," *Pattern Analysis and Machine Intelligence, IEEE Transactions on*, vol. 35, pp. 2891–2903, 2013. Copyright © 2013 IEEE. Used with permission.

Figure 1.7b   From the Corel™ image data set as permitted within the user agreement. Copyright © Corel Corporation, all rights reserved.

Figure 6.4   From: K. Barnard and D. Forsyth, "Learning the semantics of words and pictures," *Proc. International Conference on Computer Vision*, pp. II: 408–415, 2001. Copyright © 2001 IEEE. Used with permission.

Figure 6.6   From: X. He, R. S. Zemel, and M. Carreira-Perpinan, "Multiscale conditional random fields for image labeling," *Proc. IEEE Computer Society Conference on Computer Vision and Pattern Recognition*, pp. II: 695–702 Vol. 2, 2004. Copyright © 2004 IEEE. Used with permission.

Figure 7.1   From: T. L. Berg, A. C. Berg, J. Edwards, and D. A. Forsyth, "Who's in the Picture," *Proc. NIPS*, 2004. Used with permission.

Figure 7.2   From: L. Jie, B. Caputo, and V. Ferrari, "Who's doing what: Joint modeling of names and verbs for simultaneous face and pose annotation," *Proc. Advances in Neural Information Processing Systems (NIPS)*, 2009. Used with permission.

Figure 7.3a   From: K. Yanai and K. Barnard, "Image region entropy: A measure of 'visualness' of web images associated with one concept," *Proc. ACM Multimedia*, Singapore, pp. 419–422, 2005. Copyright © 2005 ACM. Used with permission.

Figure 7.3b   From: K. Yanai and K. Barnard, "Image region entropy: A measure of 'visualness' of web images associated with one concept," *Proc. ACM Multimedia*, Singapore, pp. 419–422, 2005. Copyright © 2005 ACM. Used with permission.

Figure 7.3c   From: V. Ferrari and A. Zisserman, "Learning visual attributes," *Proc. Advances in Neural Information Processing Systems (NIPS)*, 2007. Used with permission.

Figure 7.4   From: C. R. Dawson, J. Wright, A. Rebguns, M. V. Escarcega, D. Fried, and P. R. Cohen, "A generative probabilistic framework for learning spatial language," *Proc. IEEE Third Joint International Conference on Development and Learning and Epigenetic Robotics*, pp. 1–8, 2013. Copyright © 2013 IEEE. Used with permission.

Figure 8.1a   From: A. Karpathy and L. Fei-Fei, "Deep visual-semantic alignments for generating image descriptions," *Computer Vision and Pattern Recognition*, 2015. Copyright © 2015 IEEE. Used with permission.

Figure 8.1b   From: S. Venugopalan, M. Rohrbach, J. Donahue, R. Mooney, T. Darrell, and K. Saenko, "Sequence to sequence - Video to text," *Proc. ICCV*, 2015. Copyright © 2015 IEEE. Used with permission.

CHAPTER 1

Introduction

Knowledge about the world comes to us through multiple modalities, including our primary senses, and also abstractions such as illustrations and language. The different modalities reinforce and complement each other, and provide for more effective understanding of the world around us, provided that we can integrate the information into a common representation or abstract understanding. Similarly, information from multiple modalities can be exploited by intelligent computational systems. This book develops computational approaches for linking and combining the modalities implied by visual and linguistic information. In particular, automatically determining relationships between these modalities can be applied to providing better access to data, training systems to extract semantic content from either visual and linguistic data, and develop machine representations that are indicative of higher level semantics and thus can support intelligent machine behavior.

To make this endeavor concrete, we will develop our discussion in the context of image or video data that has associated text or speech. Figures 1.1 and 1.2 show six examples from this domain. Figure 1.1a shows an image of a mountain goat that has associated keywords provided a human annotator to enable searching for the image by text query. Figure 1.1b shows an image where we imagine a teacher is providing an explicit reference to what is in the image, which is achieved in this case if the learner assumes that the moving object is what is pertinent. Figure 1.1c shows an image with a caption that provides both content-related information that could be inferred from the photograph and meta-data that is meant to complement the visual information. Finally, Figure 1.2 shows three examples where images are chosen to provide key information that is spatial in nature, and thus far more efficient to provide with a figure.

Notice that in Figure 1.1a, the human annotator only had access to the image and their general knowledge about the world. Thus, their annotation is potentially derivable from the image. Of course, the image contains other information that they chose not to write about. The situation in Figure 1.1b is even more restricted where we assume the human teacher is purposefully providing text relevant to both the visual context and the focus of attention of the learner. By contrast, in Figure 1.1c, the annotation specifically provides information that is difficult or impossible to extract from the image.

In these three examples there is overlap in the two sources of information as "mountain goat" is inferable from either the images or the texts, but all the images have information that the associated text does not. Conversely, in (b) the text provides information a learner might not

Visual Data			
Linguistic Data	MOUNTAIN GOAT ROCK FOILAGE SKY	"Look at the mountain goat!"	A mountain goat in the Tantalus Range B.C. showing signs of shedding its winter coat. Photo taken by Kobus Barnard in the summer of 2011.
	(a)	(b)	(c)

Figure 1.1: Three examples of aligned visual and linguistic information. (a) Keywords for an image that could be provided by an annotator based on the image content alone. (b) An utterance that refers to the part of the scene that is moving, that could be used to learn "mountain goat" if the learner know the other words in the sentence. Motion enables effective grouping the goat pixels together in space and time (i.e., tracking the movement). This is in contrast to the other examples in this panel, where the parts of the image (if any) that the words refer to are not immediately available. (c) Information provided by the photographer.

know, and in (c) the text has information not available from the image. Further, if the interpreter of the images is a computer program instead of a human, all the texts likely add information.

In (c) both the visual information and the linguistic information include semantic components that can be dually represented (e.g., the scene contains a mountain goat), and components that are largely restricted to one modality or the other. In the case of the visual information this includes the myriad of visual details such as particular textures and patterns in the rocks, meadow, etc. In the case of linguistic information, while there are can be minor relationships between visual information and time, place, photographer, and cropping, for the most part we do not expect such meta information to be dually represented. Dual representations may have redundant and/or complementary aspects. For example, for someone familiar with mountain goats, "mountain goat" in the caption is redundant. For a computer program that confuses off-white fur coats with cumulus clouds, the two sources of information about the same thing can help each other, reducing the ambiguity about a detected fluffy white region (Figure 1.4 expands on this issue).

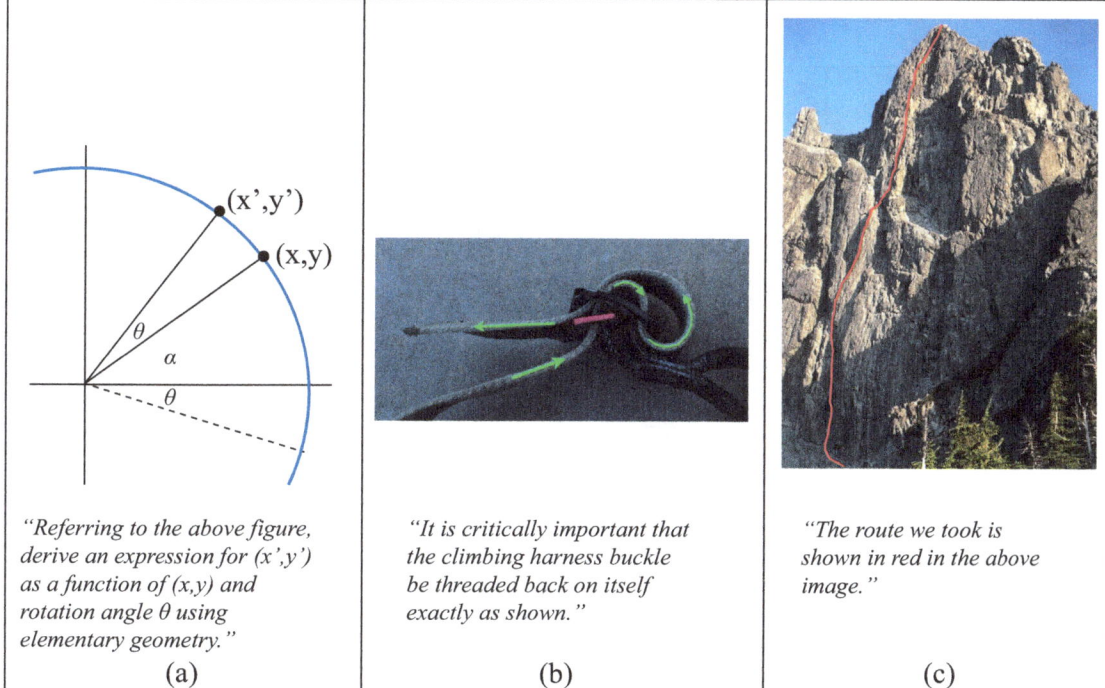

"Referring to the above figure, derive an expression for (x',y') as a function of (x,y) and rotation angle θ using elementary geometry."

(a)

"It is critically important that the climbing harness buckle be threaded back on itself exactly as shown."

(b)

"The route we took is shown in red in the above image."

(c)

Figure 1.2: Examples of text with associated images, where the text drives the need for a figure. This in contrast to Figure 1.1 where text was created in response to what was imaged. In the examples in this figure, spatial information is crucial to what is being communicated and it is more efficient to provide an illustration.

1.1   REDUNDANT, COMPLEMENTARY, AND ORTHOGONAL MULTIMODAL DATA

These examples suggest that the relation between visual and linguistic information can be considered with respect to two extremes, ranging from largely intersecting to largely disjoint. Informally we can ask the extent that two sources of information are: (1) informative about each other (*redundant*), through (2) informative about the same thing but not entirely redundant (*complementary*), to (3) completely independent from each other (*orthogonal*). Hence, we consider a continuum from complete redundancy to no interaction among modalities (Figure 1.3).

We will consider the continuum as being *relative to the capabilities of the vision and language processing systems* at our disposal. For example, while a human annotator will have no problem attaching the keyword "rose" to the image in Figure 1.3c, a machine vision system based on the color of blobs might be uncertain whether the red blob should be associated with a red rose or a

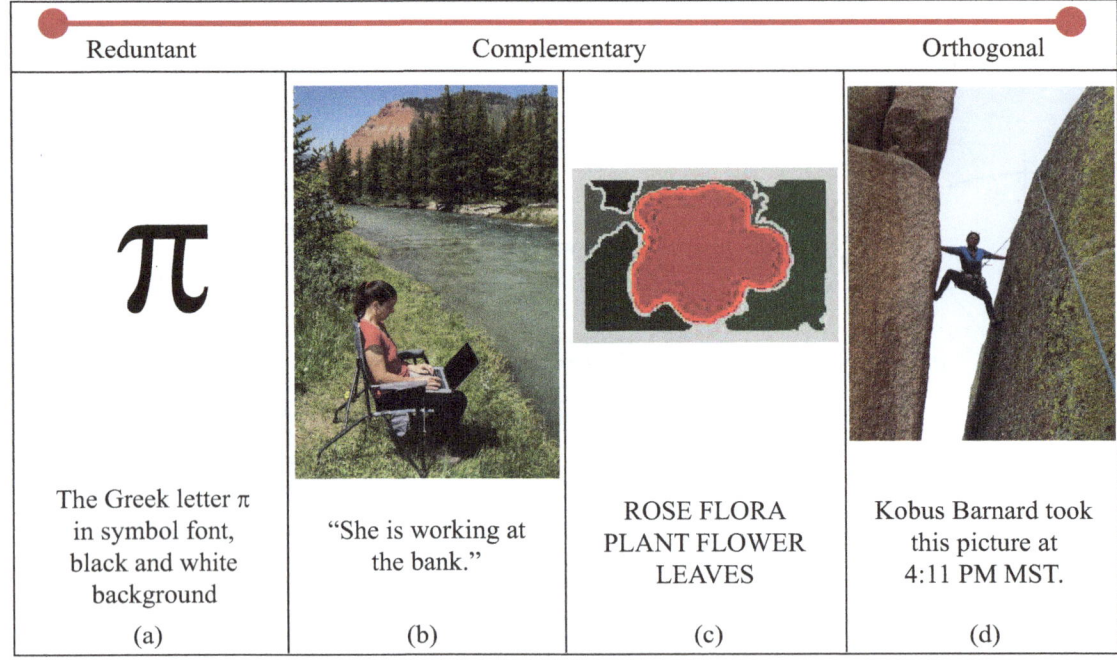

Reduntant	Complementary		Orthogonal
The Greek letter π in symbol font, black and white background	"She is working at the bank."	ROSE FLORA PLANT FLOWER LEAVES	Kobus Barnard took this picture at 4:11 PM MST.
(a)	(b)	(c)	(d)

Figure 1.3: Given a semantic subspace of interest (e.g., what is in the figure or scene), the degree of overlap between the visual information and the linguistic information lies on a continuum ranging from completely redundant to completely orthogonal. For our purposes we are most interested in information that we can extract with a computer program. Current computer vision and natural language processing are both limited, but often we can alleviate the deficiencies by considering both when the information they provide complement each other. For example, in (b), "bank" is ambiguous as it has multiple senses, but the image removes the ambiguity. In (c), a garden image is represented with colored regions to illustrate the information available to a particular computer program. In general, the red region in the middle has high probability of being a stop sign, but the addition of the keyword can push the probability toward the correct label for that region (rose)—see also Figure 1.4. Sub-image (c) was derived from the Corel™ image data set as permitted within the terms of the user agreement.

stop sign. Hence, for this simple machine vision system, the text annotation provides significant additional information (see Figure 1.4). By contrast, from the perspective of the human annotator, the text annotation is derivable from the image, and does not provide more information.

To make these notions more precise, we will take a Bayesian statistical approach where all entities are associated with random variables,[1] and we think in terms of modeling and inference

---

[1] I will be making use of basic probability and statistics, and elementary concepts from information theory. There are many resources for these topics. Useful refreshers oriented toward machine learning include Bishop [87, Ch. 1] and Koller and

Figure 1.4: A simple experiment to demonstrate how keywords and visual features constrain the semantic subspace in complementary ways using the Corel™ image database (images are reproduced within the terms of the user agreement). The text query "rose" returns rose bugs, rose windows in cathedral images, as well as some flowers. The query for similar images to one of a red rose, based on color and texture returns a variety of images with prominent red regions. Finally, a query on the conjunction of the two returns images that are both semantically associated with rose, and have regions that are visually similar to the red rose in the query image.

with respect to the joint probability distribution over those variables. In general, we anticipate reasoning about a subset of these variables, and the result will typically be uncertain, as represented by probability distributions. Mathematically, handling the uncertainty is the domain of the probability calculus.

We are particularly interested in probability distributions where the random variables from multiple modalities share information in non-trivial ways. The random variables for the problem domains of interest can include (1) potentially observable data from one or more modalities,

Friedman [331, Ch. 2]. A recommended comprehensive text on information theory, going far beyond what I will use, is Cover and Thomas [147].

and (2) additional, possibly latent, variables representing semantics or other abstract information about the world, which often conceptually span modalities. Such non-observed variables can differ in the degree to which we attach an explicit interpretation to them. For example, in a hand-built system, such variables might have very specific interpretations provided by the builder. On the other hand, in a system based on unsupervised clustering, non-observed variables might represent latent multi-modal clusters. For many tasks, the interpretation of such clusters does not matter. On the other hand, if we believe that abstractions such as semantic concepts are a good explanation of the multimodal structure of the data, then we might be able to learn such concepts. However, in this scenario, evaluation of the learned concepts is then post hoc. Notice that if we were to label the data with concepts, then the concepts would now be considered potentially observable.

Given a random variable representation for a particular domain, we can approach multiple tasks using statistical inference. For a given task we can organize our variables into three roles: (1) evidence—variables that we observe (input); (2) targets of inference—variables that we have chosen to reason about (output); and (3) variables that are neither of these. As a concrete example, we might model joint visual and linguistic data with multimodal clusters. If our task is to infer appropriate words for images, then the observed image data is the evidence, appropriate words (potentially observable) are the targets of inference, and the latent clusters (not observed) support linking images and appropriate words.

1.1.1   MULTIMODAL MUTUAL INFORMATION

For what follows, the reader may want to refer to Appendix A.1 for basic definitions.

We now consider the continuum more formally, focusing on the shared information between modalities. For simplicity, I will assume that all variables of a modality are considered together.[2] Also, to begin, I will restrict attention to observable data (extended shortly, §1.1.2). With these simplifications, the defining property of the continuum amounts to the degree of independence between the two modalities.

On the left extreme of Figure 1.3, the information provided by at least one of the modalities could be predicted from the other. As a very simple example, suppose that we have two images, one clearly of a dog and one clearly of a cat. Also suppose we have a vocabulary consisting of "dog" and "cat," and that we can classify the images accurately. Then, choosing the dog image at random, we necessarily get the "dog" label, and conversely, choosing the "dog" label at random automatically leads to the dog image. Of course, the cat image and label behave similarly. We get

---

[2]One can easily consider data components within a modality with the same analysis. For example, we can consider color and texture information as two different modalities that share some degree of information with each other and/or other modalities, despite both being visual.

(for dogs):

$$p(dog, \text{"}dog\text{"}) = p(dog) = p(\text{"}dog\text{"}) = \frac{1}{2},$$

$$\text{and thus } \frac{p(dog)\,p(\text{"}dog\text{"})}{p(dog, \text{"}dog\text{"})} = p(dog) = \frac{1}{2}.$$

(1.1)

The mutual information is then given by:

$$I[label, image] = -\sum_{x \in (\text{"}dog\text{"},\text{"}cat\text{"})} \sum_{y \in (dog, cat)} p(x, y) \log_2 \left(\frac{p(x)\,p(y)}{p(x, y)} \right)$$

$$= -\left(\frac{1}{2} \bullet \log_2 \left(\frac{1}{2} \right) + \frac{1}{2} \bullet \log_2 \left(\frac{1}{2} \right) \right),$$

$$= 1$$

(1.2)

which is distinctly greater than zero, reflecting the fact that the two data sources share information and that they are not independent.

On the other hand, for the right extreme of Figure 1.3, the information from each of the two modalities is independent. Observing one of them does not tell us anything about the other. For example, data such as the time of day, camera used, or photographer name, typically provides very little information about image content, and knowing the values of these variables only slightly changes our estimate for the distribution of the object in the center of the image. Notationally, this means that

$$p(object \,|\, time, camera, photographer) \cong p(object),$$

(1.3)

which is the definition that *object* is independent of the three other variables. In terms of information theory, the mutual information between the two variable sets is close to zero. Specifically, if we denote *meta* = (*time, camera, photographer*) then $p(object, meta) = p(object)\,p(meta)$ and

$$I[object, meta] = \sum p(object, meta) \log_2 \left(\frac{p(object, meta)}{p(object)\,p(metal)} \right)$$

$$\cong \sum p(object, meta) \log_2 (1)$$

$$= 0.$$

(1.4)

1.1.2   COMPLEMENTARY MULTIMODAL INFORMATION

The continuum would be of limited interest if we only used it to represent the degree of independence between two observable variable sets. We now consider adding random variables that represent abstractions such as semantics, which are informed by multiple modalities. It is an interesting empirical fact that different modalities can often work together in a complementary fashion, which is tied to the fact that multimodal data is common in documents. We can view abstract semantics as explaining the partial dependence (non negligible mutual information) between observables. However, we can also choose to be agnostic as to any such explanation, as long as the performance on a specific task is satisfactory.

To make the discussion more concrete, consider a random variable over semantic concepts, c, within scenes. For example, a concept could be that of a red rose. We will reason about which concept is most applicable for a particular image region,[3] and we will represent our uncertain understanding of which concepts are promising with a probably distribution over the finite set of semantic concepts. Note that while we often use text to indicate semantics, semantic entities are different from the observed text, which only gives us a partial indication of meaning. This will manifest in a number of ways in this book, including the two following. First, words in observed text are often ambiguous because words often have multiple meanings referred to as *senses*. For example, "bank" has a number of meanings including a financial institution, or a slope, or an edge. To distinguish senses of words, it is common to append a sense number to the word as in "bank_1" or "bank_2."[4] Second, words in text may be incorrect or misleading if they are naively expected to link to visual data, especially if they are extracted from captions using imperfect language processing. For example, if we simply extract nouns from "marmots are often seen in mountain goat terrain," then we might expect that the image contains depictions for both a marmot and a mountain goat, which is possible, but not likely the intent of the caption.

To simplify reasoning about semantic concepts given multiple data sources, let us suppose that the observables (A, B, C, ...) are conditionally independent, given the concept, c. We are then hopeful for two properties. First, we would like each data source to be informative about c, and thus have the potential to reduce our uncertainty about it. Second, we would like different data sources to reduce the uncertainty differently so that they all can improve our estimates of what is in the scene. In the general case, this means that any pair of data sources, A and B, tends to be in the complementary (middle) part of the scale in Figure 1.3. In particular, on the left extreme of the continuum, one of the variables (say A) implies the other (B). Hence, knowing A means that we know B, and hence subsequently learning B does not provide any more information. Thus, if all variables are helpful when considered together, we are not operating in the left extreme.

Analyzing the right extreme is more challenging. One might expect that if A and B are both informative about c, then they must be informative about each other (and thus cannot be independent). However, this is not always the case as they may be informative about different aspects of c. Hence, in this case, complementary data can also be independent. Briefly digressing, the contrapositive of this (informal) proposition claims that if A and B are independent, and we know one of them (say A) then the other (B) would not tell us anything more about c. Formally, this says that c and B can be conditionally independent given A. Then we would have

---

[3]We could also consider the probability that K labels are the K-best for the image considered as a whole (more complicated), or the probability that each label is independently appropriate for the image (simpler, but less illustrative, as it amounts to a collection of separate simple cases).

[4]This is the convention followed by WordNet [30, 210, 425, 426], which is the source of all sense-disambiguated words in this book. See also §3.1.

$p(c \mid A, B) = p(c \mid A)$ and then B would not be helpful once we have A. However, while we expect this to be often true, it is possible that $p(c \mid A, B) \neq p(c \mid A)$—see Appendix A.2. In other words, it is possible that independent data sources are not necessarily quite on the right extreme of the continuum, as they could work together to estimate c. Hence, the term "orthogonal" is better than "independent" for the right side of the continuum.

Regardless, in the ideal case, each data modality has some shared information with our inference target, and they are also diverse so that there is an advantage to including all of them. Consider getting the values of these variables one at a time. Before we know any of the observations, the entropy of the inference target (c, in our example) is simply that of its prior distribution. Then, if we are told the value of A, which is informative about c, the decrease in entropy is given by the mutual information $H[c, A] = I[c] - I[c \mid A]$. This corresponds (informally) to the degree that the posterior distribution $p(c \mid A)$ is more peaked than the prior distribution $p(c)$. Now, if we are told the value of B, we can hope for further reduction in entropy, and thus even more certainty in the posterior, $p(c \mid A, B)$. Since we assume that the observables are conditionally independent given concepts, we have

$$p(c \mid A, B) \propto p(A \mid c) \, p(B \mid c) \, p(c) \propto p(c \mid A) \, p(B \mid c), \qquad (1.5)$$

applying Bayes rule twice. In other words, ignoring constants, the posterior $p(c \mid A)$ is revised by the additional information in the likelihood, $p(B \mid c)$, which, informally, is peaked (lower entropy) in accordance with how informative it is.

Some of the possibilities are illustrated in Figure 1.5, with modalities C (camera model meta data), A (image features), and B (associated text). In this example the camera model is assumed to be at best only slightly informative about what is in the scene. By contrast, extracted image features and associative text are both substantively informative in the example. In addition, image features and associated text are complementary. The likelihood due to learning about the camera is relatively flat, whereas the likelihoods for image features and image text are more informative, and noticeably, have different shapes from each other. Even if the shapes were similar (but not uniform) across semantics, they could still mutually reinforce the same conclusion to reduce the overall uncertainty.

1.2 COMPUTATIONAL TASKS

Both joint representation and complementary representation enable interesting and important computational goals. Pragmatically, which of these aspects we focus on depends on the particular task and available data. In this section I introduce three kinds of task, with the first (translation, §1.2.1) relying on sufficient redundancy between data types, the second (cross-modal disambiguation, §1.2.2) relying on overlapping information, as does the third (grounding language, §1.2.3).

Figure 1.5: Plots illustrating overlapping information of multimodal data, inspired by the retrieval example in Figure 1.4. All curves are normalized so that quantities sum to one, as the key issue is the shape of the curves. Different evidence modalities reduce the uncertainty among semantic concepts differently. Without any evidence, the distribution over semantic concepts, c, is the prior distribution illustrated in (a). The left-hand column shows likelihood factors for concepts due to observing (b) the camera make and model, C, (d) the query image I (Figure 1.4), (f) associated text, T ("ROSE"), and (d) both I and T, assuming that these modalities are conditionally independent given c. *(Continues.)*

Note that much of what we consider in this book applies to multimodal data in general[5] although specific examples will be about visual and linguistic data.

---

[5]Examples of multimodal analysis along the lines of this book, but outside of the scope of vision and language include sounds and text [529, 544] and speech recognition and video [226–228].

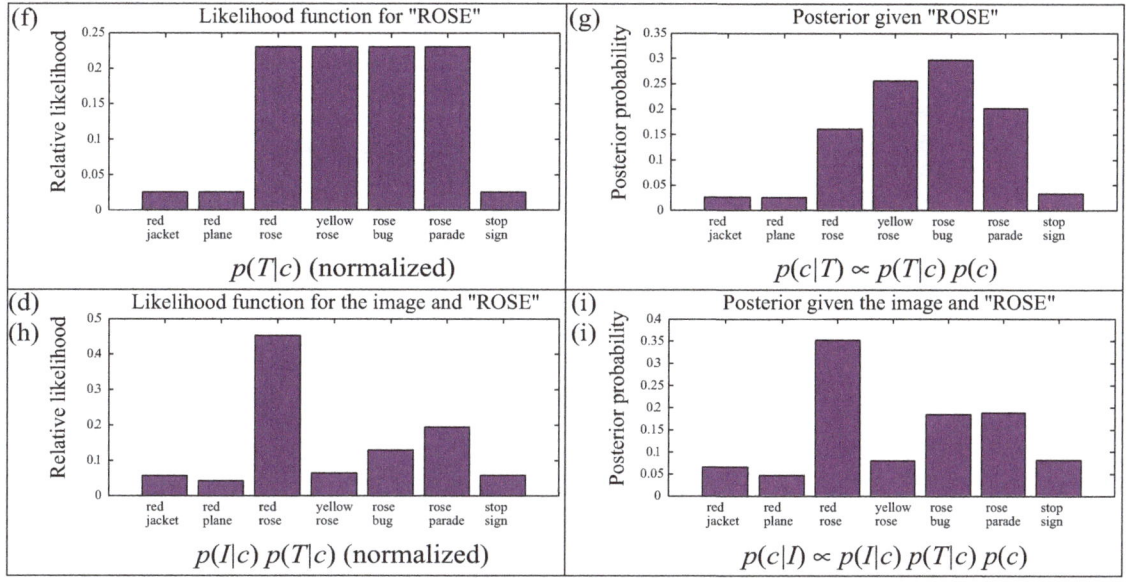

Figure 1.5: *(Continued.)* Here the choice of camera is minimally affected by the semantics reflected by the relatively flat curve (b). On the other hand, image content and associated words both significantly restrict the semantics, and do so differently, so that together they restrict the semantics more then doing so individually. The right-hand column shows the posterior distribution without any evidence (the prior, (a)), and updated beliefs after observing C, I, T, and both I, and T.

1.2.1 MULTIMODAL TRANSLATION

Figure 1.6 illustrates a significant theme for this book, namely *multimodal translation*, which concerns computationally producing linguistic representations of images, and vice versa. We refer to this task as translation in analogy with the task of automatically translating from one language (e.g., French) to another (e.g., English)[6]—see Figure 1.7. In its simplest form this amounts to having a cross-lingual dictionary that maps words from one language to words in another. The learning task then becomes automatically learning the dictionary. By analogy, each region (French word) is mapped to a label (English word), and the collection of such words becomes a set of automatically generated keywords for the image. This then supports image search by keywords, even when human provided keywords are not available. This is helpful because humans typically search for images based on semantics (§2.1), which are most efficiently provided by language. Image-to-text translation thus links the scientific goal of being able to understand images, to the practical application of image retrieval.

---

[6]This analogy was introduced by Duygulu et al. [182].

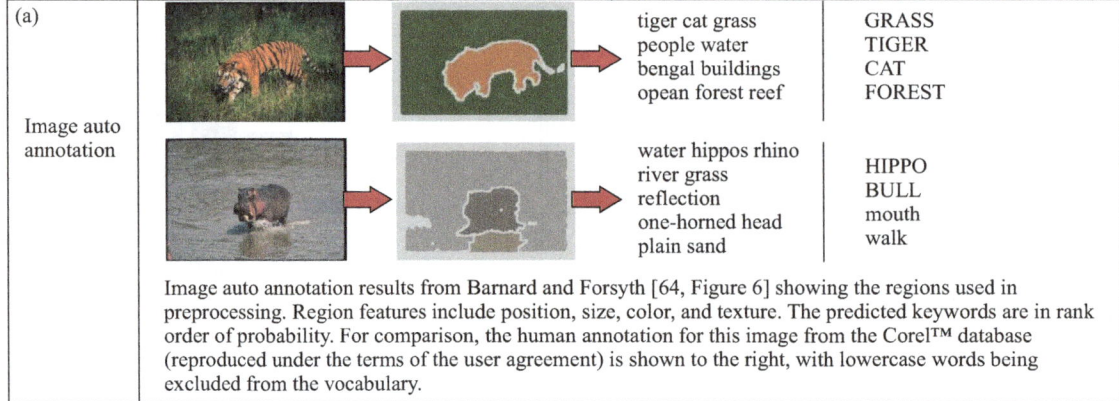

(a)

Image auto annotation

tiger cat grass people water bengal buildings opean forest reef

GRASS
TIGER
CAT
FOREST

water hippos rhino river grass reflection one-horned head plain sand

HIPPO
BULL
mouth
walk

Image auto annotation results from Barnard and Forsyth [64, Figure 6] showing the regions used in preprocessing. Region features include position, size, color, and texture. The predicted keywords are in rank order of probability. For comparison, the human annotation for this image from the Corel™ database (reproduced under the terms of the user agreement) is shown to the right, with lowercase words being excluded from the vocabulary.

Figure 1.6: Variations on the translation task. These examples are meant to be indicative of the goal, i.e., what is to be achieved, rather than how it is done in the particular cases. Multiple methods exist for each task, some of which are discussed in this book. Notice that despite being selected among better results, there are errors in every example. All figures reprinted with permission. *(Continues.)*

We will consider two simple forms of translating image data into a keyword representation. First, we can provide keywords for the image without specifying what parts of the image the keywords refer to, which is known as "auto-annotation" (Figure 1.6a). Second, we can provide words for image regions, which I will refer to as "region-labeling" (Figure 1.6b). A human annotator had no difficulty "translating" the image in Figure 1.6a into keywords, but building a computational system to do the same thing is very challenging. Chapter 6 covers machine learning approaches that use data like that illustrated in Figure 1.8 to build models or classifiers that embody relationships between image features and words. Such a system can then be applied to images that are not in the training data to generate appropriate text for these images.

Going beyond simple keywords, a full translation system would be able to encode much more about the semantics of the scene including relative sizes and locations of the objects as well as the appearance characteristics of the objects and backgrounds. Here, some labels would refer to image regions ("human face"), groups of them ("young boy"), the entire image (e.g., "birthday party"), as well as concepts that speak to object relationships, appearance, actions, and activities. Doing so would demonstrate capability on the key task in machine vision, which is to extract semantic representations from image data, as linguistic representations are close to what we commonly consider semantic information.

Chapter 7 covers methods using language models beyond keyword. One example is shown in Figure 1.6c. In organizing this quickly growing body of work, it is helpful to distinguish between the tactic of using parts of speech other than nouns to help identify and/or disambiguate objects (e.g., red car) vs. the goal of providing richer translations. The former is often most useful in

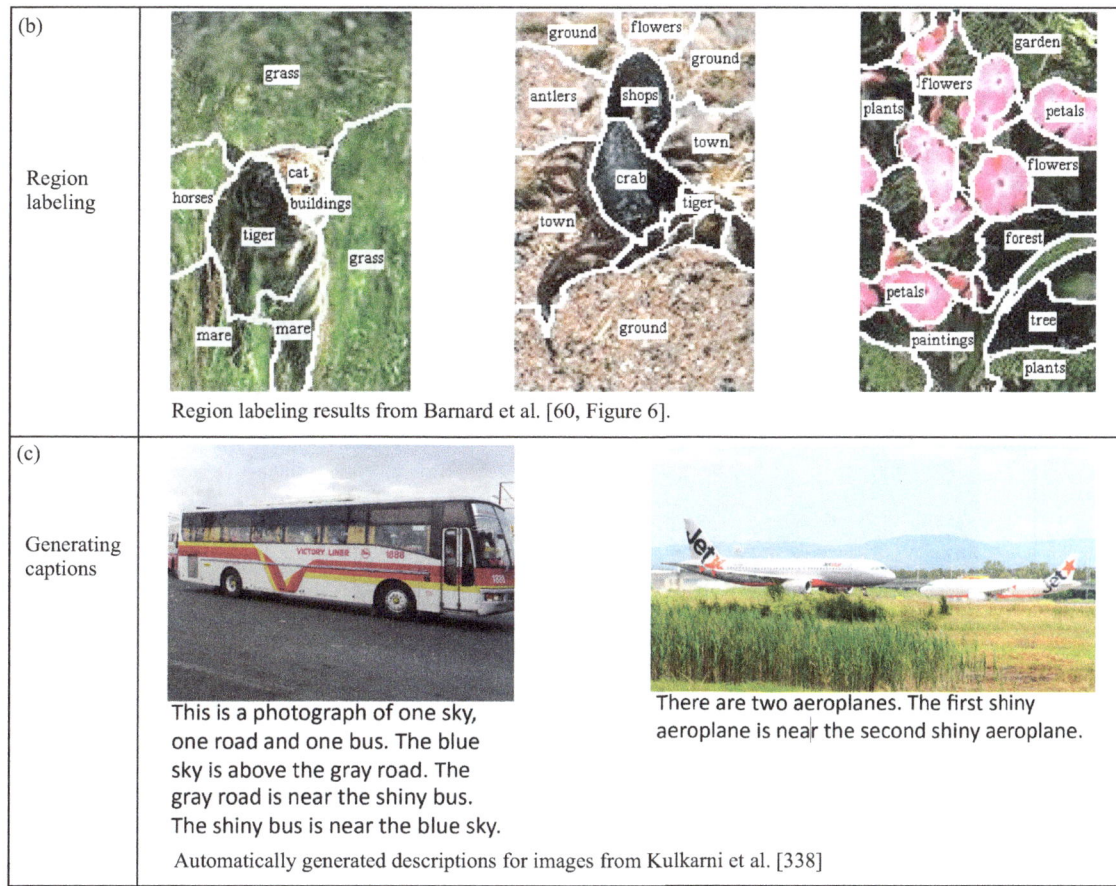

Figure 1.6:   *(Continued.)* Variations on the translation task. These examples are meant to be indicative of the goal, i.e., what is to be achieved, rather than how it is done in the particular cases. Multiple methods exist for each task, some of which are discussed in this volume. Notice that despite being selected among better results, there are errors in every example. All figures reprinted with permission.

model learning, where the additional information provided by adjectives and spatial prepositions help reduce correspondence ambiguity between visual and linguistic elements during training.[7] The visual meanings of adjectives and spatial prepositions are either supplied by system developers

---

[7]For example, Gupta and Davis [259] proposed an effective system for learning the translations dictionary which augmented nouns annotations with propositions over noun pairs for comparative prepositions (e.g., above) and adjectives (e.g., taller). They learned nouns visual characteristics and relationship jointly, as well as relationship priors that helped annotate new data. This is discussed further in §7.3.

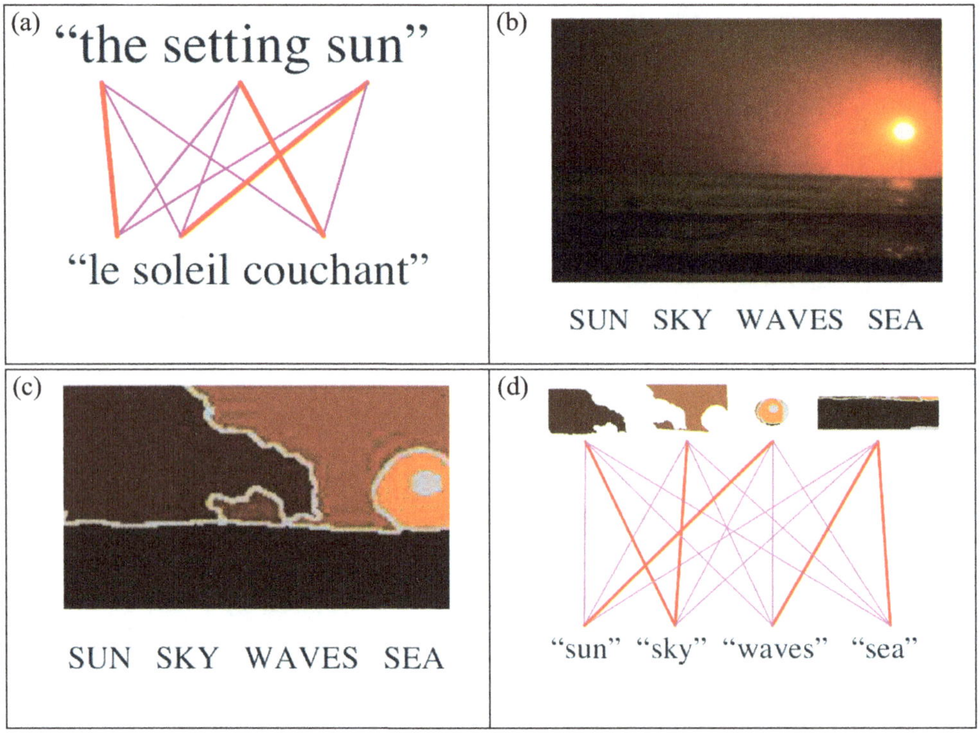

Figure 1.7: The analogy between machine translation in natural language processing, and learning to label regions in loosely labeled data: (a) translating a simple phrase from English to French. Because of differences in word ordering (as in this example), or multiple words mapping to a single word, or some words not mapping to any words in the other language, there is little information in the local ordering and the correspondence between elements is ambiguous. Each English word can conceivably map to any of the French words, i.e., any of the lines may be correct. However, with additional examples (e.g., seeing "sun" in difference contexts), our belief increases that certain matches are likely to be correct (red lines), thereby automatically creating a probabilistic dictionary. (b) A Corel™ image (reproduced under the terms of the user agreement) with associated keywords. (c) Image regions produced by a simple segmentation program. Notice that the mapping between regions and keywords is not, a prior, known, and thus the situation is similar to that in (a) as emphasized in (d). A system for image-to-text translation will typically use an extensive set of aligned data (e.g., (c), Figure 1.8) to learn a dictionary. The dictionary can then be used to attach keyword probabilities to regions in images without keywords, which then can be distilled into a list of annotation words for the image.

GOAT SNOW
(a)

GOAT ROCK
(b)

FOLIAGE ROCK
(c)

GOAT SNOW ROCK
(d)

CLIMBER ROCK NÉVÉ
(e)

CLOUD GOAT ROCK SNOW
(f)

CLIMBER CLOUD SNOW
(g)

Figure 1.8: Example images that are annotated with appropriate keywords. The red lines outline machine segmentations achieved automatically by a version of normalize cuts [518] with the cost matrix taking into account color, texture, and edges [395]. Such data is referred to as loosely labeled because, while the words are usually relevant, we do not know which part of the image should be associated with each word.

or learned together with noun meanings. Regardless, having visual meanings for non-noun words can help provide richer translations and finer grained image search.

1.2.2   INTEGRATING COMPLEMENTARY MULTIMODAL DATA AND CROSS MODAL DISAMBIGUATION

The opposite of translating from one modality to another is using both modalities together to understand their combined story. In such tasks, a computer program plays a similar role to a person who uses both the text and the figures of a document to understand it. For example, we might consider building an application that analyzes archives of news photos with captions to mine historic data for interesting trends.

Recall that a particular data component might provide completely orthogonal information to the other parts of the data (extreme right of the scale in Figure 1.3), or it might be semantically linked to other data components, but each one provides additional, non-overlapping, information (middle of the scale in Figure 1.3), or it could be highly redundant with other data. Unlike the translation task where only one modality is present, with both modalities the redundant information is superfluous. At the other extreme (orthogonal information), then there is little to do from an inference perspective, other than record the independent piece of data. For example, if the name of the photographer cannot help interpret the image, then we are limited to making the photographer name available when needed, as we would do to support image search by photographer.

Thus, from a computational perspective, we focus on the case when the two modalities provide partially overlapping information. Specifically, at least one of the modalities provides information about the other that is not otherwise available. For example, consider the image in Figure 1.3c. The region shown is likely to be one of a limited set of possibilities including a rose or stop sign. Adding the caption "rose" helps distinguish among them. Note that from the perspective of image retrieval, the keyword "rose" does not invariably lead to flowers (see Figure 1.4), and further, does not alone specify a red one. Hence, the caption and the image data complement each other. Using the complementary data to distinguish among possibilities illustrates a second important kind of task, namely *cross-modal disambiguation*.

The rose/stop-sign example illustrates that images and text can be ambiguous when considered separately, but are not necessarily ambiguous when they are considered together. This reflects how humans often arrange jointly occurring images and text—captions tend to omit what is visually obvious, and images are chosen to provide information that is awkward to provide using language. Thus, we can loosely interpret the task of building computational systems to understand such data as extracting a non-ambiguous multimodal representation of what the document creator intended, thereby reversing the creation of those artifacts. To solve this inverse problem we observe that each modality constrains the underlying semantics of the scene. When we put these complementary constraints together, they can constrain the semantics sufficiently to be useful to an information system user. In particular, ambiguities at the category level (e.g., "rose" vs. "stop sign") can be removed, thereby leading to an interpretation of the data that will be judged more semantically correct.

Figure 1.3b shows an example of a different problem, namely that words have multiple meanings, again illustrated using "bank" as an example. Human readers resolve such ambiguities using a variety of contextual information ranging from nearby words to the entire document and cultural background. The example shows how image data can also play this role.[8] In particular, the image depicting an outdoor scene can tell us that the second sense of bank is likely meant.

1.2.3   GROUNDING LANGUAGE WITH SENSORY DATA

Language is extremely valuable for agents collaborating to survive in the world, but the abstractions in a symbolic system are not inherently connected to the physical environment. Defining all symbols in terms of other symbols is circular, and results in a closed system that is not informative about anything physical. Endowing cognitive systems with language that can refer to the physical world can be achieved by associating words with sensory data (e.g., images), thereby *grounding* their meaning. For example, while a word like "snow" can be defined abstractly using other words, its physical meaning requires shared experience of snow, or the words used to define it. Without meanings eventually linking to the world through sensor input, there is no way to use language to communicate about interacting with the world.

The need for computational approaches for grounding language arises naturally in human-robot communication. For example, Roy and colleagues have developed a robot, Ripley, that learns from language/visual association, and can respond to verbal requests grounded in the world [409, 410, 491]. Consider a simple directive to a robot like Ripley: "put the red cone on top of the blue block." For the robot to accomplish this task, it needs to connect words in the directive to the visual data from the world in front of it.

These kinds of human-robot interactions can have elements of both exploiting redundant information and integrating complementary information. The existence of a "red cone" and "blue block" in the scene is implicit in the text, and is redundant information that the robot can use to learn the visual representation of the words. On the other hand, both vision and language are needed to establish the physical coordinates of the object to be moved, and where it should be moved. In other words, executing the directive requires both processing the sentence and tying the appropriated parts to the physical world through the sensory system.

The robot interaction domain shares with image understanding applications the notion of referential meaning (words referring to the world), but also relies on function meaning, which is described by Roy as "agents using language to achieve goals" [490]. In the example of moving the red cone, the intent is clearly specified as a directive. In the general case, inferring intent is very difficult. An interesting example from Roy [490] is translating the statement "this coffee is cold" into "bring me hot coffee" based on the appropriate context. In making use of multimodal data to understand such scenarios, Roy categorizes "signs," which we can define as evidence available in

---

[8]This was first studied computationally by Barnard et al. [66] (see also [67]).

data, into three groups: *natural*, *indexical*, and *intentional*. Natural signs are evidence of what is in the world. Indexical signs are also about the world, but are specific to spatiotemporal coordinates of those entities, such as object position and pose. Finally, intentional signs are evidence about the intent of agents.

Intentional signs can come from both language and the physical world. In particular, what is possible in the physical world can reduce ambiguity about what directives means [246]. For example, going back to putting cones on blocks, one can imagine a reasoning system that understands that putting cone shapes on block shapes works better than the reverse, which can further reduce ambiguity between blocks and cones, both for executing the task and learning what they are more generally.

In summary, language enables agents to cooperate by being able to represent goals compactly. However, actions needed to fulfill the goal typically are relative to the environment, which must be perceived and analyzed with respect to the goal. Hence, grounding language is an important computational task within our domain that brings in different aspects than the previous two tasks.

1.3   MULTIMODAL MODELING

Many of the models considered in this book build upon the basic model suggested by Figure 1.9. Here, concepts are treated as underlying *latent* variables that generate data for multiple modalities (e.g., words and image region features). For example, the multi-modal concept of a tiger is both associated with the label "tiger" (a human categorization) and what it looks like. Clearly, this can be extended to other text information, and other modalities. Regardless, following the graphical modeling paradigm,[9] the distribution of the data for each modality is independent, conditioned on the concept. Thus, the linkage between modalities is only through the concept. Variations within this approach include different particulars of how concepts generate data for each modality, and how the concepts themselves arise. For example, outdoor scenes have a different mix of concepts than indoor scenes, which can be modeled by adding a higher-level clustering for scene types which provides for different distributions of concepts (see §6.5).

Binding data from different modalities through underlying concepts nicely handles arbitrary sets of modalities, and does not give any of them special status. For example, visual appearance is handled symmetrically with text labels, and similarly with other modalities that one might add, such as how an object moves or how it feels to the touch. Additional modalities provide additional opportunities to learn from data. For example, consider a learned concept linked both to "giraffe" and a particular spotted pattern. Text-based collections of semantic information such as WordNet (§3.1) could then connect the underlying concept to that of a quadruped that has mobility and whose environment is often "savanna" which may be a word not yet connected to visual

---

[9]This book relies on modest familiarity with graphical models as well as basic probability and statistics. For graphical models I suggest Ch. 8 of Bishop [87], which is available on-line, or the very comprehensive book by Koller and Friedman [331]. Chapter 2 of Koller and Freidman also provides a concise review of probability for applications such as the ones in this book.

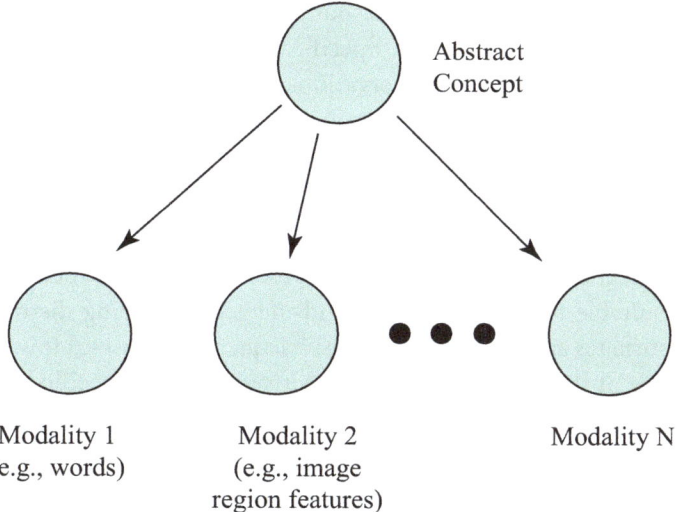

Figure 1.9: A simple model for multi-modal data. Here the multimodal data connects to a common abstract (latent) concept, rather than being directly connected. For example, images with captions could be modeled as a collection of multiple concepts, each of which gives rise to words and image region characteristics. Further, image region characteristics could be broken into sub-modalities such as color, and texture. Readers familiar with graphical models will recognize concepts as latent cluster variables and the observations of different modalities being conditionally independent given the cluster. More complex structures such as hierarchical concept hierarchies and context dependent concepts and/or data models can be constructed within this general paradigm. An alternative approach, suitable for some applications, is to build discriminative models for predicting one modality directly from the other, e.g., predicting words from image data.

information. The giraffe's spotted pattern could also be linked to video data, where segmenting out the giraffe based on its movement is easier, and where its movement reveals its articulated structure.[10] Similarly, linking the spotted pattern to video or image data could provide further understanding of the appearance of giraffes, as well as a visual understanding of its typical environment and thus the newly learned word "savanna." While a system to integrate all these sources of data in a general-purpose system has yet to be built, examples of many of the components have been explored in limited domains.

To summarize, when visual and linguistic information provide alternative representations of the same underlying concepts, we can have access to rich joint representations of those concepts. These representations can provide computational systems with some of the attributes that we associate with deeper understanding. For example, consider the concept suggested by "car."

---

[10]This strategy was first explored by Ramanan et al. [477].

Certainly we can describe cars with words, but we can also visualize them and connect them with movement and functional attributes. Specifically, the abstract semantic concept is *grounded* by sensory data, which can be strictly observational, or can include interacting with the concept (e.g., driving the car) as discussed in the human-robot interaction example.

1.3.1   DISCRIMINATIVE METHODS

The generative approach just described is intuitively appealing, as it is explicit about how our modeling constructs connect to the distribution of the observed data. The focus on the joint probability makes the model suitable for multiple tasks, and the accompanying distributional answers provide uncertainty estimates and can be useful for subsequent processes. However, providing general capabilities can come at the expense of reduced performance on specific tasks. Intuitively, if performance on a specific task such as auto-annotation is paramount, then anything in the approach that is not optimized for that task is potentially a liability. This has led researchers to consider discriminative methods for tasks that can be expressed as a classification problem. Generally, the focus of such methods is to establish what differentiates the classes in the space of features (e.g., color and texture descriptors), with less interest on why they are differentiable, or what the confidence might be. Because auto-annotation is important for practical reasons that are agnostic to how it is achieved, I include some discriminative approaches in this book (§6.4.6, §6.6.10, §6.7.2).

1.4   MUTIMODAL INFERENCE–APPLICATIONS TO COMPUTATIONAL TASKS

I now provide a taste of how we can approach some of the computational tasks introduced in §1.2. For each of the three examples that follow, we assume that we already have the model. Learning model parameters from data is covered in §1.5.

1.4.1   REGION LABELING WITH A CONCEPT MODEL

Region labeling, covered in depth in Chapter 6, maps vectors of image region features, $\mathbf{r}$, to words, w. We can imagine generating regions with labels by first sampling a concept, c, from a distribution $p(c)$, and then generating a word, w, and a region feature vector, $\mathbf{r}$, based on the concept. Formally, and $\mathbf{r}$ and w conditionally independent given the latent concept, c. Our generative model for a region-word pair is thus

$$p(w, \mathbf{r}, c) = p(c) \, p(w \,|\, c) \, p(\mathbf{r} \,|\, c). \tag{1.6}$$

To do inference on the observed variables w and we $\mathbf{r}$ marginalize out the unobserved concept:

$$p(w, \mathbf{r}) = \sum_c p(c) \, p(w \,|\, c) \, p(\mathbf{r} \,|\, c) = \sum_c p(w \,|\, c) \, p(\mathbf{r}, c). \tag{1.7}$$

Thus,

$$p(w|\mathbf{r}) = \sum_c p(c|\mathbf{r}) \, p(w|c), \qquad (1.8)$$

where

$$p(c|\mathbf{r}) = \frac{p(c) \, p(\mathbf{r}|c)}{\sum_{c'} p(c') \, p(\mathbf{r}|c')}. \qquad (1.9)$$

This provides a distribution over words for each region. To label a region we can choose the word with maximal probability, or one might take advantage of the full distribution for further processing.

The result (1.8) is very intuitive. It says that for each semantic concept, c, consider how likely it is responsible for the region under consideration, $\mathbf{r}$. To the extent that it is as measured by $p(c|\mathbf{r})$, we accordingly weight the word distribution, $p(w|c)$, associated with that concept.

1.4.2 CROSS-MODAL DISAMBIGUATION–REGION LABELING WITH IMAGE KEYWORDS

Now consider region labeling when we have the luxury of image keywords, $\mathbf{k}$. Assuming that image keywords are informative about region labels, we can improve the labeling by using this additional source of information. We consider that region labels come from $\mathbf{k}$ with high probability, but there is ambiguity in which word links to which region. Alternatively, the region labeler provides word probabilities for each region, but restricting them to $\mathbf{k}$ further disambiguates the meaning. In short, this task is an example of cross-modal disambiguation.

Notice that $\mathbf{k}$ and w are **not** conditionally independent given the abstract concept, c, and thus Figure 1.9 does not apply.[11] But we can improve the estimate of $p(w|\mathbf{r})$ using the conditional independence of $\mathbf{k}$ and $\mathbf{r}$ given w as follows:

$$\begin{aligned} p(w|\mathbf{k},\mathbf{r}) &\propto p(\mathbf{k},\mathbf{r}|w) \, p(w) \\ &\propto p(\mathbf{k}|w) \, p(\mathbf{r}|w) \, p(w) \qquad (1.10) \\ &\propto p(\mathbf{k}|w) \, p(w|\mathbf{r}). \end{aligned}$$

A simple choice for $p(\mathbf{k}|w)$ is to set it to one if $w \in \mathbf{k}$, and zero otherwise. We can also consider learning $p(\mathbf{k}|w)$ from data to better reflect how annotators choose keywords.

1.4.3 CROSS-MODAL DISAMBIGUATION–WORD SENSE DISAMBIGUATION WITH IMAGES

Finally, consider the task of word sense disambiguation with images [66, 67].[12] Here, we assume that we have distributions over senses for each word, w, based on the collection of words, W,

---

[11]To see that conditional independence does not hold, consider a tiger concept that is associated with the words "cat" and "tiger." Either could be used as the region label, but having decided on a choice, the image keyword choice is fixed.

[12]The formulation in Barnard and Johnson [66] implicitly assumed that the prior over senses $p(s)$ is uniform, which is sub-optimal. Algebraically this assumption leads to dropping the final division by $p(s)$ in (1.12).

from natural language processing. Denote this distribution by $p(s|w, W)$. We wish to improve this using an illustrative image, I, by computing $p(s|w, W, I)$. To take a similar approach to the previous two examples, we assume our learned concept model has distributions over words senses, s, instead of words themselves. Then we can compute distributions over senses, given a region, $\mathbf{r}$, by (1.8), with w replaced by s. Further, we consider that images taken as a whole—not regions— influence caption senses. Thus, we need to estimate $p(s|I)$, where the image, I, is represented by the set of regions, $\{\mathbf{r}_i\}$. To estimate $p(s|I)$ we assume that words senses for I are independently drawn by first choosing a region at random, and then choosing a sense based on the region. This leads to the image word sense distributions being the average of those for the regions. Formally,

$$p(s|I) = \frac{1}{N} \sum_{i=1}^{N} p(s|\mathbf{r}_i).$$

(1.11)

Then,

$$
\begin{aligned}
p(s|w, W, I) &\propto p(s, w, W, I) \\
&\propto p(I|s, w, W)\, p(s|w, W) \\
&\propto p(I|s)\, p(s|w, W) \\
&\propto p(s|I)\, p(s|w, W)/p(s),
\end{aligned}
$$

(1.12)

ignoring probabilities over subsets of (w, W, T) as these variables are given, and using $w, W \perp I | s \Rightarrow p(I|w, W, s) = p(I|s)$.

1.5 LEARNING FROM REDUNDANT REPRESENTATIONS IN LOOSELY LABELED MULTIMODAL DATA

To learn parameters for the concept model from §1.4.1, we nominally need examples of the concepts together with their visual features and associated words. One way to do this would be manually segment images into regions corresponding to concepts, and provide words for each region, which implicitly provide concept examples. Notice that this does not establish what the concepts actually are, as we only have a collection of examples of different ones. To proceed, we could cluster the concepts based on both their word attributes and their visual features, thereby getting concepts defined by groups of examples that are similar both in the distribution of words used to describe them and in visual appearance.

While this approach is sound, the need for a large amount of manual segmentation and annotation is problematic. As research into various aspects of image understanding has progressed, various stores of such data have accrued through significant human effort. In addition, methods for semi-supervised semantic labeling have been developed, and crowdsourcing through Amazon Mechanical Turk [3] has become increasingly popular. However, despite the hope that eventually there will be enough high quality training data, most research into linking vision and language has focused on using *loosely labeled* data (see Figure 1.8), as such data is much more plentiful and easier to create or collect from the web. In such data, images are annotated by keywords or captions, but we do not know which aspects of the image are relevant to which words. Each word is somewhat informative, but it is also ambiguous. This is an example of *correspondence ambiguity*.

Correspondence ambiguity is similar to the *data association* problem, which we would have if we take a clustering approach. Here, we do not know *a priori* which concept a word or a region comes from, and the number of possible assignments is exponential in the size of the data set, making it potentially a far worse computational issue. With loosely labeled data, the assumption that the words and regions come from the set of clusters constrains the possibilities. For example, if we assign R regions to R concepts out of C possible concepts, then the words are now constrained to come from one of R concepts instead of one of C, which is typically a much larger number. In practice, we often focus on the data-to-concept correspondence, with the data-data correspondence being implicit—if a word and a region in the same document come from the same concept, then they are linked.

Notice that these correspondence problems arise only during inference and, generally, as in this example, when we want to learn models from data. One of the strengths of the probabilistic graphical modeling paradigm is that it helps us keep modeling and inference (which includes learning) separate. Generative models for the data (e.g., (1.6)) do not need to represent the association of the data and the model because the model considers each document as an independent sample. Correspondence problems arise when we see the data, but we do not know which part of the model (e.g., which concept) is responsible for it.

1.5.1   RESOLVING REGION-LABEL CORRESPONDENCE AMBIGUITY

To develop intuition about why the region-label correspondence ambiguity can be overcome, consider Figure 1.8a. Based on this single image we are not able to judge whether the word "snow" should be interpreted as a label for one or more goat regions, one or more snow regions, or noise (not visually relevant). Without additional sources of information, this correspondence ambiguity cannot be resolved. Interestingly, multiple examples can help reduce the ambiguity. If we were able to link the goat regions in Figure 1.8a with those in Figure 1.8b based on appearance, then this would suggest that they are linked to the same concept. Since we assume that the data from multiple modalities in a single image share concepts, this would lead to the conjecture that those regions also likely link to the only common word keyword ("goat"). Further, we would also have some handle on the assignment of the snow regions in Figure 1.8a to "snow" because we expect that it is quite likely "snow" refers to some part of the image, and further that it is less likely to also refer to the goat. We refer to this kind of argument as *exclusion reasoning*.[13] This notion is important because concepts that are relatively common and are easy to link to visual features (e.g.,

---

[13]This was the term used by Barnard and Fan [62] who considered the constraint computationally. The concept was referred to as the exclusion principle by Siskind [528] who discusses it in the context of language learning in humans.

water, sky, snow) can reduce the labeling ambiguity for rare or otherwise difficult concepts (e.g., climber or mountain goat).

We see that the key leverage that we have on correspondence ambiguity is the fortuitous occurrences of subsets of concepts in various data examples. While correspondence ambiguity is generally an impediment, it is interesting to compare having N labeled regions compared with N loosely labeled images with R regions and R words. Notice that these are the same if $R = 1$. In other words, we can compare having more information that is ambiguous (e.g., if $R = 3$, we have three words that pertain to one of three regions) vs. less information without ambiguity (e.g., if $R = 1$, the data only speaks to one region, but it does so unambiguously). Whether or not we would prefer more regions at the expense of more ambiguity is difficult to analyze in general, but it is certainly a function of the statistics of the pairings. On the one extreme, if, for example, "skiers" and "snow" always occur as a pair, then we cannot distinguish them and we would prefer some single region examples of them. On the other extreme, if we assume that regions can be tokenized precisely (e.g., a snow region always matches snow and never anything else), and parings occur with uniform probability, then it is possible that multiple regions are more informative (see Appendix A.3; also of relevance is Cour et al. [146]). Of course, many concepts commonly co-occur, and so pairing with uniform probability is not a realistic assumption. Pragmatically, it is a happy accident that loosely labeled data is easy to come by in quantity, as it improves our chances of having the diverse sets of concepts in images needed to deal with the correspondence ambiguity.

In addition to linking visually similar entities across loosely labeled instances, there are several other ways to reduce correspondence ambiguity. First, rich text descriptions such as "a red car on gray pavement" (see §7.1, §7.2, §7.3) can help localize labels. Second, detectors for specific entities (e.g., "faces") can localize labels that can be associated with them (e.g., "person") [166]. Third, keyword lists can be processed using tools such as WordNet (§3.1) to merge redundant words. For example, keyword lists often include a specific terms (e.g., "f-17") and more general terms (e.g., "jet") which typically map to the same image features. Finally, words can be processed to ignore ones unlikely to have identifiable visual features because they are abstract (e.g., "religious") (see §7.2).

1.5.2   DATA VARIATION AND SEMANTIC GROUPING

Learning from data sets that have many examples of each concept is also warranted because both the linguistic and the visual evidence for concepts vary substantively. This variation, especially in the case of visual features of objects, is one reason why recognition of object categories is very difficult. With large data sets we can learn the statistics of features for concepts that are valid over a broad domain, and thus are potentially indicative of the world at large (i.e., ecologically valid). However, we also must recognize the limitations of our data domains, which are invariably biased.[14] For example, we often learn from stock photo collections or web images, which are typically chosen as canonical or aesthetic visual representations of something in the world. Images from such datasets have *photographer bias*, and what is learned from these domains may be less useful in other domains. For example, images taken by competent photographers are quite different from the images taken by a robot navigating a building.

Given data variation, to establish the word and region models associated with concepts (e.g., $p(w|c)$ and $(p(\mathbf{r}|c))$ in (1.6)), a learning process often (at least implicitly) needs to group textual and visual features in the training data.

Grouping text elements. If one assumes that keywords are synonymous with concepts, then grouping text elements is not needed (see §6.4.4 and §6.4.5 for approaches based on this assumption). However, words are not the same as concepts for several reasons. First, as I have already noted, many words have multiple senses. Second, a concept might be reasonably connected to multiple words, either because they are near synonyms (e.g., "snow" vs. "névé") or the concept needs multiple words to describe it. Hence, words in the training corpus need to be grouped, and the same word might be in different groups depending on the context. Notice that determining that two words are close in meaning might be possible using tools such as WordNet (§3.1), or can potentially be learned based on co-occurring visual similarity.

Grouping regions. Similarly, if we are using regions for visual representation, then they (at least implicitly) need to be grouped to form a representation of the visual appearance of the concept. Here features are typically represented using continuous values, and so there is at least a notion of closeness assuming that the relative weights of the features are known or learned. Since the underlying assumption is that concepts are somewhat visually homogenous, large variation might be captured using multiple related concepts (e.g., red roses and white roses). Again, the learning algorithms will at least implicitly group features in the training data into concepts, and again, similar features might be grouped differently depending on context. For example, a white region in a skiing image (with the word "snow") might be grouped with a snow concept during learning, but a second similar region in a cloud image (without the word "snow") might be grouped with a cloud concept.

1.5.3 SIMULTANEOUSLY LEARNING MODELS AND REDUCING CORRESPONDENCE AMBIGUITY

The previous discussion suggests two key processes for learning from generic multimodal data: (1) learning models for the underlying structure; and (2) learning the correspondence between data and model elements. While some methods do not break the problem down in this way, this is often the case for generative models. A key observation is that solving one of these problems

---

[14]Data set bias in object recognition is considered by Torralba and Efros [557]. See also [317]. Also relevant is mapping what is learned using from one dataset so that it is more applicable for use on another data set, which is often referred to domain adaptation or transfer learning (e.g., [245, 337, 499]).

helps solve the other. For the first, knowing which data elements correspond to a given concept enables the building the textual and visual model for the concept. For example, if we know that the snow regions in the images in Figure 1.8 are connected to the snow concept, we can aggregate all these observations into a visual model for snow. Similarly, if we know the word instances that correspond to the concept (e.g., "snow," "névé"), then we can learn a distribution for the use of the words given the concept. For example, since "névé" is more specific than "snow," we expect that it might be used less on average.

For the second, if we know the model, we can compute the data-model correspondences. For example, given a good visual representation of the snow concept, we can link regions in Figure 1.8a to snow, and, given a language representation of snow, we can then attach the word "snow" to the concept as well. Exclusion reasoning could then further reduce the correspondence ambiguity between "snow" and "goat."

Since neither the correspondences nor the models are typically known, but either one can be used to estimate the other, we have a classic "chicken-and-egg" situation that is common in computer vision. This suggests the algorithmic approach of learning them iteratively. For example, we could compute initial noisy models ignoring correspondence ambiguity, and then use those models to reduce the ambiguity. On subsequence iterations, improved models can be computed from the data with reduced ambiguity, and those models can further reduce the ambiguity. This simple iterative approach can be formally defined as an instance of the Expectation-Maximization (EM) algorithm,[15] which is a common method for learning models for images and text (first discussed in detail in §6.3.5).

---

[15]Expectation Maximization (e.g., [111, 113, 122, 169, 412]) is commonly used for missing value problems. In computer vision, the missing values are often the correspondence between data elements and model components during learning.

CHAPTER 2

The Semantics of Images and Associated Text

The term semantics refers to the study of meaning and how it relates to representations. While it is beyond the scope of this book to delve into the philosophical discourse on the topic, it is helpful to consider what meaning people attach to images and associated text. In particular, for information retrieval and data mining applications, the question is clearly relevant, as designs for systems to address these needs should be focused on what people actually want such systems to do. It has even been argued that images to not have meaning outside of such contexts [502–505, 607]. Regardless, categories of meaning (not necessarily disjoint) that are relevant to linking words and pictures include the following.

- Images and associated text are both evidence about the physical world as it was when and where the image (or video clip) was created. While the choice to create an image is never completely random, this subjective bias interacts minimally with the particulars of the image as evidence. As discussed previously (§1.1), associated text might be derivable from the image by a human annotator, or some of the text might add information about the scene that is not visually available. As also discussed previously (§1.1), text that is derivable by a human annotator might not be reliably extracted by computer programs, and, from the perspective automatically inferring what was in front of the camera when the picture was taken, it adds complementary information.

- Images and associated text together communicate objective message. Here images typically take a secondary role, illustrating parts of the meaning that are more effectively conveyed using images. See Figure 1.2 for examples.

- Images and associated text communicate subjective meaning. Here associated text provides a subjective interpretation of the image. For example, the image might be described as "compelling," "dark," or "scary."

- Text associated with images provides objective information about the image as an artifact. Such meta-data might include the time, the GPS location, the camera and lens used to take the picture, and who the photographer was. Typically, the meta-data is largely orthogonal to the visual data as discussed previously (§1.1), but modest mutual information between the visual information meta-data is possible.[1]

2.1   LESSONS FROM IMAGE SEARCH

Studies into image search confirm that people searching for images generally want access to the underlying physical world depicted in the image [47, 193, 244, 403, 404, 451–453, 473, 603]. This is not surprising because the search will often be initiated for a specific reason such as illustrating a point or verifying a claim. Typically, the criteria for what is being searched will be thought about in linguistic terms, as opposed to visual features or similarity with image examples. In other words, the searching studied in the cited work is typically driven by semantic concerns. As a very simple example, someone searching for a picture of a tiger in water absolutely requires the presence of both a tiger and water visible in the image.

Given results faithful to the requested objective semantics concerning the physical world, further choices about how suitable the image is can be made by the user. It seems reasonable that user queries will be biased by what they expect library services or computational systems are able to provide, which tends to rule out queries requiring subjective agreement (e.g., "an exciting image"). It is unclear from the cited work to what extent such attributes would be used if users thought that retrieval systems could compute or encode such judgments that were consistent with their own interpretations. However, there is a rapidly growing body of work attempting to provide such capability (see §2.3, §7.2.3–7.2.7).

2.1.1   CONTENT-BASED IMAGE RETRIEVAL (CBIR)

Finding suitable images satisfying queries is often referred to as content-based image retrieval (CBIR). CBIR systems have been proposed that support queries based both on visual and textual input and combinations thereof.[2] Visual input methods include queries using: (1) an example image (where the user provides an image in the hopes of finding similar ones); (2) a sketch by the user indicative of shapes of interest; and (3) selected patches of color and texture.[3]

Most research in content-based retrieval (CBIR) assumes that image semantics is what the user wants. In fact, for this endeavor, this essentially defines semantics. This notion is built into the common phrase, "the semantic gap," which is used to express the main difficulty in image retrieval. According to the survey paper (dated December 2000) by Smeulders et al. [530]:

---

[1]Clearly, there can be some mutual information between the image and the time of day or the location, especially for outdoor images. However, the impact on knowing the time of day on understanding images is likely to be minimal. GPS location has been connected to image content in particular cases. See, for example, work on inferring the location of an image, based on appearance [270, 651, 653] as mapped to already geotagged images, or mountain skylines that can be matched to topographic data [49, 50, 384, 471, 554]. Finally, the mutual information between GPS location and words has been looked at by Yanai et al. [623].

[2]Early systems that experimented with using both text and visual features include Blobworld [75, 111, 112] and others [500, 501].

[3]An early example of the first method (query by example image) was reported in Pentland et al. [467]. All three of these methods were included in the QBIC system [148, 461].

"The semantic gap is the lack of coincidence between the information that one can extract from the visual data and the interpretation that the same data have for a user in a given situation."

Notice that there are two elements of the semantic gap. First, there are limitations on extraction, and second, the notion that the meaning of retrieved image is a function of the user and their current needs. The second element underscores that the interface between the user and the CBIR system is critically import. The first element—limitations on extraction—can be addressed in multiple ways. First, we can improve our ability to extract information from visual data, and much progress has been made on this task in the intervening years. Second, we could augment visual data with text, and such imagery is now common on the web due to ubiquitous captioned and tagged images. Finally, we could push extraction of semantics onto the user as well, which was argued as necessary at the time.[4]

Important elements of user interaction include displaying of a range of candidates, and having a mechanism for the user to indicate more relevant and less relevant examples. The later is referred to as relevance feedback, which has a long history of study.[5] Such interaction can help user guide the system to what the user wants, and also circumvent some of the difficulties with automated image understanding. If the system, by whatever process, can find an image with some of the elements the user is seeking, that can be leveraged to find images that are closer to what they really want. In fact, Smeulders notes that an important observation during the "early years of CBIR" was the realization that "image retrieval does not entail solving the general image understanding problem" [530]. However, despite this reduction in difficulty by appropriate user interfaces, CBIR systems at that time (2000) that relied on image features alone were still too far below the bar to be adopted by users. Part of the reason was that finding initial images, and then leveraging them, relied on relatively low-level features that were hard to link to what the user wanted—even with their help.

By contrast, image search based on text alone, or text together with image features, is sufficiently effective for many tasks that most readers will have already used it (e.g., Google™ image search). We often want to find web images that can communicate something that is both semantically specific (due to our task) and visual (otherwise we would not be seeking an image). In this use case, image search often works reasonably well, and does so partly due to the development of methods along the lines discussed in this book.

Historically, the focus on image features and query by example was partly motivated by a lack of annotated images, and the effort needed to annotate them. But the lesson learned was that even the very noisy text associated with web pages that became available a few years later trumps naïve use of image features. The reason is that our primary notion of semantics—what was in front

---

[4]See, for example, the discussion on the USNFS 1992 workshop in the introduction of Smeulders et al. [530], as well as the first section of Flickner et al. [229] which includes the following statement: "One of the guiding principles used by QBIC is to let computers do what they do best—quantifiable measurement—and let humans do what they do best—attaching semantic meaning." (QBIC—Query by Image and Video Content—refers to their interactive system for image and video retrieval).
[5]See, for example [119, 138, 148, 276, 286, 318].

of the camera when the picture was taken—is paramount for most image searches. Associated text can provide this, and if text is not available, then some fraction of the computer vision problem does need to be solved to respond to many queries. Interestingly, having images with text supports both searching for them, as well as learning the mapping between image content and text, which is a key topic in this book.

Coming back to the characterization of the semantic gap from Smeulders et al. [530], we can summarize the image retrieval problem as simultaneously interpreting the needs of a particular user at a given time, with being able to find images with the appropriate meaning. In general, translating user needs in detail is a challenging user interface problem, but we are still left with the basic issue of finding images that match approximations of that need. This later task aligns with key goals in computer vision, especially since commonly a perquisite for fulfilling user need is a characterization of what was in the physical world when images were created.

2.2   IMAGES AND TEXT AS EVIDENCE ABOUT THE WORLD

In light of the previous discussion, this book will focus mostly the semantics of images and text as being the physical attributes of the world present in the scene as captured by a camera (the first meaning category listed in the begining of this chapter). Specifically, an image can record which entities were present, where each entity was (to the extent that can be inferred from a 2D image of the 3D world), and their physical attributes such as shape, texture, and color. We assume that observations such as images and text are evidence regarding underlying physical structure that can be connected to abstract symbolic meaning (semantics). It is intuitive that such structure exists, at least in the way that our own cognitive experience organizes information about the world. Using abstractions, such as those for an object or its category, provide an efficient way to assimilate data about the world to support inferences that are important for survival. More pragmatically, if we are to learn about the world from multimodal data, then extracting these abstractions is helpful, and the link to language provides access to the collective understanding of them.

A key facet of the physical world accessible to vision system is spatial information, which includes location, extent, configuration of connected entities, and context provided by non-connected entities. Thus, an important consideration is the spatial grouping of elements into the abstractions just described. This grouping is hierarchical, and the semantics of a scene spans several logical scales, ranging from object parts and their configuration, to objects, to the scene considered as a whole. As an example of the later, humans might label a scene as "sunset" or "birthday party." It is a difficult open problem to computationally parse an image into regions for each of the 3D semantic components that the scene is composed of. The difficulty is due to multiple related reasons including the loss of information from projecting the 3D world into the 2D image, the huge variance on what constitutes a component, and ambiguity between component boundaries and internal surface variation and illumination effects.

However, notice that associated text is largely concerned about those components. Hence, a key ingredient that text brings to computationally understanding images is implicit information about the appropriate groupings. This relies on the assumption that they are shared across scenes, and therefore across images. Put differently, data sets of images with associated text encodes information about how to group pixels within images so that the groupings are semantically relevant. With such grouping, and associated semantic labels (e.g., the orange stripy region is a tiger), each image with text also contains other information such as the particular location of each named item, and the particular characteristics of each of their appearances. Thus, the image-text combination is generally more informative than the text alone, as a complete visual description would only be provided by an exceptionally pedantic caption.

2.3   AFFECTIVE ATTRIBUTES OF IMAGES AND VIDEO

Affective image attributes such as "compelling," "beautiful," and "terrifying" describe the experience of humans interacting with images, and thus are subjective by definition.[6] Thus, we expect substantially more variation among such judgments compared with opinions about more objective information such as what was in the scene when the picture was taken. Nonetheless, most research into inferring affective qualities of images has assumed that there is enough agreement among viewers that treating affective properties of images as universal is an acceptable simplification.[7] Early work in including affective properties in CBIIR are summarized by Wang and He [596] (see also Datta et al. [162]). Recent work in inferring affective properties of images includes inferring induced emotion from images (§7.2.3) and video (§7.2.4), visual sentiment analysis (§7.2.5) where the polarity (negative-to-positive) of opinion is estimated for a large number of subjective concepts, and estimating how aesthetically pleasing images are (§7.2.6).

In all these meaning systems, the semantic notions are generally related to an image or a video clip taken as a whole. While it is interesting to consider which pieces of visual information contribute to a particular affective property, this "localization" is not generally considered integral to the semantics. (Contrast this to the physical content of scenes, where the existence of particular objects and their spatial arrangement is relevant.) Similarly, in the case of video, affective properties are reasonably analyzed at the level of short clips. If we consider what someone might write about an image or video clip, his or her basic affective response might be mentioned, and if so, expanded upon to provide nuances. In addition, affect might also influence overall word choice in their description. Finally, the commentator might attempt to analyze which visual elements led them to feel a particular way when looking at the image. So far, only the first of these (basic affect response) has been addressed computationally. In what follows we further consider visual meaning with respect to emotion induction.

---

[6]The definition of "subjective" commonly listed first in dictionaries is along the lines of this example from `www.dictionary`
`.com`: "existing in the mind; belonging to the thinking subject rather than to the object of thought (opposed to objective)."
[7]One recent empirical study supports this assumption in limited context [168].

2.3.1   EMOTION INDUCTION FROM IMAGES AND VIDEO

Consider finding images that make people feel a particular way such as happy or fearful. Naively attempting this with simple image search does not necessarily work as expected. For example, currently (2015) using Google^{TM} image search reveals that "scary" is a visual synonym for Halloween masks, and "joyful" is highly associated with people jumping in the air. While the relationships between the images and words are clear, Halloween scary is not really scary, and images of joyful people in a canonical pose do not necessarily make one feel joyful. More generally, many emotion word queries return images of people who appear to have that emotion, not images that might lead you to have that emotion.

We consider machine learning approaches to link visual features to emotion words in §7.2.3 and §7.2.4 for images and video data, respectively. Naturally, these approaches rely on datasets that are labeled with characterizations of emotion. Some the available data sets are described in §3.3. The characterization of emotion has been extensively studied and debated in psychology (see Gross for a modern integrative view [252]). We limit the discussion here to two broad, related approaches that have been adopted by computational researchers interested in inferring emotional responses from visual data. The first representation maps emotion into a continuous three-dimensional space with axes commonly described as valance-arousal-control (VAC)—or interchangeably pleasure-arousal-dominance (PAD) [349, 413, 495, 599]. Valance refers to the degree of negative versus positive affect (e.g., unpleasant through pleasant). Arousal ranges from calm to excited. Control ranges from feeling controlled by others to feeling in control of one's circumstances. Often this third dimension (control) is dropped, as the bulk of emotion variation is captured in valence and arousal. The second representation assumes that emotional states are discrete (e.g., surprise, interest, joy, rage, fear, disgust, shame). Emotion categories have been studied both as discretizations of the VAC space (e.g., [418]), as well as independent of such spaces [190, 470].

Acquiring characterizations of induced emotion with the appropriate semantics is more challenging than labeling physical objects due to individual variation in interpreting the labeling task, as well as genuine variation in induced emotion. In building the International Affective Picture System (IAPS) Lang et al. [349] used their Self Assessment Manikin (SAM) [94] to pictorially establish a scale for VAC, which was linked to physiological data in a preliminary study [350]. Such care is rare in subsequent data collection for various image retrieval driven experiments, and for early video retrieval work, despite early studies on emotion induction using video [253, 468]. However, recent work has looked at linking affective response to physiology [430, 534, 535], and the recently released DEAP dataset [327, 328] makes such grounded affective data readily available.

In contrast to grounded data, researchers are also building large-scale datasets for computationally inferring induced emotion (e.g., LIRIS-ACCEDE [72, 74]) that are annotated by crowd sourcing (e.g., using the Amazon Mechanical Turk system [3]). This approach has the advantage that large numbers of annotated image or video clips can be acquired inexpensively, but the lack of grounding is a problem. Annotators might, for example, be asked to compare video clips as to which one is more frightening than the other. One can imagine an annotator making superficially reasonable choices without feeling any fear, or having any real knowledge that some, many, or most people would feel fear. Nonetheless, the information can be valuable for retrieval applications, where somewhat reasonable tags are better than none, and the user is in the loop to select among choices.

Regardless of how grounded the emotion characterizations are in a particular dataset, the issue of individual differences remains. Some sources of variation can conceivably be accounted for. For example, experiments with the IAPS data have found differences in psychophysiological measures due to gender [71], established personality traits (e.g., sensitivity to punishment vs. reward [33]), habituation [609] (and, as moderated by sleep [455]), and regulatory efforts [71]. Hence, modeling the users of a system has promise for improving our ability to understand their relationship between visual content and affective language (see [556] for a relevant study using the IAPS data).

2.3.2 INFERRING EMOTION IN PEOPLE DEPICTED IN IMAGES AND VIDEOS

A different computational problem is inferring the emotion experienced by a person depicted visually. To state the obvious, a person in an image might have been happy or sad when the picture was taken, but that does not mean that the viewer will necessarily tend to feel happy or sad. Computationally, the two distinct problems are inferring emotion induced by visual content that *people look at* (§2.3.1) vs. inferring emotion of people based on *how they appear* (or what they do). Notice that the effect on linguistic description is potentially quite different. For example, if we consider annotating an image with respect to whether people are happy or sad, we immediately see that localization is part of the semantics. For example, there may be three people in the image but it could be the case that only one of them is sad. Historically, computationally estimating human emotion from their appearance (e.g., facial expression) has largely been driven by human computer interface (HCI).[8] Directly applying similar methods to linking linguistic and visual data is rare, and we leave further discussion for future editions.

---

[8]The literature on integrating affective information into human computer interfaces is substantive (for a start, see [460, 469]). Most estimates of the affective state of humans are based on facial expression and/or audio tone [647], but research using physiological sensors is also common (e.g., [380]). Applications range from educational games [144] to driver safety [180, 202].

CHAPTER 3

Sources of Data for Linking Visual and Linguistic Information

The data available for researchers interested in studying the integration of visual and textual data has rapidly increased over the last 15 years. Here I catalog many of the data sets that have been used. I begin with the WordNet text resource, which is commonly used to anchor text in datasets with respect to semantics, as well being used for preprocessing (Chapter 5) and joint learning. I then describe datasets that provide images or videos together with semantics in linguistic form, organized across two dimensions. The first dimension is whether data items are annotated with a single word applicable to the entire scene as a category (e.g., sunsets), multiple keywords (usually nouns), or complete descriptions which are typically in the form of sentences. The second dimension is the degree to which relevant labels have been localized. Here the common choices are no localization (e.g., the standard loosely labeled data as illustrated in Figure 1.8), bounding boxes or polygons for pertinent objects within the images, and relatively complete region level segmentations covering most the major elements of each image with a single semantic label for each region. The breakdown also applies to video, except that the textual information might be limited to the speech signal.

3.1 WORDNET FOR BUILDING SEMANTIC VISUAL-LINGUISTIC DATA SETS

The WordNet lexical taxonomy [30, 425, 426] has been adopted for much research in linking visual and linguistic information. As developed further later (§5.5), the WordNet system is used extensively to bridge text and semantic spaces. From the perspective of building datasets, a key feature of WordNet is that entities are encoded by senses, which is important because many words have multiple possible senses. An example already used in the Introduction (Ch. 1) is the word "bank," which has meanings (senses) that include a financial institution and an edge or discontinuity in terrain (e.g., "snow bank"). Such words are referred to as *polysemous*. WordNet provides a sense number as a suffix for each word (e.g., bank_1, bank_2), or alternatively for computer programs using the WordNet libraries, these are indexed (e.g., bank[1], bank[2]). The sense numbers are roughly in order of decreasing frequency in common usage. Many of the datasets described in this chapter, especially the more recent ones, use WordNet senses for text associated with visual data. Since the text usually comes from sources that do not provide senses (e.g., user tags or crowd-sourced captions), this entails additional manual input, but the effort to do so is relatively modest [494].

Having provided terms labeled with respect to the WordNet system, words indicative of visual content can be linked to other words using WordNet facilities. For example, WordNet groups senses into sets of similar meaning (*synsets*)—the words in a synset are synonyms. A second relation important for linking vision and language is *hyponymy* (the "is-a" relation), which identifies subordinate class structure. For example, using this relation, we can find out that "sparrow" (both senses) is a bird (first three senses). Formally, "sparrow[1-2]" is a hyponym of "bird[1-3]," and "bird[1-3]" is a hypernym of "sparrow[1-2]." More generally, WordNet provides semantic hierarchies for various sets of terms. A third relation useful for linking visual and linguistic content is *meronymy*, which tells us about parts of objects.

Exploiting these relations improves datasets by reducing the number of categories at a given level of generality, and, conversely, increasing the number of examples within them. For example, there are many different words that can be considered as indicative of a person, which is a reasonable level of abstraction for basic visual understanding. However, relevant images may not initially be associated with "person"—an image containing a person could be labeled with "dancer." Thus, the WordNet system can be used to aggregate disparate labelings. In general, WordNet enables effective integration of input from multiple sources or annotators (e.g., [82, 494, 645]).

WordNet is also often used to provide search terms to construct datasets with reasonable semantic coverage for a variety of broad categories such as scenes in the case of the SUN dataset [611, 612] (or animals [347, 348]). The broadest example is ImageNet (§3.2, [9, 172, 492]), which provides an illustrated version of WordNet. ImageNet is constructed by using WordNet concepts as search terms for images, followed by manual checking and refining of the labels.

Extensions to WordNet.   SentiWordNet [51, 198, 199] extends WordNet for sentiment analysis. In particular, it provides ratings for positivity, negativity, and neutrality for the WordNet synsets. SentiWordNet is built automatically using classifiers, but validation on small subsets has been done. The related dataset, SentiStrength [551, 552], which is not tied to WordNet, provides ratings for 298 positive terms and 465 negative terms.

3.2   VISUAL DATA WITH A SINGLE OBJECTIVE LABEL

Collections of images with a single label fall into several groups. First, the label might label scenes holistically (e.g., sunset, mountain, or beech scenes). Often the label set is limited to binary choices such as indoor vs. outdoor, vertical vs. horizontal, or graphically created vs. photographs. These data sets serve scene classification work (§6.1), but only weakly link vision and language, as there is limited structure in a single a label.

Second, images linked through a single word can be found by simple web searches. Here images can be found that depict adjectives (e.g., "yellow") [220, 621], general attributes of specific classes (e.g., animals) [347, 348], or object categories. For object categories, data sets differ by the amount of irrelevant, distracting background the images typically have. For example, in the important object recognition data sets Caltech-6 [219], Caltech-101 [207, 208], and Caltech-256 [251], the images returned by the web search were manually pruned to generally contain only good examples without too much clutter. Bounding boxes and object contours are also available for Caltech-101.

One issue with images found by simple web search is that the indexed terms are not sense disambiguated. For example, the search term "mouse" returns images of an animal, a computer pointing device, and a cartoon character (i.e., "Mickey"). This issue is normally dealt with through human intervention; however, Saenko et al. [498] suggested automated approaches. In particular, they consider both words surrounding the search term, as in classic word sense disambiguation (discussed in §5.4), and visual information, capitalizing on the significant visual difference that often exists for disparate senses. This was further extended to filter out abstract senses by using the WordNet hypernym structure to include only senses that are from broad physical categories (e.g., animal) [497].

Scaling up image collection based on searching the Internet for images with single-word queries has led to the ImageNet [9, 172, 492] system for organizing images by semantics. ImageNet provides a large number of examples (of the order of 1,000) for most WordNet nodes. Image candidates are retrieved for each node, and workers from the Amazon Mechanical Turk system [3] are recruited to filter the results. In addition, bounding boxes for the relevant part of the image are provided for many of the images, as are image features. ImageNet respects the copyright holders of the images (as well as saving storage), by only saving image thumbnails and the ULR for the image. Currently, over 14 million images have been indexed. Finally, a subset of ImageNet (688,000 images) has been extended to support attributes such as `eats_anything` (one of the attributes of bear image), `is_oval` (egg plant), and `made_of_metal` (bicycle) [27, 523].

For research into the visual understanding of scenes, the Scene Understanding (SUN) database [26, 611, 613] provides a relatively complete coverage of images of scenes. In particular, there are 899 categories (397 are relatively well sampled) across 130,519 images. In this work, a "scene" is defined as "a place where humans can act within, or a place to which a human being could navigate." Hence, it is similar in spirit to ImageNet, but the context is quite different due to the difference in selection criterion.

In the case of video, the Mind's Eye year one video dataset [15] consists of thousands of clips produced with the intent of enacting 1 of 48 verbs. However, the best verb for each clip is not necessarily the one intended, and hence the data set comes with additional annotations from crowdsourcing using Amazon Mechanical Turk (AMT) [3].

3.3   VISUAL DATA WITH A SINGLE SUBJECTIVE LABEL

Orthogonal to the largely physically based image labels just discussed, there are datasets that provide characterizations of emotional responses to images. As discussed in §2.3.1, this meaning space is typically about the image taken as a whole, and so labels at the image level make sense. An early dataset used for this task is the International Affective Picture System (IAPS) [10, 349, 418], already introduced (§2.3.1). Here, valence-arousal-control (VAC) (§2.3.1) is available for 700 images [94, 349], and discrete emotion category data is available for 390 images [418]. The discrete category data targets positive and negative valance, but excludes images close to neutral. The set of negative emotion labels were fear, sadness, and disgust, and the positive emotion labels were awe, excitement, contentment, and amusement. Importantly, the IAPS system is grounded in physical response [350], and many subsequent studies have linked viewing of IAPS images to multiple modalities including electromyography [71], degree of startle response [52], and electroencephalogram (EEG) [290]. The IAPS has inspired a second dataset along the same lines, namely the Geneva affective picture database (GAPED) [157, 158], which addresses some issues with the IAPS dataset, and provides alternatives for experiments where unfamiliar images are better and the anticipated participants are likely to be familiar with the IAPS images.

Emotion induction in movies has been studied by Gross and Levinson [253] and Philippot [468], but the datasets studied are small and not conveniently available. However, the recently developed DEAP dataset [327, 328] provides ratings, physiological signals, and videotaped faces of participants while they watched 40 movie clips. Exchanging quantity for detail, large scale annotation of data is now available either implicitly through tagging, or explicitly through crowd sourcing (e.g., Amazon Mechanical Turk [3]). Notably the Liris ACCEDE dataset [72–74] has valance annotations for 9800 video clips. However, the lack of grounding in psychology in such datasets make the semantics of the emotion words less clear as discussed previously (§2.3.1).

For more general sentiment estimation, Borth et al. [91] used both tag analysis and crowd sourcing to create the Visual Sentiment Ontology dataset [28]. Finally, Murray et al. [438, 439] constructed a large database for aesthetic visual analysis (AVA) from the tags and peer votes on photo-sharing sites.

3.4   VISUAL DATA WITH KEYWORDS OR OBJECT LABELS

Early work linking text and image features relied substantially on the Corel^{TM} dataset. This was a commercially produced dataset hundreds of groups of 100 images (originally distributed on CDs with one group per CD), each taken by professional photographer. The images have been distributed in a variety of sub-collections, and images have 3–5 keywords.[1] Now that researchers have a much greater choice in datasets, the Corel^{TM} data has lost favor because it is not open

---

[1]The images all have distinct numbers, and seem to be consistent across the various sub-sets. In one version there are images from 392 CDs, and each image has a short title as well as 3–5 keywords. The title text could be used as in addition to the keywords, but in general, researchers stick to the keywords. There is also a version with 592 CDs which partly overlaps the one with one with 392 CDs and more than 800 CDs in total is mentioned in [434].

and is no longer available.[2] Further, the data has been criticized for being too amenable to simple approaches for image annotation.[3] Nonetheless, it was one of the first large-scale loosely labeled data for learning to link image features to words. Examples of images from this dataset can be found in Figures 1.4, 1.6a,b, and 1.7.

The task of providing keywords for images has been integrated into the on-line ESP "game with a purpose" [584]. Here players are paired with an anonymous collaborator. They both guess an appropriate word for the image, and they are successful when they agree. The game then moves onto another image. While, as described, the output is only one word for an image, the image can be reused, and, in this case previously found words are "taboo." Some of the data collected using ESP is readily available on-line [23].

The growing popularity of photo-sharing websites such as Flicker [6], which include infrastructure for tagging images, provides opportunities for very large-scale gathering of images with labels through their API services (e.g., [7]). Many datasets constructed by web search will include photos from photo-sharing sites, but they do not necessarily make use of the tag structure other than to find the images. Datasets that use multiple tags from Flickr to provide loosely labeled data include MIR-FLICKR-2500 [17, 288] with 25,000 images, NUS-WIDE [136] with 269,648 images, and MIR-FLICKR [16, 289] with 1,000,000 images.

Finally, the Aesthetic Visual Analysis (AVA) dataset [439], consists of images pulled from amateur photography sites, and notably includes aesthetic data along with the semantic labels along the lines of the Flicker-based data sets just described. The aesthetic data are the distribution of scores for the image as related to a photographical "challenge" (e.g., "make the sky the subject of your photo this week"). The number of scores ranges from 79 to 549 for each challenge. AVA has over 250,000 images participating in 1,447 challenges. While the scores are from a peer group, they capture some of the variation expected due to the subjective nature of the task. The AVA dataset also includes images from 14 image style categories (e.g., "complementary colors," "motion blur," "silhouettes").

3.4.1 LOCALIZED LABELS

Data sets with multiple objects with bounding contours include various datasets from the pattern analysis, statistical modeling, and computational learning (PASCAL) visual object class (VOC) challenges [18, 200, 201] and the LableMe dataset [11, 493, 494]. The VOC datasets provide bounding boxes and some pixel-level labelings for a large number of images with respect to a modest number (typically 20) of object categories. The image collection procedure emphasized

---

[2]The reproduction rights for the data set are relatively reasonable for academic use, but currently legitimate copies of the data set are only available second hand (e.g., through eBay).

[3]Jiayu et al. [300] analyzed issues with the fact that the Corel™ images come in groups of 100 images, and that often the visual features in the groups are similar. However, this work did not consider holding out CDs as done in [60], or region labeling where localization of the words is required. Muller et al. [434] reported on the range of content-based image retrieval results due to different research groups evaluating on different subsets of the Corel™ data. This is partly due to the images being distributed in various collections, and different research groups have access to different ones.

preventing biases that could be exploited for scoring well on the challenge. The VOC group provides test/train splits and evaluation protocols.

The bounding contours for the LableMe dataset range from simple bounding boxes for small and/or simple objects to relatively tight polygonal contours. Many images have multiple regions labeled, and some labelings are close to a semantic segmentation of the image. Data regarding multiple objects within a scene enables learning and exploiting contextual information—e.g., mice (the computer variety) tend to be found near keyboards. The annotators nominated needed labels, as opposed to having to choose them from a pre-specified list. This resulted in a large number of labels (of the order of 4,000), which have been manually mapped afterward to WordNet terms, which then enables adding additional labels using the WordNet system to add synonyms and hypernyms. For example, user labels such as "seagull" can also be labeled with the superordinate category "animal."

Providing localized image keywords has also been integrated into an on-line game with a purpose (Peekaboom [585]). This game presents image-word pairs found using the ESP game to pairs of participants, who again collaborate anonymously. The goal here is to extract how the word relates to the image, such as which area it occupies. Here one player (boom) knows the word, and tries to have the other player (peek) able to guess the word by exposing parts of the image to them. Once peek guesses the word, the round is complete. The data collected over such interactions can be used to develop localizations for the word within the image. A subset of the data collected using Peekaboom is available on-line [20].

The Microsoft COCO (common objects in context) dataset [13, 377] consists of 328,000 images with all instances of 91 common objects segmented at the pixel level with the appropriate annotations. As the name suggests, it was designed for developing systems to understand objects visually in the context of complex scenes. In addition, each image has five natural language captions, and the website has an interface for caption evaluation.

3.4.2   SEMANTIC SEGMENTATIONS WITH LABELS

A long-standing dataset of images with localized semantics is the Sowerby data set [24, 284] which provides 214 driving-related images which have been segmented into 11 semantic regions (sky, trees, road surface, road border, building, object, road sign, telegraph pole, shadow, car). This has been used to train and evaluate image classifiers [582], and semantic pixel labeling algorithms [272, 273].

Datasets with localized labels have also been created from subsets of the Corel™ data to support evaluation of region labeling methods that were trained on the loosely labeled data. This can be done by using choosing words from the keyword sets for the same machine segmentations used by the algorithms being tested as done by Duygulu et al. [182]. Clearly, this limits the use of the data to the particular circumstance. Another approach is to make use of human curated segmentations of the data (e.g., from [408]), and have annotators choose words from WordNet (§3.1), as done by Barnard et al. [63] with 1,014 images. This way, all pixels, except those that are part of very small semantic regions, are labeled correctly with sense-disambiguated words. He et al. [272] also labeled 100 Corel^{TM} images from arctic and African wildlife scenes for training and testing their pixel-labeling approach (§6.6.7).

A key dataset for work in semantic pixel labeling using supervised methods (§6.6) is the Microsoft research Cambridge (MSRC) dataset [14, 520]. The dataset provides 591 images (240 in version one) segmented at the pixel level into regions for 23 categories (9 in version one). The dataset many regions for each category (compared with [63]), and diverse categories (compared with [272]), which makes it especially suitable for supervised approaches.

Recently, significantly larger datasets along these lines have become available. First, 16,873 images from the SUN dataset [26, 611, 613] have been fully annotated at the pixel level. While labeling simple images is conceptually easy, labeling complex scenes such as depicted in many SUN images has significant challenges which are aptly described by Barriuso and Torralba [70]. Second, the Lotus Hill Institute image database [12, 629, 630] provides images and video frames that are annotated hierarchically. Specifically, scene type is at the top level, then scenes contains objects within, and objects might be broken down further into parts (e.g., a car might have wheels, windshield, and license plate labeled as well). The number of annotated still images is in the tens of thousands. Finally, the PASCAL-context dataset [19, 433] has 10,103 training images from the PASCAL VOC 2010 challenge which are semantically segmented at the pixel level and labeled with one of 540 categories. Like LableMe [11, 493, 494], the annotators could add categories. However, unlike many recent datasets which rely on Amazon Mechanical Turk [3], the research team directly provided the annotations. The data collection protocol was thus designed for high-quality extensive labeling.

3.5   VISUAL DATA WITH DESCRIPTIONS

It is possible to collect a large number of news photos with captions from sources such Associated Press and Reuters. For example, Edwards et al. [189] reported collecting from 800 to 1500 such documents every day from these two sources. While the photographs can be of almost anything that is newsworthy, they are mostly of people. The format of the captions is relatively structured. Edwards et al. [189] reported that captions average only 55 words and generally begin by identifying people in the image followed by the activity depicted, and then optionally followed by additional context. Work using this kind of data is described in §7.1.1 and §7.1.2.

A comprehensive data set for evaluating algorithms linking images to words is the segmented and annotated IARP (SAIARP) TC-12 data set [196, 197] which has 20,000 natural images. The images have descriptions in up to three languages (English, German, and Spanish), as well as semantic segmentations with labels.[4] Hence, this dataset can be used for research into

---

[4]The SAIAPR TC-12 data set is an extension of the IAPR TC-12 data set [254, 255] which provided the natural language descriptions but not the segmentations and their labels.

image annotation, region labeling, and making use of free form captions.[5] Figure 3.1 provides an example of the kind of data available.

Figure 3.1: An example of a pedantic caption for an image that has been manually segmented. The spatial location of some of the caption words is indicated. Notice, however, that there are many complexities. The girl's face is labeled as girl, but one can easily consider the clothing as part of the girl. In other words, there is typically overlap in the spatial extent of visual information corresponding to associated caption words. This example is taken from the SAIARP TC-12 data set [196, 197] which provides both free text image descriptions and semantic segmentation with labels.

Interest in providing full captions for images (§8.1) has driven the construction of a number databases for this purpose. Multiple captions are available for a portion of the PASCAL dataset [203, 204, 480] and the Flickr 8K dataset [481] and Flickr 30K dataset [638]. The Stony Brook University (SBU) captioned photo dataset [449, 450] consists of URLs for 1 million images from Flickr with captions that were minimally screened to be descriptive (e.g., of sufficient length, containing at least one spatial preposition). Kong et al. [333] provided captions and noun-object alignments for the NYU Depth Dataset V2 (1449 densely labeled pairs of aligned RGB and depth images of indoor scenes) [524, 525]. Finally, as already mentioned, the Microsoft COCO dataset [13, 377] has five natural language captions for each of its images.

In the case of video, the Microsoft research video description corpus [124, 125] provides about 120,000 sentences for more than 2,000 video snippets that were composed by AMT workers. In the particular domain of cooking, the YouCook dataset [160, 614] provides detailed annotations for 88 YouTube videos showing people cooking. In the domain of movies, Rohrbach

---

[5]For some images there is some inconsistency between the descriptive text and the label words.

et al. created the MPII Movie Description dataset (MPII-MD) [486, 487]. This leverages descriptions of movies created for the visually impaired, which are very appropriate for the task of automated video captioning. The data set provides 68,000 sentences aligned with video snippets from 94 movies.

3.6   IMAGE DATA WITH QUESTIONS AND ANSWERS

The recent interest in automatically answering questions about images (§8.4) has driven the creation of datasets for training and evaluating on this task. Malinowski and Fritz created DAQUAR (DAtaset for QUestion Answering on Real-world images) [396, 397] that provides questions and answers for the NYU Depth Dataset V2 [524, 525]. The VQA (Visual Question Answer) data set [39, 40] provides questions and answers for both the Microsoft COCO dataset [13, 377] and images created from clip art to enable VQA research without low-level vision issues. Finally, the visual madlibs dataset [642, 643] provides fill-in-the-blanks questions and answers for a large number of images.

CHAPTER 4

Extracting and Representing Visual Information

This chapter covers methods for representing visual information so that it captures semantic content. Relevant semantic content has a range of spatial scope. For example, semantics can pertain to the entire scene (e.g., birthday, sunset, frightening), objects within (cars, people, dogs), parts of objects, backgrounds (e.g., sky, water), and even spatial relations between objects or backgrounds. Given appropriate localization, the appearance of objects or backgrounds provides further semantics. Notice that spatial arrangement carries significant meaning, and that even simple co-occurrence (e.g., perhaps the scene has people and cars) carries meaning. By contrast, a single pixel or region does not tell us much about what was in front of the camera when the picture was taken. In short, for many tasks, our representations need to support localization and context.

Research in computer vision and related fields has provided many methods for extracting visual information indicative of semantic entities and attributes at disparate levels of abstraction. In general, structure and regularity in the world leads to corresponding structure and regularity in captured images. For example, an object with a component made of a particular material with a specific color and texture will typically yield a region in the image with multiple image pixels that can be grouped together as likely semantically related because of their shared appearance. Further, the boundary of the component will often be associated with an observable spatial change in the image because the appearance of the component is likely to be different from that of the background. To the extent that such intermediate representations can be reliably extracted, they will be more compact and more informative than the raw data (i.e., pixels). If components could be assembled into groups associated with an object category, then the representation would be yet again more compact and informative. In particular, the agglomeration of data from the grouped pieces provides more discriminative information about what the object is. This can be combined with data from the spatial configuration of the pieces—which one is connected to which—for additional discriminative power.

Similarly, aggregating image pixels into regions corresponding to semantically relevant backgrounds (e.g., sky, forested mounted side), leads to more compact and semantically relevant descriptions. If the pixels can be grouped, then the data can work together to exclude distracting noise effects, understand the appearance of the region as texture, and extract size, shape, and boundary information. Further, effective grouping provides semantically specific relationships between regions and objects. For example, we can represent that a region that is potentially part of a mountain is bordered by region that might be sky.

Inferring the semantics of a scene is generally assumed to benefit from both bottom-up and top-down processing. In a strict *bottom-up* paradigm, evidence from raw data (e.g., pixels) is aggregated locally to provide mid-level representations (e.g., regions), when are then used as the basis for inferring even higher levels of representation (e.g., objects and backgrounds). This protocol will often fail because the task is fundamentally ambiguous. Hence, integrating *top-down* information, such as global information (e.g., context) or information about the world in general, will often lead to a better answer. For example, as objects are identified with reasonable certainty, this can resolve ambiguity in grouping. As a second example, low-level processing might be used to determine scene type (e.g., indoor scene with people), but scene type can then further inform details of the specific instance. In the extreme, we might imagine dispensing with bottom-up processing altogether, and simply look for evidence for hypotheses. However, even if this were possible, bottom-up processing is normally needed to keep the overall process computationally tractable. In general, interaction between the two kinds of processing is warranted.

The set of methods for extracting meaningful structure from images and video is vast and continuously growing.[1] In what follows I discuss basic tools available for creating initial representations of visual data that are commonly used in linking language and vision. I also include object recognition (briefly), as methods for linking vision and language (e.g., [166, 222, 338, 339, 632]) have also made use of the significant recent progress in this area of computer vision. I begin with extracting low-level features including color (§4.1.1), edges (§4.1.2), texture (§4.1.3), and histograms of oriented gradients (§4.1.4). We then consider mid-level representations including regions of constant appearance (§4.2, §4.3). We then consider representing images as whole (§4.4) and detecting objects (§4.5).

4.1   LOW-LEVEL FEATURES

Raw image data consists of a spatial array of values indicative of sensor responses from one or more channels—e.g., three channels for a standard color camera. Bottom-up processing can extract low-level feature information such as edge strengths, edge directions, corner locations, and texture signatures. Color and texture can be used to group together pixels into regions of similar color and texture, providing convenient building blocks for assembling semantic patterns. First, we consider features defined at or around a single pixel.

4.1.1   COLOR

At the level of pixels, the only information available is the color (e.g., RGB or gray level). Here we will assume RGB from a common color camera. While three sensors provide an economical way to capture a large fraction of what the human vision system can see, having only three sensors

---

[1]Textbooks for computer vision include Forsyth and Ponce [232] (closest to the discussions in this book), Szeliski [542], and Shapiro and Stockman [516].

looses a significant amount of information about the light that was present when the picture was taken. Further, the mapping from the light energy to RGB is a function of the physical camera, the camera settings, and, for many images on the Internet, unknown post processing. Without information to the contrary, the best assumption is that the RGB values are from the standard sRGB space [29, 35, 478, 538]. In particular, this means that the sRGB values are not linear, having an associated gamma of 2.2. Finally, because RGB values are correlated through overall brightness, it is common to map the sRGB values into a different color space that decorrelates the three dimensions, with the perceptually oriented L*a*b color space being a common choice.[2] A second common choice is to linearize the sRGB to RGB, and define $S = R + G + B, r = R/S$, and $g = G/S$.

A non-trivial issue with color in general is that the RGB captured by the camera is confounded by the illumination—a red patch might be white sand under the reddish light from a sunset. In some cases it might be appropriate to preprocess the images to reduce this confound using a *color constancy* algorithm.[3] However, most work on linking visual and linguistic information makes the reasonable simplifying assumption that images are taken with appropriate color balance.

4.1.2   EDGES

Most of the information content in images is captured by changes in the signal (e.g., either brightness or color). Edge points linked into longer contours can be indicative of object boundaries, or material changes within objects, or changes in background. There is a significant literature developing a number of ways of extracting edge points and contours in the face of inherent difficulties that include noisy data, significant variation in the strength of edges of interest, and ill-defined behavior at corners. A typical edge detector for gray-scale images (e.g., [104], [232, §5.2.1]), applies smoothing at a chosen scale, then estimates the gradient, and then applies some form of thresholding and linking of candidate edge locations. For what follows, edges are helpful for creating regions (§4.2) and constructing descriptors of neighborhoods around locations (§4.1.4), although those methods typically use the raw gradients rather than the linking, which is part of standard edge detection.

4.1.3   TEXTURE

Texture captured in images is a function of the scale associated with the perspective projection—leaves, trees, and forests can exhibit different texture, even though the source of the light is the same in the three cases. Further, since texture captures local patterns, it requires spatial extent to be meaningful. Hence, texture associated with a pixel necessarily incorporates information from pixels around it, with the extent of influence being a tunable parameter.

---

[2]An alternative reason often given is that since the human vision system is so effective, working in a color space that is closer to the one we use is likely to be advantageous.
[3]There is a large literature on color constancy. Some basic algorithms are described and referenced in [58, 65].

A typical approach [395] used in much of the work cited in this book begins by computing the response of the image at each pixel to a set of localized filters that respond, for example, to edges of various widths and angles, and bright/dark regions surrounded by dark/bright regions at various scales (see [395, Figure 4] or [232, Figure 6.4]). The vector of filter responses can be used as a texture descriptor, and we can capture the texture in a predefined region by averaging the vectors over the region (e.g., as done in [60, 61, 64, 182]). However, because the number of filters is relatively large (e.g., 40), the resulting feature vector for each pixel has a relatively large number of correlated dimensions. Further, only part of this space is represented in our data. Hence, we might cluster these feature vectors to get discrete elements of texture (*textons* [307, 395]). One can think of an example texton as being like a polka dot of a given size. Texture can then be defined in a window around the pixel by the occurrence (histogram) of textons. This histogram provides a pixel anchored feature vector which encompasses significant information from nearby pixels, which can be used as a segmentation cue with the distance between texton histograms being computer by the χ^2 test[4] as done by Malik et al. [395]. Notice that the texture descriptor, and measures to compare them (if any) when used in segmentation, is logically distinct from whatever measures we use to aggregate texture information for the resulting regions (see §4.3 for further discussion), and often texture is handled differently in these two parts of standard pre-processing pipelines.[5]

4.1.4   CHARACTERIZING NEIGHBORHOODS USING HISTOGRAMS OF ORIENTED GRADIENTS

Effective methods for characterizing the spatial distribution of edges have had significant impact on many standard computer vision tasks. There are two broad schools of thought (or categories of tasks) on defining which neighborhoods to characterize—sparse, and dense, which are commonly associated with SIFT (scale invariance feature transform) [315, 387, 419] and HOG (histograms of oriented gradients) [156]. Sparse methods define neighborhoods around distinct and localizable points (interest points or keypoints), and, at least in the canonical case of SIFT, the neighborhoods are designed to be scale covariant (if the image size doubles, so does the neighborhood of the interest point). Dense methods define neighborhoods that cover the image or detection window.[6] In the canonical case of HOG as defined by Dalal and Triggs [156], neighborhoods are overlapping grid blocks. Defining neighborhoods and characterizing them are logically distinct,

---

[4]For histograms h_1 and h_2, $\chi^2 = \frac{1}{2} \sum_{k=1}^{K} \frac{(h_1(k) - h_2(k))^2}{h_1(k) + h_2(k)}$ (from [395]; see also [474]).

[5]For example, Barnard et al. [60] segmented images along the lines of Malik et al. [395], with the texture cue (one of three cues) relying on textons. However, they represented regions by feature vectors that were concatenations of values from multiple feature types, and the features for texture were averages and standard deviations of filter responses. They used a modest subset of the filters used for segmentation for region characterization.

[6]The use of the terms sparse and dense can be confusing because often images have many keypoints with highly overlapping neighborhoods—in this context sparse refers to selective samples, but not necessarily few of them.

and it is possible to independently use methods developed for each task, although the SIFT and HOG combinations both work well for particular sets of tasks.

Defining scale invariant keypoints with canonical orientation.   The SIFT approach [387] for finding keypoints is based on the scale space representation [329, 379, 604] of an image which considers many convolutions of the same image with Gaussian kernels of increasing standard deviation parameter, σ, leading to increasingly smoothed images. Images at successive scales are then subtracted to produce a different of Gaussian (DOG) function, $D(x, y, \sigma)$. Keypoint candidates are proposed as extrema, $(\hat{x}, \hat{y}, \hat{\sigma})$, of $D(x, y, \sigma)$. This approach naturally provides scale invariance of the location $(\hat{x}, \hat{y})$, as well as a specific scale, $\hat{\sigma}$, for the point. A second important step is to exclude edges that are essentially unidirectional. In other words, a corner makes a good keypoint, but a keypoint on a single strong edge would be arbitrary—a similar point can be found nearby, depending on noise and other irrelevant factors. This is implemented by considering the ratio of the eigenvalues of the 2×2 Hessian matrix of $D(x, y, \sigma)$ evaluated at $(\hat{x}, \hat{y})$. If a keypoint passes this test, then a circular neighborhood for the keypoint is constructed of radius $\hat{\sigma}$. Finally, an orientation for the keypoint neighborhood is established based on the dominant edge direction of the neighborhood, which is defined as the peak in the histogram angles for edge points in the neighborhood. If there are multiple good peaks, multiple keypoints with differing orientations are output.

Scale and rotation invariant histograms of gradients.   Given a location and scale, $\hat{\sigma}$, the SIFT descriptor [387] is constructed as follows. First, an orientation for the keypoint neighborhood is established based on the dominant edge direction of the neighborhood, which is defined as the peak in the histogram angles for edge points in the neighborhood. If there are multiple good peaks, multiple descriptors with differing orientations are output. The histogram of edges that comprises the descriptor is computed using the coordinate system implied by the orientation, which makes the histogram invariant to rotation of the image. The descriptor itself is a concatenation of 16 histograms for a 4×4 grid block with respect to the coordinate system. Each of these histograms counts the number of edges in the grid block quantized into 8 values. Hence, the overall descriptor is 128 dimensions. Fortunately, software for computing both keypoint locations and the descriptor is available on-line [386, 574].

The HOG region descriptor.   The HOG descriptor defined by Dalal and Triggs [156] is similar to the SIFT descriptor. A key difference already mentioned is that in common practice neighborhoods are grid blocks. The descriptor is not intended to be either scale or orientation invariant. Rather, in the inaugural application of detecting pedestrians, the detector is applied at multiple scales. Further, given upright images, pedestrians are all aligned roughly the same way. To compute the HOG descriptor for a grid block, the gradient strengths are normalized over the block (reported as important). Each block itself is composed of a grid of cells. Like SIFT, the descriptor itself is the concatenation of histograms of orientations computed for each cell. In the pedestrian detection application, each detection window is broken into overlapping grid blocks, which are concatenated to give a final feature vector for classification.

4.2 SEGMENTATION FOR LOW-LEVEL SPATIAL GROUPING

Grouping adjacent pixels with similar appearance together into contiguous regions is a natural first step in many image analysis pipelines, and is a common part of computational systems for linking vision and language. This has the immediate advantage of reducing computational complexity, as images with hundreds of thousands of pixels can be represented by a much more modest number of regions. In addition, regions begin to define boundaries, provide units for texture, provide averaged feature quantities (thereby reducing noise), and also provide the variance of feature quantities, which can be informative. In short, because spatially contiguous objects and backgrounds play a major role in determining semantics, adjacency can be very helpful for aggregating features for intermediate representations.

Researchers interested in region-based representations can leverage a very large body of work on low-level image segmentation, and several good software implementations are available (e.g., [45, 143, 212]). Segmentation methods typically combine choices of cues (e.g., color, texture, contours) and how to combine them with choices of inference (e.g., normalized cuts [518]). Further, hierarchal or overlapping segmentations can be provided. Finally, parameters can adjust the degree to which segments are large (optimistic) or small (conservative).

Given that users of segmentation tools inherit many of the possible choices as a package, low-level segmentation methods used in work on computationally linking vision and language fall into three broad, overlapping categories. For relatively large segments, methods that integrate color, texture, edge strength, and contour information can group together pixels somewhat semantically, although semantically coherent but distinctly different pixels (e.g., pixels from the black and white parts of a penguin) will still need to be merged by higher level processing. Methods commonly considered for optimistic segmentation in the context of linking vision to language include [44, 112, 378, 395, 407]. Second, many researchers have used super-pixels which are regions of coherent color and texture that are purposely defined conservatively. In other words, the variation in appearance across a super-pixel is kept small. The super-pixel approach has some attraction when the rest of the method is designed to group regions based on higher-level information. Methods commonly used for super-pixel segmentations include [143, 212]. Finally, some researchers dispense with segmentation altogether and simply use a grid to divide up the image, often with overlapping cells (e.g., [107, 272]).

4.3 REPRESENTATION OF REGIONS AND PATCHES

Strategies for representing region appearance are influenced by the obvious assumption that they are relatively uniform in appearance due to segmentation criteria. Hence, region color and texture is typically computed by averaging values across the region. However, if texture is considered as a histogram of textons during segmentation, re-computing the histograms once region boundaries are established makes sense. We can add geometric properties to region representation, such as size, position, and shape descriptors (e.g., convexity and roundness).[7]

4.3.1   VISUAL WORD REPRESENTATIONS

It is common to further distill the data by clustering the feature vectors found in the training portion of the data. Then each region is associated with a discrete token [182] (sometimes referred to as a visual word, or visterm). This makes visual representation immediately amenable to algorithms initially developed for language. This quantization process is also often used with patches[8] around keypoints (e.g., [151, 316, 536]). Notably, Cao and Fei-Fei [105] integrated region appearance visual words, with keypoint visual words to an advantage. Notice that texture representations for segmentation are somewhat different than (say) the SIFT descriptor, which also has different spatial scope. This speaks against tying the two representation together at a low-level, and Cao and Fei-Fei [105] instead used the two representations as difference sources of evidence for a higher level of abstraction.

4.4   MID-LEVEL REPRESENTATIONS FOR IMAGES

Simple methods for classifying images by scene types (e.g., indoor, sunset) typically aggregate local features using histograms (e.g., color histograms). This can be extended to many features by concatenating histogram vectors. However, spatial co-occurrences of feature types cannot be captured without using a multidimensional histogram space, which is not feasible for more than a few dimensions. Instead, histograms of the tokenized representation just discussed (§4.3.1) provides the feasible (and popular) bag of visterms (BoV) (or just bag of words (BoW)) representation (e.g., [475]). Here "bag" reminds us that spatial relationships between the quantized features are ignored.

4.4.1   ARTIFICIAL NEURAL NETWORK REPRESENTATIONS

The BoW representation is relatively powerful and simple, but spatial structure is lost. Further, the heuristics to compute them are not necessarily grounded in any particular task, although it is common to tune options such as the number of clusters for better performance. An alternative, which is rapidly becoming the preferred method for many vision tasks, is convolutional neural networks (CNNs) [79, 239, 297, 336, 353–355, 527]. As in artificial neural networks (ANNs) in general,[9] these consist of artificial neurons with inputs from the data or other neurons, and

---

[7]It is less clear if detailed shape is helpful, and it has not been studied in depth. Possible detailed representations of region shape include a Fourier representation of the boundary, or shape context [76] computed from the boundary and interior edges.

[8]Here "patches" is meant to suggest spatially contiguous parts of images that often overlap, where regions are usually associated with a partitioning of the image. This is consistent with many papers, although almost surely not all of them.

[9]There are many sources for the basics of artificial neural networks including standard pattern recognition texts, e.g., [87, Chapter 5], [181, Chapter 6], and [11, Chapter 11]. For recent developments, see, for example, [78, 79, 275, 336, 463].

outputs going to other neurons or classification outputs. The neurons in each layer compute a response based on a weighted sum (i.e., a linear function) of the neurons feeding into it, followed by nonlinear transformation (activation function).[10] CNNs are feed-forward networks with multiple convolutional layers, followed by a handful of fully connected layers, with the activations of the last layer providing strengths of beliefs for each category. The convolutional layers maintain the spatial organization of the input image, and each neuron takes input from a local subset of the previous layer (or the image in the first layer). Importantly, the weights are shared by all neurons in the layer, which implements a convolution kernel, and makes the response of the network to a stimulus translationally covariant (i.e., a shift of the stimulus leads to an analogous shift in the response). Typically, as one goes up the levels in a CNN, the representation of the image becomes more semantic and less localized, culminating in a single non-localized output layer in the space of categories. All weights of the neurons are set based on the categories of training examples using (typically) variants on back-propagation.[11] A key observation is that the middle layers of the network can provide image representations for other purposes, as features learned for the classification task can be good ones for general image understanding.

Convolutional neural networks have impacted computationally integrating vision and language in several ways. First, they have lead to object detectors with impressive performance that can be used to an advantage (e.g., [312]). Second, the network hidden layers provide useful mid-level representations, often in conjunction with a second network for learning to generate text (e.g., [179, 578, 617]) or answer questions (e.g., [40, 235, 483]). Here, the CNN is typically trained on a classification task such as image categorization (e.g., using networks such as [313, 336] on a subset of ImageNet [492]), which makes the mid-layer representation effective, and a mid-level convolutional layer is used for image representation. Finally, they can be trained simultaneously (end-to-end) with connected recurrent neural networks (RNN) for associated text (e.g., [179, 577]). For end-to-end training it is common to pre-train the CNNs on image categorization, and then further optimize the combined network on the joint visual-text task.

4.5   OBJECT CATEGORY RECOGNITION AND DETECTION

As objects are key players in semantics, the extensive body or work on recognizing objects in images is relevant to integrating vision and language. For this task, *object category recognition* is most important (e.g., recognizing cars in general as compared with looking for your own car). Significantly, due to the development of sophisticated discriminative machine learning methods, and the ever-increasing availability of training data, methods for linking vision and lan-

---

[10]Common choices for the activation function f as a function of the input x include the log sigmoid where $f(x) = (1 + e^{-x})^{-1}$, hyperbolic tangent where $f(x) = (e^x - e^{-x}) / (e^x + e^{-x})$, or even a simple thresholding at zero where $f(x) = \max(0, x)$ [440].

[11]See references listed in footnote 9 for standard methods for training neural networks and recent advances.

guage can now include high-level evidence from object category detectors for a relatively large number of object categories. Most state-of-the art object detectors are based on variations of CNNs [239, 514, 541]. Building object detectors for complex images in the spirit of using CNNs to classify images of a single concept adds the complexity of having to choose the location and size of the objection region. This can be achieved simply by sliding windows of multiple scales as done in early work on specific detection tasks, or using methods that propose good object region hypothesis [239], or using the final layers of the network for regression estimation of bounding box coordinates [514, 541]. Regardless, most object detection methods only provide bounding boxes around the object, and the detections tend to be noisy as the problem is inherently difficult.[12] When used for joint understanding of images and text, detections are generally integrated with other sources of evidence including region boundaries and appearance [166], context [222, 632], and as part of models that co-train on image and caption data [312].

---

[12]Difficulties include: (1) significant variation across features from examples within categories making establishing category boundaries difficult; (2) variations in pose—even when the structure is similar, each image of the object examples can be from a different angle; (3) background features (clutter) pollute the learned representation, and generally needs to be identified as not relevant through integrating multiple examples; and (4) alternatively, background features associated with typical context of the object can mistakenly emerge as key features for the object, leading to a detector which can exploit context, but can also be mislead by it.

CHAPTER 5

Text and Speech Processing

Linguistic representations associated with visual data are available in the form of single labels for scene type (§3.2) or image or video affect (§3.3), tags and keywords (largely concrete nouns) for images (§3.4) and video frames, natural language captions for images (§3.5), text found near images in multimodal documents (e.g., Wikipedia pages), closed captioning for audio-video data available as a text stream (§5.1), text extracted from the speech signal in audio-video data using automatic speech recognition (ASR) (§5.1), and text embedded in images and video such as street signs or bill-board text in images, informative titles inserted into broadcast news, or even embedded text from closed captioning, when the text stream version is not available (§5.2). These sources vary with respect to overall complexity, prevalence of errors, and number of irrelevant words. We can improve representations of the semantics in linguistic data using conventions about language structure, information from lexical resources (§5.5), and context from world knowledge in general. Even in the case of images with keywords, pre-processing can be used to remove less useful words, flag proper nouns, identify redundant or highly correlated words (e.g., the keywords "tiger" and "cat" often refer to the same image entities), and link visual representations based on semantic connections (e.g., we can posit that characteristics of "tiger" and "leopard" be shared if we can lookup the fact that they are closely related animals).

Natural language captions generally contain more information than keywords, but making use of them is more difficult. However, toolkits for implementing a natural language processing pipelines (§5.3) are rapidly improving with respect to features, accuracy, and ease of use. Some simplifications are possible if the text is domain specific, and thus has restricted structure (e.g., news captions (§7.1.1)). If the text has been extracted from multi-modal documents with multiple images, then determining which parts of the text share information with which images will incur additional challenges. In videos, much of the linguistic information comes from what people say, which often has little to do with the physical content of the scenes captured visually (§5.1). Also, if transcripts are produced automatically, then there is generally a great deal of noise. Fortunately, for researchers wanting to focus on the temporal nature of visual semantics without some of these complexities, video data with informative semantics are becoming available. In what follows, we briefly cover extracting text from generic videos with audio (§5.1), work on recognizing text embedded in visual data (§5.2), tools available for language processing (§5.3), word sense disambiguation (§5.4), and integrating information from the WordNet lexical resource (§5.5).

5.1   TEXT ASSOCIATED WITH AUDIOVISUAL DATA

Text encoding the semantics of what is depicted visually in video data is becoming increasingly available from ground truth efforts. However, such data is logically distinct from the language that naturally accompanies much video data in the world such as what is spoken in broadcast news, sports coverage, and movies. In such cases, the language content often has little to do with what is visually available. For example, in broadcast news, the main visual entity is often the anchorperson. In this domain, it is common to consider both modalities together in support of information retrieval (e.g., [267–269, 282, 620]). Similarly, in movies, both modalities might contribute to the narrative in different ways. In both cases, linking linguistic and visual information is more typically in the context of complementary information (§1.1.2) and multimodal disambiguation (§1.2.2).

It is natural to begin by extracting a speech transcript, although sound attributes such as changes in pitch have been considered, largely in the case off inferring affect (e.g., [263, 299, 431, 445, 512, 548, 592, 647]). The speech transcript itself might be available from the text stream for closed captioning, or through manual transcription, or the audio signal can be processed by automatic speech recognition (ASR) software. There are a number of commercial products and open source tools for extracting transcripts from audio signals (e.g., [4, 170, 287, 326, 356, 357, 472, 587, 639]). If the signal is clear, and the system is trained to a particular speaker, or the vocabulary is limited (e.g., numbers or choices in audio driven interfaces), then accuracy can be quite high. However, much work on linking language to video cannot make these assumptions, and the result generally has many errors. From the perspective of providing search terms, it can be argued that noisy text is better than none, as users are accustomed to picking what they want from a list of hits [230]. For video understanding, the negative effects of noise words in transcriptions can be reduced by integrating visual information (also noisy) (e.g., [120, 267, 268]) as well as world knowledge from resources such as WordNet (§5.5).

5.2   TEXT EMBEDDED WITHIN VISUAL DATA

Text appears directly in images and video through captions superimposed during the creation of multimedia content (e.g., hockey team names with scores), scanned text documents, or text occurring in natural scenes (e.g., signs, advertisements, historical markers). Superimposed text in broadcast news and sports coverage is common, and is likely to be related to semantic content that should be exposed to search applications. In addition, the synthetic construction of the text reduces the difficulty of the task (still far from easy). Hence, much early work focused on this case (e.g., [507]). Additional sub-domains of early interest include non-standard scanned document text (e.g., color book covers and advertisements in newspapers) and scene text in restricted domains such as license plates, cargo containers, and CD covers. Jung et al. [308] and Lienhart [375] provided surveys of such early efforts. Most approaches considered follow a pipeline consisting of detecting text in images, extracting appropriate regions for the text (e.g., a bounding box that does not clip too much text) while ensuring temporal consistency (in the case of video), extracting and enhancing the text (often resulting in a binary image with 0 for non text pixels and 1 for text pixels), and then recognizing characters, often using standard optical character recognition software (OCR). This is also followed by Chen and Yuille [130] (see also [605]), who focused on the broad problem of recognizing content in street signs targeted at technology for the visually impaired. They used a boosted classification system to find text regions and then spatially extended them to include likely missed character pixels, followed by adaptive binarization and processing with commercial OCR. They reported reasonable performance which was not possible using OCR alone. More recently, there has been interest in interpreting arbitrary scene text more directly as a computer vision problem, often with additional information provided by lexicons (e.g., [164, 194, 444, 594, 595, 602]). These more general approaches to recognizing text "in the wild" show more promise than adapting commercial OCR software to do so.

5.3   BASIC NATURAL LANGUAGE PROCESSING

With readily available tools it is possible to reduce natural language text passages to forms that are far more amenable for inferring semantics, and thus linking to visual representations. For example, the Stanford CoreNLP toolkit [25, 399] implements a pipeline that can: (1) extract tokens; (2) extract sentences; (3) identify parts of speech (i.e., verbs, adjectives, adverbs, prepositions) as described in Toutanova et al. [562] (see also [96, 142]); (4) map words to their base (dictionary) forms (i.e., lemmatization) so that, for example, plural and singular forms, or past and present tense forms, are normalized to the same token; (5) identify gender; (6) identify named [224, 225] and numeric entities [116]; (7) provide a syntactic parse (using [165, 325]) of each sentence so that the relations between entities is exposed; (8) tag parse sub-trees with sentiment (expressed negative to positive affect) [533]; and (9) provide coreference resolution so that multiple references to the same entity are made explicit (using [358]). Toolkits such as this one (see also [8, 139, 152, 153, 221]) enable relatively sophisticated use of natural language text by researchers who are not expert in natural language processing.

Natural language processing for ungrammatical texts.   Inevitably, researchers will want to link vision to less formal and less grammatical language as this ubiquitous in social media data, which is an extremely fast-growing and rich source of data. Fortunately, natural language processing tools tuned to this source are becoming available. Notably, TweetNLP [86, 238, 334, 454] provides tokenizing, parts of speech tagging, word clustering, and parsing for language found in typical tweets.

5.4   WORD SENSE DISAMBIGUATION

As discussed in §3.1, the same word can often mean multiple semantic concepts depending on context (e.g., financial bank vs. snow bank). Such words are referred to as *polysemous*. The notation for word senses is commonly adopted from WordNet (§3.1). Automatically assigning the correct sense to words in free text—word sense disambiguation (WSD)—is a long-standing problem in natural language processing that has inspired the development of a number of approaches. Given that word senses point more strongly to the underlying semantics than naked words, it seems that using text-based WSD as pre-processing should be helpful for linking vision and language. However, there has been little empirical work verifying this.[1]

Text-based word sense disambiguation methods leverage a variety of cues to estimate the correct sense. The simplest cue is the relative frequency of the senses, and simply using the most common sense, especially together with part-of-speech estimation, does surprisingly well compared to early methods [565]. The next most obvious cue is associated context words. For example, in the case of the word "bank," nearby words related to financial transactions or physical buildings can help push the sense toward financial institution. Going further, Gale et al. [233, 633] proposed exploiting the observation that senses for multiple uses of the same polysemous word in larger units of discourse (e.g., paragraphs) tend to be the same.

Co-occurrences indicative of semantic similarity can be learned from data [311, 416], determined by a semantic distance defined using WordNet [32], both [352], or extracted using Wikipedia [415]. WordNet has also been used to extend the set of words that might indicate semantic concurrence with the nearby target word [137]. Many other variations and improvements are available. (See Miller et al. [424] for an early, commonly used, ground truth data set, Navigli [441] for a survey, and Lee and Ng [360] and Traupman and Wilensky [565] for empirical evaluations. Additional influential work not already mentioned includes [417, 442, 634].)

5.5   ONLINE LEXICAL RESOURCE FOR VISION AND LANGUAGE INTEGRATION

This section covers the use of lexical resources in the integration of vision and language. For the most part, work in this domain has used WordNet, but other potentially useful lexical resources are becoming available, awaiting ingenuity of researchers to find uses for them.[2] Notably, using continuous vectors to represent words has recently become an important tool in natural language processing, and is emerging as a useful tool for vision and language integration as well.

5.5.1   WORDNET

Using WordNet in the construction of datasets has already been discussed (§3.1). To review, the main uses for data set construction discussed were: (1) providing semantics through sense specification and inherited infrastructure for relations between words; (2) integrating data from multiple

---

[1]Barnard et al. [59] used word sense disambiguation as part of a text processing pipeline going from descriptions of museum pieces to keywords, but the efficacy of doing so was not rigorously tested. Russell et al. [494] reported that automatic WSD methods are too noisy for distilling the non-sense-disambiguated input from multiple annotators, which is not surprising as ground truth data should be relatively error free, and automatically improving upon it is a bit risky.
[2]For example, tools for information extraction (IE) are able to infer relations from natural language such as place of birth.

annotators; and (3) providing a semantic structure for choosing images with good semantic coverage for a given domain.

Evaluation.   WordNet has been used in evaluating annotation systems as it makes it possible to compare a broader set of annotation words to ground truth data. For example, suppose an annotation system correctly provides the word "cat" for a tiger region in an image. Clearly, the more specific word, "tiger," would be better, but "cat" or even "animal" is technically correct. To properly score annotation words, we could consider them correct if their synset contains the ground truth word below them in a hierarchy, but this would make it advantageous for systems to use non-specific words (e.g., animal, or even physical entity). To properly account for the tradeoff, we could score annotations words in the correct WordNet branch in proportion to how common the ground truth word is relative to the superset of entities represented by the annotation word [63]. For example, if the number of cats in the training data is ten times that of the number of tigers, then the score for "tiger" should be ten times more (if correct). This ensures that there is no advantage in comparative evaluations in naively using WordNet to provide a more general, and thus more likely correct, term.

Semantic similarity.   Perhaps the most common algorithmic use of WordNet is indirectly through supporting semantic similarity measures for pairs of words. Software for six measures based on WordNet is described by Pedersen et al. [464] (see also [99, 573]). It is natural to use a semantic similarity for multimodal clustering, where a number of approaches use a joint distance that includes contributions from both visual features and words. The addresses the issue that the naive distance between two labels is binary (either they are the same or they are different), and that naive distances between sets of labels are thus limited to measures of the degree of overlap. However, semantic similarity functions for word-pairs enable more graded multimodal distance functions. Multimodal clustering with words as one of the modes has been used for multimedia summarization [80], image classification [81], video retrieval [48], generating language for video [617], and grouping scene words for videos [553].

Semantic similarity also has been used for cleaning up output from methods that provide words for images (image auto annotation). In auto annotation, multiple words are typically emitted independently, and thus a set of annotation words can be in conflict, or at least not likely to appear together [302]. The basic idea is that the words in an annotation should be semantically related, and that outliers from this assumption are likely annotation errors. However, as noted by Tousch et al. [561], WordNet does not help with all conflicts among words. They provide the example of "taxi" and "ambulance" being in conflict, but "taxi" and "station wagon" not being in conflict, with the two cases not easily distinguishable using WordNet.

In the case of video, Hoogs et al. [282] used visual descriptions and news topics extracted from transcripts to annotate clips from broadcast news enabling fine-grained search. WordNet is used heavily to integrate the global context and various sources of information into a more consistent and accurate annotation.

Semantics and visualness.   Semantic similarity has also been used to estimate the semantic density of visual datasets, which is found to correlate with the difficulty of distinguishing between the examples using appearance [171]. This corroborates that there is some correlation between visual and semantic distances. However, the relation is often weak. First, two semantically close synsets might be visually quite different. Hence, researchers interested in hierarchies (or networks) that are both semantic and visual combine information from WordNet with visual representation [55, 90, 370]. Second, a WordNet synset might not have inherent visual properties at all. Hence, researchers have also considered estimating visualness of synsets [174, 175, 610] or filtering out abstract ones [497]. Finally, semantic similarity has also been used to segment images through intermediate labels from a learned classifier [281]. This strategy boosts visual dissimilarity when associated estimated labels are semantically dissimilar.

Aggregating output from multiple classifiers.   Similar to aggregating results from multiple human annotators [82, 494, 645], Torralba et al. [560] aggregated results from multiple nearest neighbors to provide a single scene label for highly down-sampled (tiny) images. Here the ground truth labels for the 80 appearance-based nearest neighbors each vote for their labels and the labels of all of their ancestors (i.e., they use all labels above the ground truth label in the tree branch). The aggregated votes can then supply labels at any chosen semantic level.

Creating vocabularies for linking vision and language.   It is relatively common to use WordNet in a preprocessing stage to remove junk or rare words [53], or restrict attention physical concepts only [114, 115, 117, 366, 369, 531], or more specifically to objects [497], or even more specifically to humans [160]. Preprocessing to remove junk or rare words is often combined with expanding word sets from captions or automatic speech recognition (ASR) to include synonyms, hypernyms [183], and meronyms [183].

Bridging internal representations and natural language.   Many applications benefit from constrained internal representations for semantics. These representations might be the result of classifiers trained for disjoint concepts, meta-data annotations from a limited vocabulary, or simply the result of the vocabulary in a particular training data set. WordNet provides for mapping such internal representations to natural language. For example, if index terms are limited, many user queries might come up empty. Hence, semantic similarity has been used to expand text queries for images and video to include semantically similar words. The results from Yan et al. [620] suggest that blindly applying this method in the case of broadcast news reduces retrieval performance. On the other hand, Aytar et al. [48] reported improvement if the query term does not exist in the database. Similar in spirit, Fergus et al. [217] used WordNet for general sharing of labels for visual representations based on semantic similarity. Here a base set of labels and associated features is expanded into features for a much larger labels set. More specifically, feature data for a given label is constructed from that for base labels by using the semantic similarity between the label and the base labels as weights.

Del Pero et al. [166] integrated a modest set of object detectors into a region labeling system trained on aligned data with a large vocabulary. Here, a detector for a general label (e.g., "bird") is assumed to be a useful detector for synonyms and subordinate words (e.g., "sparrow"), assuming some correlation between visual similarity and semantic similarity, especially for synset words and hyponyms. Others have used semantic similarity to choose sentences for captioning images or videos consistent with extracted symbolic representations (e.g., [204, 279, 335], see §8.1.1). Finally, WordNet has been used to map free text to database terms in the context of creating virtual 3D scenes from text [114, 115, 117, 149].

5.5.2   REPRESENTING WORDS BY VECTORS

Semantically similar words occur in similar contexts [427]. Put differently, if two words are semantically similar, then the distributions of words around them tend to be similar. This simple notion has led to a number of methods to encode the distributions into vectors where vector closeness, such as Euclidean distance or cosine similarity, maps into semantic similarity. Many of methods for achieving this have been surveyed by Erk [195], and recently Baroni et al. [68] experimentally compared what they see as the two main approaches: ones based on co-occurrence counts and ones that use neural network representations trained on predictive tasks (e.g., predicting nearby words for each word in a large corpus [420]). They found that the later methods performed significantly better, but this result is somewhat mitigated by subsequent work by Pennington et al. [466] described briefly within the next paragraph.

Ideally, as reported in recent work by Mikolov et al. [420–422], the semantic space can have a semblance of semantic uniformity. To clarify, letting $vec(\bullet)$ map its argument (a word) into the space, Mikolov et al. reported findings such as

$$vec(\text{"king"}) - vec(\text{"man"}) \simeq vec(\text{"queen"}) - vec(\text{"woman"}) \tag{5.1}$$

and

$$vec(\text{"apple"}) - vec(\text{"apples"}) \simeq vec(\text{"car"}) - vec(\text{"cars"}), \tag{5.2}$$

which is surprising, given that the vector representation was not trained on this task. Consequently, Pennington et al. [466] developed an algebraic method (GloVe) for mapping words to vectors motivated by modeling displacements between words being treated symmetrically with words themselves. This led to substantive improvements in tasks such as word analogy tasks (i.e., filling in an answer to A is B as C is to **what**?). Fortunately, for those that want to experiment with modern word vector representations, perhaps in place of WordNet based similarity measures, implementations and trained vectors are available both for neural network based methods [1], and the GloVe system [465]. Vector representations of words have already been used in several efforts on integrating vision and language (e.g., [312, 564, 616]), and increased use seems likely. In addition, similar ideas have recently been developed for sentences [323] which have already been used for aligning books and movies [655].

CHAPTER 6

Modeling Images and Keywords

We are now prepared to study in detail computational methods that focus on the joint modeling of vision and language. Organizing these methods is challenging. The underlying goal—no less than jointly understanding vision and language—is vast, and progress reflects the need for researchers to focus on manageable sub-problems. Historically, one clear trend is increasingly sophisticated language modeling, which is our first organizing principle. This chapter considers image and video data with associated non-ordered collections of keywords, which are invariably nouns. Chapter 7 goes beyond simple keywords, considering proper nouns (§7.1), adjectives and attributes (§7.2), noun-noun relationships (§7.3), and vision helping language (§7.5). Chapter 8 considers sequential structure in language, as exemplified by the application of generating descriptive natural language text for images and video clips (§8.1).

This chapter begins by briefly considering nouns that apply to the entire scene (e.g., birthday), typically categorizing them into disjoint sets of types of scenes (§6.1). Section 6.2 then introduces the natural assumption that most nouns refer to particular elements of the scene (e.g., backgrounds and objects, often referred to as stuff and things [231]). Section 6.3 then develops semantic concepts as generators of both image regions and words. This is followed by instantiations of the translation metaphor (introduced in §1.2.1) where localized visual representations such as region features are translated into linguistics representations (here keywords) (§6.4). Section 6.5 considers how scene types provide context for the expected content (e.g., birthday party scenes typically include kids and often there is a cake with candles). These methods provide a holistic approach to integrating scene type and scene components. Then, going beyond such co-occurrence assumptions, §6.6 considers the spatial arrangement of the content. Finally, §6.7 discusses methods for providing keywords for images without any attempt to localize them.

6.1   SCENE SEMANTIC–KEYWORDS FOR ENTIRE IMAGES

Keywords such as "birthday party," which refer to images as a whole, link the semantics of scenes to language. Hence, they provide high-level linguistic representations. Further, the semantics of scenes also influence the components we expect to find within them, as well as how we might choose to write about them. Hence, combining these two levels of representation makes sense (see §6.5). Here we focus on inferring scene type from image features alone, without explicitly considering components. We exclude related work where the images are of single objects, possibly with some clutter, where the "scene" category is simply the label of the foreground object.[1]

Scene type includes abstract categories such as indoor/outdoor or photo/synthetic [81, 236], more visual categories such as beech scenes, mountain scenes, and sunsets, or geographical land use categories in aerial or satellite images (see [388] for an overview). Much early work considered this as a supervised learning problem where each image in training dataset had one scene oriented label. A common representation for this task is feature vectors consisting of color and/or texture histograms (e.g., [121, 264, 484, 570, 571]). Such distributions of localized appearances ignore global spatial structure. Integrating various kinds of local features can be achieved by concatenating histograms, but the spatial concurrence of the features can be preserved by first grouping multimodal features into discrete appearance categories (visual words, or visterms (§4.3)), and then using the histogram over visual words as the representation (e.g., [475]).

Alternatively, filter responses to the entire image at different orientations and scales or Fourier analysis can represent the image with a large dimensional feature vector [257]. The dimension can be reduced with methods like PCA. An extension is to map this kind of data into a lower dimensional space of perceptual properties such as naturalness, openness, roughness, expansion, and ruggedness [390, 447]. This reduction is often referred to as the image *gist* [559].

To encode the spatial structure of scenes it is common to use features from fixed blocks in order [131, 132, 135, 570, 608], or hierarchically arranged as with the pyramid matching kernel [248, 351]. Others classify the semantics of blocks, and then use the intermediate semantics for image scene classification [515, 543, 583], or use Multiple Instance Learning [34, 177] to learn which regions are helpful [625, 649]. More flexibility with regard to the location and contributions of sub-images can be implemented with topic model approaches (e.g., [69, 93, 209, 324]). Alternatively, integrating image spatial structure through relations between image blocks or overlapping windows has also been shown to be beneficial [135, 365, 608]. Finally, others have combined visual representations with text data (e.g., caption words or non-scene oriented keywords) [81, 236, 262, 456].

6.2   LOCALIZED SEMANTICS–KEYWORDS FOR REGIONS

Consider again the canonical words-and-pictures data shown in Figure 1.8. Specifically, each image is associated with keywords which are typically nouns referring to objects or background textures. Further, the order of the keywords does not matter—this is sometimes referred to as a "bag of words." Finally, the images are divided into regions, which is a convenient way to establish the localization of those objects and backgrounds.

Recall that the words and region features can embody both redundant and complementary information extractable by computer programs. To the extent that the information is redundant, knowing the joint distribution enables us to predict words based on image region features and

---

[1]There are a number of datasets for work on object recognition where the single label refers to the prominent foreground object (e.g., [18, 172, 206]). Examples from the large body of work in this domain include [92, 593, 626].

vice versa. Hence, many of the methods discussed in this chapter are inspired by, or at least can be evaluated by, the task of providing keywords for images that do not have them (auto-annotation), or the task of labeling image regions. To the extent that image region features and keywords reflect complementary information, this supports tasks such as image clustering, search by both image features and keywords, and region labeling when it can be assumed that keywords are also available.

While some of the models consider image regions and keywords symmetrically, there are asymmetries that help explain some of the modelling choices.

- There is generally no information in the order of keyword lists, but image regions have spatial structure, which we can reason about (§6.6). However, word order can play a role when we go beyond keywords (Chapter 7), and even more explicitly when we consider sequential structure (Chapter 8).

- Unless we specifically discretize region features, they are typically represented by continuous values, which naturally support standard measures of closeness between region feature vectors. Distances between words have been proposed (§5.5), but are less often used in this setting. While it might be advantageous to estimate the likelihood that two similar keywords (e.g., "tiger" and "cat") refer to the same part of an image, this is not generally done.

- Human annotators generally provide keywords while they are looking at the images. Hence, a keyword will generally have a representation in the image. However, the converse is not necessarily true. Of course, as we move from keywords to free text, many words will not have any corresponding elements in the visual data.

- Regions from automatic segmentation methods are relatively noisy compared to keywords. While segmentation can provide regions with similar appearance (super-pixels) that are likely to be part of the semantic entity, typically many regions will then be needed to cover each semantic component. Further, since semantic components often have parts with distinctive appearance (e.g., black and white areas of Penguins), low-level segmentation methods will not be able reliably extract a single region for a single keyword.[2] The converse—multiple keywords linking to one region—is less common and more easily addressed (again language tools like WordNet (§5.5.1) can help).

- The previous two points also mean that we generally will have more regions than keywords.

- Most methods have been driven by the task of inferring semantic markers (words) from image data. There has been less effort on the converse task (images for words).

---

[2]The Penguin example shows the danger assuming that our concepts are necessarily natural semantic ones. While an ideal representation for a penguins would include spatial structure (e.g., familiar configuration), relying on simple localized appearance models leave us with concepts that are better described as pieces of penguins. Assembling regions into structure is considered later (§6.6).

6.3   GENERATIVE MODELS WITH INDEPENDENT MULTI-MODAL CONCEPTS

Inspecting the data in Figure 1.8 suggests that entities in the world (e.g., mountain goats) lead to both visual and linguistic data. This further suggests a model where multiple abstract concepts generate data from both modalities. In this section we will make the simplifying assumption that the concepts themselves are generated independently. This assumption is relaxed in §6.5 and 6.6.

6.3.1   NOTATIONAL PRELIMINARIES

In what follows, let c denote one of C concepts. When summing over all C concepts (in contrast to the concepts specific to a given document) we will index them by k (i.e., c_k). Let w denote one of V words. When iterating over all words in the vocabulary (in contrast to the words specific to a given document) we will index them by v (i.e., w_v). Our data has D documents indexed by d. Each document has R_d observed regions, indexed by i, each of which has F features in a feature vector, $\mathbf{r}_{d,i}$. We will denote the collection of R_d region feature vectors by $\mathbf{R}_d$. These regions are associated with a list of concepts, $\mathbf{c}_d$ (in order), each chosen from the entire concept set of size C, with repeats allowed. Each region, i, comes from a single (unknown) concept, which we write as a function of the region index as $c_d(i)$ abbreviated by $c_{d,i}$ when clarity is not lost. Each document also has a set of W_d observed keywords, $\mathbf{w}_d$, indexed by j (i.e., $w_{d,j}$). Alternatively, if we assign keywords to regions, we will index them by i. We will denote the data for each document by $\mathbf{x}_d = \{\mathbf{R}_d, \mathbf{w}_d\}$. Finally, we will often focus on single document, or all documents taken together, and then we will drop the index d from each of the denotations.

6.3.2   SEMANTIC CONCEPTS WITH MULTI-MODEL EVIDENCE

A natural building block for modeling the joint statistics is the directed graphical model[3] shown in Figure 6.1, which is a specific instantiation of the informal representation in Figure 1.9. We assume that there are latent "concepts" such as the notion of a tiger, which are linked to both textual evidence (e.g., keywords such as "tiger" or "cat") and image region features (e.g., orange-stripy texture). Intuitively, concepts are about the world (i.e., what was physically in the scene when the picture was taken), as opposed to being about the data. In this concept model, words and image features are conditional independent given the concept. This means that the only influence between the words and image features is through the concept. Informally, if the concept is known, then knowing the region features provides no further information about likely associated words, and vice versa. Formally, we have:

$$p\left(w \mid \mathbf{r}, c\right) = p\left(w \mid c\right) \qquad \text{and} \qquad p\left(\mathbf{r} \mid w, c\right) = p\left(\mathbf{r} \mid c\right), \tag{6.1}$$

---

[3]Directed graphical models, also called Bayes nets, represent factorizations of probability distributions. There are excellent texts (e.g., [87, 331, 435]) that develop them in detail.

or using the alternative definition of conditional independence,

$$p(w, \mathbf{r}, c) = p(c)\, p(w \,|\, c)\, p(\mathbf{r} \,|\, c).$$ (6.2)

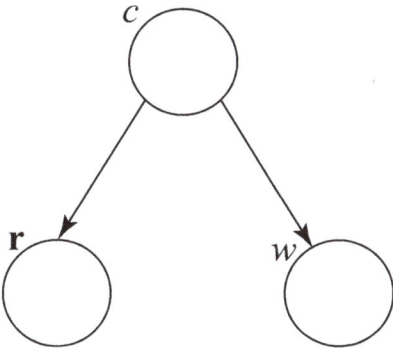

Figure 6.1: Graphical model representation for the joint probability distribution of region features, $\mathbf{r}$, and words, w which forms the building block for more complex models for images with keywords. Circles (nodes) represent random variables are represented as circles, and arrows a node indicate all the variables that the node depends on. So, the above figure is equivalent to $p(w, \mathbf{r}, c) = p(c)p(w|c)p(\mathbf{r}|c)$, i.e., $\mathbf{r}$ and w are conditionally independent given c. From a generative modeling perspective, we first sample c from $p(c)$, and then sample w from $p(w|c)$ and $\mathbf{r}$ from $p(\mathbf{r}|c)$.

The simple directed graph in Figure 6.1 is a generative model for the joint data distribution $p(w, \mathbf{r}, c)$. Intuitively, representative samples from the data set are generated by *ancestral sampling*. Here we sample a concept from the distribution, $p(c)$, and then we sample a word according to the distribution, $p(w \,|\, c)$, and region features from $p(\mathbf{r} \,|\, c)$. Additional word-region feature pairs are generated independently, starting with a new concept sample. Note that each concept is sampled independently, which is overly simple for many purposes. Correlations between concepts are considered in §6.5.

Word emission.   The concept model requires choices for $p(w \,|\, c)$ and $p(\mathbf{r} \,|\, c)$. A common simple choice for $p(w \,|\, c)$ is a *multinomial* distribution where, for each sampled concept c, only one word is chosen. Thus, each word has a probability of being the sole word being emitted, and these probabilities sum to one. The values for $p(w \,|\, c)$ can be stored as a matrix with a row for each concept, with the values for each row summing to one.

A less explored choice is to consider the observed words as the result of a Bernoulli process, as introduced by Feng et al. [213] for word generation conditioned on entire images (see MBRM in §6.7.1). With the Bernoulli approach, the probability of the occurrence of each word is considered independently, and thus occurrence probabilities do not need to sum to one. Feng et al. [213] argued that this is a more appropriate word emission model if the goal is to estimate the probability of a word being relevant, instead of how likely it is to be in a (roughly) fixed length keyword list. While we do not use this approach in the concept based models in this section, the argument is relevant to evaluating whether the multinomial model is best for particular circumstances. Hence, we include it for completeness. Since current uses of Bernoulli approach do not use concepts specifically, I will specify the probability of the observed word as being conditioned on arbitrary variables, indicated by •, instead of concepts. Then the Bernoulli model for the probability of a set of words is given by

$$p(\mathbf{w}\,|\bullet) = \prod_{v \in \mathbf{w}} p(v\,|\bullet) \prod_{v \notin \mathbf{w}} (1 - p(v\,|\bullet)), \quad \text{where} \quad v \in V. \tag{6.3}$$

Region feature emission. A common choice for $p(\mathbf{r}|c)$ is a multivariate normal distribution with diagonal covariance matrix. This simplifies to a product of normals for each feature, and also means that features are conditionally independent given the concept. Formally,

$$p(\mathbf{r}|c) = \prod_{f=1}^{F} \mathcal{N}\left(r_f; \mu_{f,c}, \sigma_{f,c}^2\right), \tag{6.4}$$

where

$$\mathcal{N}\left(r_f; \mu_{f,c}, \sigma_{f,c}^2\right) = \frac{1}{\sigma_{f,c}\sqrt{2\pi}} \exp\left(-\frac{(r_f - \mu_{f,c})^2}{2\sigma_{f,c}^2}\right), \tag{6.5}$$

where r_f is the value of component f of the region feature vector, $\mu_{f,c}$ is the mean specific to feature f and the concept c, and $\sigma_{f,c}^2$ is the variance. While a block diagonal covariance matrix could be used to capture correlations between selected variables (e.g., among color channels), a full covariance matrix generally has too many irrelevant parameters to learn effectively due to significant over-fitting.

An alternative to using a probability density for $p(\mathbf{r}|c)$ is to convert regions into tokens using clustering as introduced in §4.3. Common choices for clustering include K-means or a Gaussian Mixture Model (GMM).[4] Having done so, each region is assigned to a cluster whose identity becomes their token. In the simplest case we consider (§6.4.2), regions become synonymous with the concept c.

6.3.3 JOINT MODELING OF IMAGES AND KEYWORDS (PWRM AND IRCM)

To model multi-region images with keywords, we might be tempted to apply the region concept model (6.2) repeatedly to generate word-region pairs, assuming that differences in the numbers of words and regions is the result of repeats.[5] For example, an image of a horse on grass may be

---

[4]K-means clustering and Gaussian (or normal) mixture models are covered in most pattern analysis texts (e.g., [87, 181, 265]). Additional resources for this topic include the comprehensive book in mixture models by McLachlan and Peel [412] and Carson et al. [111] on using GMMs for segmentation.
[5]This is the base case of the "correspondence" model (C-0) in [60], and evaluated more thoroughly tested in [63].

segmented as three horse regions and one grass region. Then the multiple horse regions would be associated with "horse" which would be generated from a generated concept three times and collapsed into one mention of "horse." Note that this model forces all regions to be linked to word generation, which means that any regions that are not aligned with any keyword can be a significant source of noise.[6] We will refer to this model as the pairwise word region model (PWRM).

The PWRM implicitly assumes that word and region generation is symmetric. However, as already addressed (§6.2), this is often not the case for data like that in Figure 1.8. This is because we assume a noisy segmentation, and segments might not be associated with any word, or the word might require multiple regions (e.g., "penguin"). As also mentioned previously, the converse situation is less likely to be a problem, especially when the text data is a few keywords.

An alternative model,[7] which better respects these asymmetries, assumes that the words are generated from the *collection* of concepts that generate the region features. Here each word is generated independently from one of those concepts. If we assume that the image concepts are equally likely to generate the word, then this is equivalent to generating words according to be average of the distributions over words given each of the concepts associated with the R regions. Formally,

$$p(w \mid \mathbf{c}) = \sum_{i=1}^{R} p(w \mid c_i) p(c_i) = \frac{1}{R} \sum_{i=1}^{R} p(w \mid c_i).$$ (6.6)

Note that multiple regions might be associated with the same concept, and repeated concepts play a larger role in word generation. We illustrate this model using graphical notation in Figure 6.2. We will refer to this model as the image region concept model (IRCM) to emphasize that regions come directly from concepts.

The simplest process to generate multiple words is to independently sample (6.6) until we get the desired number of words, ignoring any duplications. Then

$$p(\mathbf{w} \mid \mathbf{c}) = \prod_{j=1}^{W} p(w_j \mid \mathbf{c}),$$ (6.7)

where $p(w_j \mid \mathbf{c})$ is computed from (6.6).

Aside.   This approach is convenient, but note that the independence assumption has the consequence that the same semantic concept can be consulted multiple times for word emission via $p(w|c)$. This is counter to the intuition that each concept in an image should be linked to single word (assuming some semantic preprocessing to deal with synonyms). Concepts can be consulted multiple times either due to repeated sampling of the same region-concept (6.7), or sampling of different region-concepts that happen to be the same through one sampled via $p(c)$ in (6.6). To

---

[6]This could be addressed by introducing a probability that a concept does not emit any word (or emits a special "NULL" word), as considered in Duygulu et al. [182] for the simple region translation model (RTM) (§6.4.2).
[7]This is the base case of the "dependent" model (D-O) introduced in [61], and further evaluated in [63].

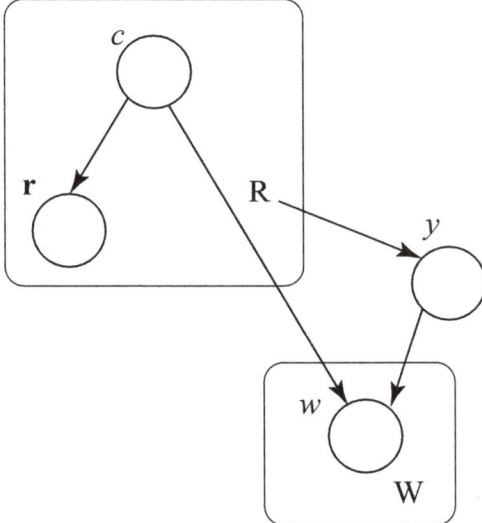

Figure 6.2: A graphical representation for the basic image region concept model (§6.3.3) with multi-nomial distributions for word generation. As in Figure 1.9, concepts are generated from $p(c)$, and then region features, $\mathbf{r}$, are generated according to $p(\mathbf{r}|c)$. Rectangles denote repetition ("plate" notation) and the rectangle around the c and $\mathbf{r}$ nodes indicates that this is repeated R times. Each generated concept can also generate one or more words with probability $1/R$, which necessitates the arrow from R to y. Here y encodes how many times the generated concept also generates a word. This is usually 0 or 1, but if $N_w > N_r$ then one of the values of y needs to be larger than 1. Alternatively, we could ensure that $N_w \leq N_r$ with preprocessing.

see how this might be less than ideal, consider an image with one tiger region, and 19 instances of a generic background region (e.g., savanna) which has many related words (e.g., "grass") and many noise words (e.g., other animals associated with this kind of background). Then, on average, we would have to draw many samples to have our generative model emit "tiger." Notice that this is partly due to the asymmetries listed in §6.2—from the perspective of the annotator, the single tiger region is as important as all the background, which only happens to be 19 regions simply because of the segmentation method used. To mitigate such effects we could merge segments based on their word distribution (§6.6.4), or, more generally, integrate segmentation and region labeling (§6.6).

Regardless of whether we use independent word emission for $p(\mathbf{w}|\mathbf{c})$, the complete joint distribution of image regions, key words, and concepts is given by

$$p\left(\mathbf{c}, \mathbf{w}, \mathbf{R}\right) = p\left(\mathbf{c}\right) p\left(\mathbf{w}\,|\mathbf{c}\right) p\left(\mathbf{R}\,|\mathbf{c}\right), \tag{6.8}$$

where

$$p(\mathbf{c}) = \prod_{i=1}^{R} p(c_i),$$ (6.9)

as concepts are generated independently, and

$$p(\mathbf{R}|\mathbf{c}) = \prod_{i=1}^{R} p(\mathbf{r}_i|c_i).$$ (6.10)

6.3.4   INFERRING IMAGE KEYWORDS AND REGION LABELS

We can use this model to semantically label image regions (region labeling), or provide keywords for the image as a whole (image annotation). In both cases we assume that the image has been segmented and features have been extracted for each region. For region labeling we are interested in the posterior distribution over words for each region, given the features. Words come from concepts, and region features indicate which concepts are likely associated with the region. As we are now describing inference (as opposed to data generation), the concept that generated a given region is unknown, and so we marginalize over all concepts:

$$
\begin{aligned}
p(w|\mathbf{r}) &= \sum_{k=1}^{C} p(w|c_k, \mathbf{r})\, p(c_k|\mathbf{r}) \\
&= \sum_{k=1}^{C} p(w|c_k)\, p(c_k|\mathbf{r}) \quad (\text{as} \quad w \perp \mathbf{r}|c_k),
\end{aligned}
$$ (6.11)

where we compute $p(c_k|\mathbf{r})$ by applying Bayes' rule:

$$p(c_k|\mathbf{r}) = \frac{p(\mathbf{r}|c_k)\, p(c_k)}{\sum_{k'=1}^{C} p(\mathbf{r}|c_{k'})\, p(c_{k'})}.$$ (6.12)

(These two equations are (1.8) and (1.9), respectively, as this model was used as an example in the introduction.) Having computed $p(w|\mathbf{r})$, we can label each region with the word with maximum probability, perhaps omitting ones where there is too much ambiguity as indicated by the maximum probability being relatively low. Indeed, an advantage of this approach is that we have access to the distribution over words to exploit for a variety of subsequent computations.

In order to use the model for image annotation we compute the distribution over words resulting from all image regions together, assuming that words come from regions with equal prior probability by:

$$p(w|\mathbf{R}) = \frac{1}{R} \sum_{i=1}^{R} p(w|\mathbf{r}_i).$$ (6.13)

One can also derive (6.13) directly from the joint model (6.8) (and (6.6)) by marginalizing out all possible concept assignments (see Appendix A.4). Now plugging in the expression for $p(w|\mathbf{r})$ from (6.11) into (6.13) we get

$$p(w|\mathbf{R}) = \frac{1}{R}\sum_{i=1}^{R}\sum_{k=1}^{C} p(w|c_k)\, p(c_k|\mathbf{r}_i), \qquad (6.14)$$

and bringing the sum over R inside we get:

$$p(w|\mathbf{R}) = \sum_{k=1}^{C} p(w|c_k) \underbrace{\left(\frac{1}{R}\sum_{i=1}^{R} p(c_k|\mathbf{r}_i)\right)}_{\substack{\text{image-dependent}\\\text{concept distribution}}} \qquad (6.15)$$

$$= \sum_{k=1}^{C} p(w|c_k)\, p(c_k|\mathbf{R}).$$

The interpretation of the last line is very intuitive. It says that the collection of regions provides a distribution over concepts for the entire image, $p(c_k|\mathbf{R})$, which then provides a weighting over the word probability distributions, $p(w|c_k)$.

From regions to multiple words.   In the usual case where images are associated with multiple keywords, a common simplifying assumption [60, 61, 63] is that the words are generated by independent draws, ignoring duplicates as we go. This is similar to the method (6.7) for generating multiple words assuming the set of concepts, $\mathbf{c}$, is known. So, if the image has W keywords, then:

$$p(\mathbf{w}|\mathbf{R}) = \prod_{j=1}^{W} p(w_j|\mathbf{R}). \qquad (6.16)$$

This can also be derived pedantically by marginalizing over concept assignments similar to how (6.13) is derived from (6.8) and (6.6) in Appendix A.3.

[Aside].   Again, the independence assumption is convenient, but incurs similar approximations and consequences to those discussed previously with respect to (6.7). For example, we might prefer that two different words modeled as coming from the same region due to independent draws in (6.16) would also come from the same underlying latent concept, as we model regions as coming from a single concept. And, in particular, if the concept is only associated with one word, we would have excluded it as a duplicate. However, this is not enforced in this model. Consider a three concept model (dog, cat, grass) and two regions, one which is clearly grass and one which can be confused as to whether it is a dog or cat. Suppose we want two distinct words. This model supports the emission of all pairs of words, including ("dog," "cat"), which, in this example, must come from the same region. If the preference just stated was observed, this would not be a possible annotation.

6.3.5   LEARNING MULTI-MODAL CONCEPT MODELS FROM LOOSELY LABELED DATA

So far we have assumed that the model parameters are available. In the case of the image-concept model, the model parameters are $p(c)$ for all c, $p(w|c)$ for each combination of w and c, and parameters for the region feature models $p(\mathbf{r}|c)$ (e.g., means and variances for normal distributions). Denote the set of all parameters by Θ. To learn these parameters from training data we take an optimization approach where we seek values of the parameters that make the likelihood of the training data as high as possible. This yields a maximum likelihood (ML) estimate of the parameters. If we have usable prior probabilities for the parameters, we would instead seek a maximum a posteriori (MAP) estimate. However, to begin, we will assume that we do not, and set $p(\Theta) = 1$ for convenience. The data, $\mathbf{X}$, consists of D documents, with the data for each one denoted by $\mathbf{x}_d = \{\mathbf{w}_d, \mathbf{R}_d\}$. We assume that documents are generated independently. Applying Bayes rule with $p(\Theta) = 1$, and ignoring the absolute probability density of the data, $p(\mathbf{X})$, we get:

$$p(\Theta|\mathbf{X}) \propto p(\mathbf{X}|\Theta) = \prod_{d=1}^{D} p(\mathbf{x}_d|\Theta), \tag{6.17}$$

where $p(\mathbf{x}_d|\Theta)$ depends on the particular model. For the basic image concept model,

$$p(\mathbf{x}_d|\Theta) = p(\mathbf{w}_d, \mathbf{R}_d|\Theta) = p(\mathbf{w}_d|\mathbf{R}_d, \Theta)\, p(\mathbf{R}_d|\Theta), \tag{6.18}$$

where $p(\mathbf{w}_d|\mathbf{R}_d, \Theta)$ is given by (6.16) together with expressions for the components for particular sub-models.

Regardless of the details, for a wide range of circumstances, maximum likelihood learning of models can then be considered as finding parameters, Θ^{ML}, with the goal of making (6.17) as large as possible, i.e.,

$$\Theta^{ML} = \underset{\Theta}{\operatorname{argmax}} \left(\prod_{d=1}^{D} p(\mathbf{x}_d|\Theta) \right). \tag{6.19}$$

Alternatively, for conditional models such as the simple translation model discussed in §6.4.2, parameter learning takes place in the context that some of the data is given, and in the case that our models translates from region features to region words, (6.19) becomes

$$\Theta^{ML} = \underset{\Theta}{\operatorname{argmax}} \left(\prod_{d=1}^{D} p(\mathbf{w}_d|\mathbf{R}_d, \Theta) \right). \tag{6.20}$$

Missing data formulation and expectation maximization (EM).   Consider the data available for training the image concept model, as illustrated in Figure 1.8. Each region and each word comes from one of C concepts, but we do not know which one. If we knew the association between regions and concepts, we could then easily compute the maximum likelihood estimates for all the parameters. In particular, we could estimate $p(c)$ by counting how often each concept occurred and normalizing. Similarly, we could estimate the parameters implicit in $p(\mathbf{r}|c)$ (e.g., means and variances) by considering the regions for each concept in turn, and computing the parameters each concept using those regions. Having done so, we could also estimate $p(w|c)$ by counting word-concept co-occurrences in each image, since the region-concept mapping would be known.

Similarly, if we knew the model parameters, Θ, we could estimate the probability that each concept is associated with a given region because the model tells us the relative likelihood that each concept generates the region. In addition, we can evaluate the probability that each of those image concepts generates each of the keywords by combining those probabilities with the word generation probabilities $p(w|c, \Theta)$. In other words, given model parameters we can compute probability estimates for the unknown correspondences.

This suggests an iterative process whereby we alternately estimate the correspondence probabilities from the parameters, and the parameters from the correspondence probabilities. These two steps correspond, respectively, to the expectation (E) step and the maximization (M) step of an EM algorithm [15]. The EM formalism can be used to derive the steps (see Appendix A.5). In the case of the E step, we compute the probabilities that concepts correspond to (are associated with) regions in images using (6.12):

$$p\left(c \,\middle|\, \mathbf{r}_{d,i}, \Theta^{(old)}\right) = \frac{p\left(\mathbf{r}_{d,i} \,\middle|\, c, \Theta^{(old)}\right) p\left(c \,\middle|\, \Theta^{(old)}\right)}{\displaystyle\sum_{k=1}^{C} p\left(\mathbf{r}_{d,i} \,\middle|\, c_k, \Theta^{(old)}\right) p\left(c_k \,\middle|\, \Theta^{(old)}\right)}. \tag{6.21}$$

These probabilities for the missing values are often referred to as *responsibilities*. In addition, we can compute the probability that each concept occurs in a particular image by summing over the regions assuming the uniform probability of $1/R_d$. Thus,

$$p\left(c \,\middle|\, \mathbf{R}_{d,i}, \Theta^{(old)}\right) = \frac{1}{R_d} \sum_{i=1}^{R_d} p\left(c \,\middle|\, \mathbf{r}_{d,i}, \Theta^{(old)}\right). \tag{6.22}$$

Based on this, we can compute the probability that concepts are associated with each image word by:

$$p\left(c \,\middle|\, w_{d,j}, \mathbf{R}_d, \Theta^{(old)}\right) = \frac{p\left(w_{d,j} \,\middle|\, c, \Theta^{(old)}\right) p\left(c \,\middle|\, \mathbf{R}_d, \Theta^{(old)}\right)}{\displaystyle\sum_{k=1}^{C} p\left(w_{d,j} \,\middle|\, c_k, \Theta^{(old)}\right) p\left(c_k \,\middle|\, \mathbf{R}_d \Theta^{(old)}\right)}. \tag{6.23}$$

Here $p\left(c \,\middle|\, \mathbf{R}_d, \Theta^{(old)}\right)$ acts like a prior on the concepts for image d, which is combined with $p\left(w_{d,j} \,\middle|\, c, \Theta^{(old)}\right)$ to provide the relatively probability for the correspondence $w_{d,j} \Leftrightarrow c$, which is normalized by the denominator to yield the absolute probabilities.

We then use the estimates (6.21) and (6.23) for correspondence probabilities as weights to compute new parameter estimates, $\Theta^{(new)}$, in the subsequent M step. For example, assuming that $p(\mathbf{r}|c)$ is given by independent normal distributions for the features, f, we can compute the means for those distributions by:

$$
\mu_{c,f} = \frac{\displaystyle\sum_{d=1}^{D}\sum_{i=1}^{R_d} r_{d,i,f} \bullet p\left(c\,\Big|\mathbf{r}_{d,i}, \Theta^{(old)}\right)}{\displaystyle\sum_{d=1}^{D}\sum_{i=1}^{R_d} p\left(c\,\Big|\mathbf{r}_{d,i}, \Theta^{(old)}\right)}.
\tag{6.24}
$$

Notice that if we knew the correspondences, this would reduce to an average over the feature vectors for each concept. Since we do not, we compute a weighted average, where the weights are the expected values of those correspondences. Variances for the distributions are computed similarly:

$$
\sigma_{c,f}^2 = \frac{\displaystyle\sum_{d=1}^{D}\sum_{i=1}^{R_d} \left(r_{d,i,f} - \mu_{c,f}\right)^2 \bullet p\left(c\,\Big|\mathbf{r}_{d,i}, \Theta^{(old)}\right)}{\displaystyle\sum_{d=1}^{D}\sum_{i=1}^{R_d} p\left(c\,\Big|\mathbf{r}_{d,i}, \Theta^{(old)}\right)}.
\tag{6.25}
$$

The emission probabilities for each word given each concept are computed by summing over all counts (usually just 0 or 1 since we typically ignore duplicates) of that word across the documents, weighted by the word-concept correspondence probabilities. We get:

$$
p\left(w\,\Big|c, \mathbf{R}, \Theta^{(old)}\right) = \frac{\displaystyle\sum_{d=1}^{D}\sum_{j=1}^{W_d} \delta\left(w, w_{d,j}\right) p\left(c\,\Big|w_{d,j}, \mathbf{R}, \Theta^{(old)}\right)}{\displaystyle\sum_{v=1}^{V}\sum_{d=1}^{D}\sum_{j=1}^{W_d} \delta\left(w_v, w_{d,i}\right) p\left(c\,\Big|w_{d,j}, \mathbf{R}, \Theta^{(old)}\right)}
$$

$$
= \frac{\displaystyle\sum_{d=1}^{D}\sum_{j=1}^{W_d} \delta\left(w, w_{d,j}\right) p\left(c\,\Big|w_{d,j}, \mathbf{R}, \Theta^{(old)}\right)}{\displaystyle\sum_{d=1}^{D}\sum_{j=1}^{W_d} p\left(c\,\Big|w_{d,j}, \mathbf{R}, \Theta^{(old)}\right)},
\tag{6.26}
$$

where the simplification of the normalizer results due to the interaction between the sum over V and $\delta\,(\bullet)$—all words in the collection of documents are accounted for. Finally, we need revised estimates for the concept prior probabilities, which are given by:

$$
p\left(c\,\middle|\,\Theta^{(old)}\right) = \frac{\displaystyle\sum_{d=1}^{D} p\left(c\,\middle|\,\mathbf{R}_d, \Theta^{(old)}\right)}{\displaystyle\sum_{k=1}^{C}\sum_{d=1}^{D} p\left(c_k\,\middle|\,\mathbf{R}_d, \Theta^{(old)}\right)}
$$

$$
= \frac{\displaystyle\sum_{d=1}^{D} p\left(c\,\middle|\,\mathbf{R}_d, \Theta^{(old)}\right)}{\underbrace{\displaystyle\sum_{d=1}^{D}\sum_{k=1}^{C} p\left(c_k\,\middle|\,\mathbf{R}_d, \Theta^{(old)}\right)}_{\text{Evaluates to one}}}
\tag{6.27}
$$

$$
= \frac{\displaystyle\sum_{d=1}^{D} p\left(c\,\middle|\,\mathbf{R}_d, \Theta^{(old)}\right)}{D},
$$

where the normalizer is D because for each document the sum over concepts is 1, and we can reverse the sums over C and D as shown in the intermediate step.

Since these update equations can be derived more formally using the EM paradigm (see Appendix A.5), we are assured that the value of the objective function, (6.19), always increases (precisely, it does not decrease). Thus, the iterative process will converge to a local maximum, which is a function of the initialization, as we do not expect to find the global optimum in a real problem.[8] To investigate the influence of initialization (as well as training/testing data splitting), we can multiple runs and compute the variance of performance measures using image annotation or region labeling scores.

Alternative inference methods.   We differentiate between the tasks of specifying models, and estimating their parameters (inference).[9] Separating these logically distinct issues avoids having inference concerns unduly influence modeling, and makes it clear which approximations we are making. Hence, we emphasize that the maximum likelihood estimate (6.19) is a particular choice, as is using EM to attempt to find a good approximation for it. EM is often used for such problems as the missing data formulation tends to map onto it nicely, and it converges relatively quickly. However, since the method heads directly to a local maximum, there will be uncertainty regarding to the extent that the performance of a system is suffering due to a poor ML estimate as compared with modeling issues or whether a ML estimate is appropriate. In addition, as our models

---

[8]Notice that solving this problem is equivalent to exploring the space of all possible correspondences, which is exponential in the number of documents.
[9]See [331, Ch. 1] for a concise discussion on this issue.

become more sophisticated, EM often becomes awkward, intractable, or not applicable. Hence, alternatives should be considered.

Problems involving correspondence are usually intractable, and thus we generally rely on approximate inference. Alternatives to EM include variational methods[10] and Markov chain Monte Carlo (MCMC) sampling.[11] MCMC sampling is very general, but typically requires problem specific implementation, such as data driven proposals [654], to be effective.

6.3.6   EVALUATION OF REGION LABELING AND IMAGE ANNOTATION

Evaluation of models like ICRM has a number of subtleties. As described previously (§6.3.4), ICRM can be used for two different tasks, namely region labeling and image annotation. Measuring performance on these tasks is discussed next, but note that since learning model parameters generally requires approximate inference (such as the EM-based method described in the preceding section), it is often unclear whether poor performance is due to a poor model or poor learning.

To evaluate image annotation, we can compare keywords generated from the model (e.g., from (6.16)) to keywords for images not used for training (held out data). This begs the question of how many keywords should be generated. A conservative approach is to simply evaluate the best keyword the system can generate, but this is unsatisfactory as the approach assumes that images have multiple keywords, which are all relevant. A pragmatic solution is to simply generate the same number of keywords as available for the held out image, and count the number that coincide, as initially used by Barnard et al. [60, 64]. This measure rewards methods that do well for common words (e.g., "sky," "water"), which tends to be the case for generative models such as ICRM. This consideration is not relevant if the dataset is balanced (like many classification datasets), or the examples are weighted to make occurrence statistics more uniform.

An alternative measure, which does not have this issue, is to treat word generation as preparation for image retrieval, and then compute information retrieval measures such as precision and recall,[12] as introduced for this task by Duygulu et al. [182]. We can plot the tradeoff between these two measures by varying the number of keywords generated to produce precision-recall (PR) curves. In a well-behaved system, as we increase the number of predicted words, recall increases, but precision suffers. Because each word is considered as equally important, this measure is less favorable to methods that are sensitive to the more common cases.

In region labeling, it is reasonable to assume that each region should have only one label, and probabilistic region labeling methods will invariably label each region with the maximal probable label. Since the task then becomes predicting a single word per region, evaluating correct predic-

---

[10]For an introduction to variational methods see [87, Ch. 10], and [303]. Variational methods have been used extensively for LDA models such as those discussed in §6.5.2.

[11]Good references for MCMC include [38], [87, Ch. 11], and [237, 249, 250, 443].

[12]Precision is the number of correct results for query divided by the total number retrieved. Hence, if we query on "tiger," and receive 10 images (because "tiger" was an inferred keyword for each of them), 5 of which are correct (because "tiger" is an actual "keyword"), then precision is 50%. Recall is the number of correct results divided by the total number of relevant items in the dataset. So, if there are actually 50 images with the keyword "tiger," then recall is only 10%.

tions can easily be averaged over regions ("frequency correct") or words ("semantic range") [63] for studying getting more common cases correct more often vs. doing better on more cases, respectively. Evaluation of region labeling typically proceeds in one of two ways. First, we can inspect the labels assigned to regions in held out images [182]. If the regions are automatically generated, then their label will not necessarily be well defined, and thus evaluation requires judgment. More problematic, every time the method is changed, the process needs to be repeated, which is labor intensive. This issue is overcome by the second approach, which is to construct a ground-truth test set which consists of semantically segmented images that are labeled using WordNet senses [63]. Then the overlap between the segments used by the algorithm and the ground truth segments can be used to weight the score of the label. Further, by using a controlled vocabulary (e.g., WordNet senses), alternative words (e.g., synonyms or hypernyms) can be evaluated as described previously (§5.5). To recap, good synonyms of the ground truth word should score the same as the ground truth word, but hypernyms should be scored less; specifically, the score should be scaled by their frequency of occurrence relative to the ground-truth label. For example, "cat" for "tiger" should score less than "tiger" [63].

6.4   TRANSLATION MODELS

We will use the term "translation models" for approaches that map elements in one modality (e.g., region feature vectors) to another modality (e.g., region labels), without latent concept structure. There is some room for confusion because models with such latent structure (e.g., IRCM) can often be used for translation tasks. However, translation models will typically be expressed as being conditioned on elements in the one modality (the "from" modality). Hence, they are not necessarily generative models for the data as a whole, but might be generative given one of the modalities.

Multimodal translation models for images to keywords have been developed in analogy with machine translation between human languages.[13] Statistical models for this task can be learned from parallel text corpora. For example, the Canadian Hansard corpus [2] used by Brown et al. [97, 98] provides English sentences with French counterparts and vice versa. However, the corpus does not specify which French word(s) correspond to which English one(s). Automatically extracting an English-French dictionary presents a similar learning problem as for the IRCM. The analogy between statistical machine translation and region labeling is illustrated in Figure 1.7.

6.4.1   NOTATIONAL PRELIMINARIES (CONTINUING §6.3.1)

For some models that follow, we will cluster regions into K groups based on training data, and represent regions by their cluster index. This is referred to as tokenization or discretization or vector quantization, and the resulting tokens are sometimes called visual words or visterms (§4.3).

---

[13]In specific, ideas from Brown et al. [98] were applied by Duygulu et al. [182] to images with keywords to learn a "lexicon" for translating regions to words. Cognitive psychologists have also used similar approaches to model language learning in children (e.g., [54, 205, 640, 641]).

In addition, since regions are then represented similar to words, in this representation regions are often referred to as visual words. We will use $q = q(\mathbf{r})$ for the quantized representation, where $q(\bullet)$ is the quantization function (usually assignment to the nearest cluster center found by K-means clustering). We denote the token for the i'th region of document d by $q_{d,i}$, and all tokens for document d by $\mathbf{q}_d$. Following our general convention, we drop the subscript d when the tokens are for an arbitrary unspecified document.

6.4.2 A SIMPLE REGION TRANSLATION MODEL (RTM)

Instead of referring directly to an analogous machine translation method, we will develop the translation in Duygulu et al. [182] as a simplification of IRCM where we cluster the regions into tokens as a pre-processing step. Then there is no need to marginalize over concepts in (6.11), as each region, i, is assigned to a specific region token $q_i = q(\mathbf{r}_i)$. These visual words take the place of the latent concept in some of the IRCM formulas. To be more formal about the connection,

$$p(q|\mathbf{r}) = \begin{cases} 1 & \mathbf{r} \Leftrightarrow q \quad \text{by cluster assignment} \\ 0 & \text{otherwise} \end{cases} \tag{6.28}$$

and (6.11) becomes

$$p(w|\mathbf{r}) = p(w|q), \text{ where } \mathbf{r} \Leftrightarrow q \text{ by cluster assignment.} \tag{6.29}$$

To use this model for image annotation, we can apply (6.13) to get

$$p(w|\mathbf{R}) = \frac{1}{R} \sum_{i=1}^{R} p(w|q_i) \text{ as } \mathbf{r}_i \Leftrightarrow q_i \text{ by cluster assignment.} \tag{6.30}$$

This simple model emphasizes the region labeling and image annotation tasks. Unlike the image concept model, it is a conditional model rather than a generative one as it assumes the tokens are always available and it does not model their statistics. Put differently, a prior on concepts is not needed for the translation task. However, we lose the possibility of having the words help cluster regions into semantically relevant groups. In addition, the hard assignment to tokens can lead to errors when region features lead to ambiguity of the tokens, whereas the image-region concept model marginalizes the ambiguity.

As always, we keep modeling separate from inference, which we consider next. We could learn the lexicon (i.e., $p(w|q)$) easily from labeled data if it was available, but typically we wish to learn the lexicon from data with correspondence ambiguity (e.g., Figure 1.8). One approach is to assume that each region inherits all keywords for an image, and then compute the conditional probabilities by counting word occurrences for each region and then normalizing.[14] However, having done so, one could improve the estimates by using the current lexicon to reduce the correspondence ambiguity, which is the basis of the EM algorithm discussed next.

---

[14]This approach was used by Mori et al. [432].

Expectation maximization (EM) for the simple region translation model.   The region translation model is a special case of the image region concept model (IRCM), and we could develop it as such. However, the EM equations for RTM are even simpler and relatively intuitive, and I will discuss them independently. As with IRCM, if we knew the association between image words and concepts (now synonymous with regions), then we could compute a table for $p(w|q)$ by aggregating word—concept co-occurrence counts, and normalizing the values so that they sum to one. This is the M step.

Similarly, if we knew the model parameters (i.e., $\Theta^{(old)} = p^{(old)}(w|q)$, we could estimate the association between words and regions in the training data. Notationally, for each word, $w_{d,j}$, we can estimate the probability that it corresponds to (comes from) region $\mathbf{r}_{d,i}$ with index $q_{d,i}$. Intuitively, $p^{(old)}(w|q)$ provides the relative association of $w_{d,j}$ with each of the concepts associated with regions in document d. More specifically, the E step estimates the probability that a given word comes from each of the image regions by:

$$p\left(w_{d,j} \Leftrightarrow \mathbf{r}_{d,i} \middle| \Theta^{(old)}; \mathbb{C}_d\right) = p\left(q_{d,i} \middle| w_{d,j}, \Theta^{(old)}; \mathbb{C}_d\right)$$

$$= \frac{p^{(old)}\left(w_{d,j} \middle| q_{d,i}\right)}{\displaystyle\sum_{i'=1}^{R_d} p^{(old)}\left(w_{d,j} \middle| q_{d,i'}\right)}, \tag{6.31}$$

where $\mathbb{C}_d = \{q_{d,i}\}_{i=1}^{R_d}$ are the pre-defined token assignments for the regions from the clustering pre-processing step.

For the M step we use the probabilities (expected values) to weight co-occurrence counts. Hence,

$$p\left(w \middle| q, \Theta^{(old)}; \mathbb{C}\right) = \frac{\displaystyle\sum_{d=1}^{D}\sum_{j=1}^{W_d}\sum_{i=1}^{R_d} \delta\left(w, w_{d,j}\right)\delta\left(q, q_{d,i}\right) p\left(q_{d,i}\middle| w_{d,j}, \Theta^{(old)}\right)}{\displaystyle\sum_{v=1}^{V}\sum_{d=1}^{D}\sum_{j=1}^{W_d}\sum_{i=1}^{R_d} \delta\left(w_v, w_{d,j}\right)\delta\left(q, q_{d,i}\right) p\left(q_{d,i}\middle| w_{d,j}, \Theta^{(old)}\right)}$$

$$= \frac{\displaystyle\sum_{d=1}^{D}\sum_{j=1}^{W_d}\sum_{i=1}^{R_d} \delta\left(w, w_{d,j}\right)\delta\left(q, q_{d,i}\right) p\left(q_{d,i}\middle| w_{d,j}, \Theta^{(old)}\right)}{\displaystyle\sum_{d=1}^{D}\sum_{j=1}^{W_d}\sum_{i=1}^{R_d} \delta\left(q, q_{d,i}\right) p\left(q_{d,i}\middle| w_{d,j}, \Theta^{(old)}\right)}, \tag{6.32}$$

where we restrict our attention to words and concepts that occur at least once together in a document. Here $\mathbb{C} = \{\mathbb{C}_d\}_{d=1}^{D}$ reminds us that we have pre-specified the values of $q(\mathbf{r}_{d,i})$. The function $\delta(\cdot)$ evaluates to 1 if the two arguments are the same, and 0 otherwise. Hence, the inner sums over W_d and R_d combined are restricted to co-occurring c and w. As in (6.26), the simplification of the normalizer is due to the interaction between the sum over W_d and $\delta(\cdot)$.

Again, since Equations (6.31) and (6.32) are derivable from the EM methodology, we know that each iteration increases (precisely, does not decrease) the quantity (6.20), and thus the procedure converges to a local maximum. Interestingly, this is a rare case where EM converges to a global optimum, provided that the initial values for $p\left(q_{d,i}\,|w_{d,j}\right)$ are non-zero,[15] and hence the usual problems with initialization are immaterial.

6.4.3   VISUAL TRANSLATION MODELS FOR BROADCAST VIDEO

Models similar to RTM have been applied to informational video with associated text. In particular, Duygulu et al. [184, 185] consider the case of text automatically extracted using speech recognition,[16] which was then further processed with parts of speech tagging[17] to restrict the words to nouns. While some popular video is close captioned by humans, most video on the web is not, and thus automatic extraction is necessary to take full advantage of it. In addition to the challenge of dealing with noise due to difficulties with automated speech-to-text, applying translation methods to video is different than image annotation because words are not necessarily spoken exactly when the visual counter parts (if any) occur. In the extreme case, in broadcast news the anchorperson may describe events in detail while the visual data is simply that of the anchorperson talking. In addition, in order to create the appearance of smooth motion, videos are composed of frames that are designed to be shown in quick succession, with 24 or 30 frames for each second being common. Thus, in the time it takes to say a single word, many visually similar frames can go by. A common way to handle this in the video retrieval community is to break the video into shots, and represent each one by a keyframe. To build a pragmatic system, Duygulu and Wactlar [186] chose to align keyframe regions with nouns extracted in the window of time within 5–7 shots around the given keyframe using a model very similar to RTM.

A second translation model for broadcast video [184] uses the shots themselves as being representative of semantic entities making up a story. Here, shots are analogous to regions, and stories are analogous to the images in RTM. To build the system, Duygulu and Hauptmann [184] relied on story segmentation achieved with relatively robust heuristics. In particular, they began by identifying commercials, anchorperson and other in-studio segments, and distinctive and reoccurring graphics and logos used in broadcast news as separators. They then extracted shots by assuming that stories were delimited by breaks to commercials, anchorperson to non-anchorperson transitions, and changes in inserted graphics. They then visually characterized shots by a set of descriptors including the output of classifiers for faces, cars, and building. Finally, they used a translation model similar to RTM to link shots with words in the story segment. The result was

---

[15]This is shown in [98].
[16]Specifically, Duygulu et al. [184, 185] used the open source Sphinx-III system [4, 587].
[17]Specifically, Duygulu et al. [184, 185] used the Brill tagger [95].

that each shot was translated into words that were more likely to be appropriate for retrieval than words spoken within a necessarily arbitrary time window around the shot.

6.4.4   A WORD TRANSLATION MODEL (WTM)

While the simple RTM provides a mechanism for region labeling and image annotation, it requires a commitment to the region cluster assignment provided by the pre-processing. In that model, regions were proxies for concepts, and the key quantities were the region-to-word translation probabilities, $p(w|\mathbf{r})$. An alternative is to use the words as the proxy for concepts, and consider the reverse translations, $p(\mathbf{r}|w)$. This need not rely on tokenized regions, and a probability density over the continuous region features makes more sense. For example, we can consider normal distributions with independent features[18] or a mixture of such distributions (see SML considered next).

As a word translation model, this is naturally suitable to generating region features based on words. On the other hand, to rank words for each region, we simply apply Bayes' rule:

$$p(w|\mathbf{r}) = \frac{p(\mathbf{r}|w)\,p(w)}{\displaystyle\sum_{v=1}^{V} p(\mathbf{r}|w_v)\,p(w_v)}, \tag{6.33}$$

where the normalizing denominator is constant across word choices and can be ignored for simply ranking words for a single region. To annotate whole images based on multiple regions, $\mathbf{R}$, we could again assume that each keyword comes from regions with uniform prior probability of $1/R$, leading to:

$$p(w|\mathbf{R}) = \frac{1}{R}\sum_{i=1}^{R} p(w|\mathbf{r}_i). \tag{6.34}$$

Finally, to provide multiple words for the image, we could again assume that words are emitted independently (as in (6.16)), and choose words in rank order of the posterior (6.34).

To train this model we could use EM, with similar update equations to what we have seen already. This model shares with the pairwise word-region model (PWRM) the problem that every region must be associated with a word, which means that common region types that are not well represented in the training annotations can create significant noise.

6.4.5   SUPERVISED MULTICLASS LABELING (SML)

Similar to the simple WTM model just discussed, the SML approach [109] models image features conditioned on each word (class) independently. SML was developed in the context of retrieval applications, where words are assume to provide the appropriate proxy for semantics, which makes sense when using words to search for images. The philosophy emphasized by the SML work is

---

[18]This is essentially the model Carbonetto et al. [108] used to test Bayesian feature selection, but without the shrinkage priors.

that the words themselves, rather than latent concepts, should be the underlying states of the system. While this property is shared with WTM, SML goes much further in execution,[19] and hence it does not have some of the problems that WTM does.

For each word, w, SML trains a model for image features using training images that have w in their keyword list. The features proposed are texture features for each color from relatively small overlapping tiles. While these tiles simply describe small neighborhoods, rather than attempt semantic spatial groupings, we will still refer to them as regions. The regions in a document are modeled as being conditionally independent given the word, so

$$p\left(\mathbf{R}_d \,|w\right) = \prod_{i=1}^{R_d} p\left(\mathbf{r}_i \,|w\right), \tag{6.35}$$

with the model for $p\left(\mathbf{r}\,|w\right)$ being a mixture of Gaussians. If there was only one Gaussian, then it would be very diffuse (large variance) because it would then need to incorporate feature vectors from many regions that are unrelated to the word. A key idea from SML is that some of the mixture components will have large variance to absorb the irrelevant regions, whereas mixture components that are associated with the word will come from a more constrained set, and thus be more peaked. Since all the Gaussians integrate to one, the diffuse components will have relatively low density. Hence, simply fitting mixtures should provide a probability density that is high for relevant regions and low for irrelevant ones.

In training, the neighborhood features for each image are clustered into a fixed number of mixture components. This can be understood as a soft, non-contiguous segmentation,[20] but this facet of the representation is not used explicitly, and a strength of the approach is that it does not commit to a segmentation. The components from each image having the given word w in the caption are then clustered, hierarchically into a mixture model for the word.[21]

Providing words for images based on the feature vectors for the tiles proceeds by computing (6.35) for the tile features separately for each word using its learned top level mixture model. Then words can be ranked by their posterior probabilities computed by

$$p\left(w\,|\mathbf{R}_d\right) = \frac{p\left(w\right)p\left(\mathbf{R}_d\,|w\right)}{\sum_{v=1}^{V} p\left(w_v\right)p\left(\mathbf{R}_d\,|w_v\right)} = \frac{p\left(w\right)\prod_{i=1}^{R_d} p\left(\mathbf{r}_i\,|w\right)}{\sum_{v=1}^{V} p\left(w_v\right)\prod_{i=1}^{R_d} p\left(\mathbf{r}_i\,|w_v\right)}. \tag{6.36}$$

---

[19]Historically, the simple WTM was not developed much beyond the one by Carbonetto et al. [108] (which evolved into a different method [106]), and SML was likely developed independently of that.

[20]Using Gaussian mixtures for segmentation forms the bases for the early Blobworld system [111]. Note that Blobworld uses position as one of the features, which promotes (but does not enforce) contiguity.

[21]Specifically, the tiles are 8×8 pixels, and each one is shifted 2 pixels from the previous one either horizontally or vertically as appropriate. The features are the loadings of a discrete cosine transform (DCT) for each of Y, B, or R in a YBR color space representation. The number of mixture components per training image is 8, which are aggregated into 64 for each word (i.e., for $p(\mathbf{r}_i\,|w)$).

If we only need the relative posterior, we can ignore the normalizing denominator, as this is constant over words. However, the complete form provides an absolute measure, which we would need, for example, if we wanted to refrain from word prediction when the probabilities for all words were below a threshold (i.e., "uncertain" or "refuse to predict").

Again, neighborhoods that are best explained by diffuse mixture components will be essentially ignored in the product, and words where some of the neighborhoods are explained by peaked components will have high posterior probability. Notice, however, that the form (6.36) has a bias in favor of words whose visual evidence spans a greater area, as there will be more neighborhoods with similar high likelihood (see (6.41)). This bias may be welcome under some circumstances, but it is also a symptom of the assumption that neighborhood features are conditionally independent given the word, which is sensitive to spatial correlations. Consider an image with a large forest area. Conditioned on "forest" there may be a mixture component with forest like texture and color with some variance. However, a given image is likely to be more consistent, having perhaps just one forest color and texture, with small variation. Hence, even if we condition on "forest," knowing some of the neighborhood features reduces the uncertainty of others, in contrast with true conditional independence where "forest" carries all the information about neighborhood features. This is even more clearly the case if we consider adjacent overlapping regions, which are likely to be similar. Nonetheless, under suitably simple assumptions,[22] word ranking will be the same whether we use (6.36) as is, or whether we aggregated similar tiles into an average over them. Finally, notice that the bias due to potentially numerous factors over neighborhoods also affects the relative strength of the evidence $\prod_{i=1}^{R_d} p\left(\mathbf{r}_i \mid w\right)$ compared to the prior, $p\left(w\right)$. Despite these potential issues, SML as proposed performs well on the image annotation task.[23]

While SML is mostly focused on image level annotation, its construction permits sensible computations for localized semantics.[24] Hence, we consider it here, instead of grouping it with methods focused on image annotation (§6.7) without localization. For SML, for each small region defined by the tiling, we could rank words using essentially the same formula as (6.36) applied to each region to get

$$p\left(w \mid \mathbf{r}_i\right) = \frac{p\left(w\right) p\left(\mathbf{r}_i \mid w\right)}{\sum_{v=1}^{V} p\left(w_v\right) p\left(\mathbf{r}_i \mid w_v\right)}. \tag{6.37}$$

---

[22]For example, suppose that there are K distinct neighborhood features, $\mathbf{n}_k$ each one highly correlated with one distinct word, so that for a word, w, one of the K is part of peaked component, and the others are part of diffused components. Further suppose that dividing the neighborhoods into regions based on neighborhood features gives regions of equal size. Finally, suppose that $p(w)$ is uniform. Then words with higher $p(\mathbf{n}_k \mid w)$ will be ranked higher in both scenarios, although the actual values of $p(\mathbf{n}_k \mid w)$ would be different.

[23]When it was introduced, SML [109] exhibited clear state-of-the-art image annotation performance, improving upon the effective MBRM method (§6.7.1), which itself performed substantively better than a model similar to RTM.

[24]See, for example, Figure 6 of the SML paper [109].

The form (6.37) emphasizes one last instructive difference between WTM and SML, which is how evidence from multiple regions combines for image level annotation. For SML we compute the image based posterior by (6.36), whereas methods that focus on words coming from regions work with $p(w|\mathbf{r}_i)$. When $p(w|\mathbf{r}_i)$ is a multinomial, we have considered that words come from one of the regions with uniform probability as in (6.13) and (6.34). Consider the difference between computing $p(w|\mathbf{R})$ using (6.36) vs. a region-based approach using (6.34) together with (6.37) so that

$$P(w|\mathbf{R}) = \frac{1}{R_d} \sum_{i=1}^{R_d} P(w|\mathbf{r}_i).$$

(6.38)

Normalizing for each neighborhood limits the contribution of each neighborhood to $1/R_d$, as probabilities are between 0 and 1. This is in contrast with computing the overall likelihood first, where the probability from a single region can dominate all others.

A simple example will clarify. Suppose that there are two regions, $\mathbf{r}_1$ and $\mathbf{r}_2$, with very high likelihood for words w_1 and w_2, respectively. In other words, $p(\mathbf{r}_1|w_1) \gg p(\mathbf{r}_1|w_2)$ and $p(\mathbf{r}_2|w_2) \gg p(\mathbf{r}_2|w_1)$. We assume that are $p(\mathbf{r}_1|w_2) \cong p(\mathbf{r}_2|w_1)$ are small as they both come from flat noise distributions. Further suppose that $p(\mathbf{r}_1|w_1) = C \bullet p(\mathbf{r}_2|w_2)$. We will also simply matters by assuming that the word priors are the same (i.e., $p(w_1) = p(w_2)$). Using (6.34) we get

$$\begin{aligned} p(w_1|\mathbf{r}_1) &= \frac{p(w_1)p(\mathbf{r}_1|w_1)}{p(w_1)p(\mathbf{r}_1|w_1) + p(w_2)p(\mathbf{r}_1|w_2)} \\ &= \frac{p(\mathbf{r}_1|w_1)}{p(\mathbf{r}_1|w_1) + p(\mathbf{r}_1|w_2)} \cong 1. \end{aligned}$$

(6.39)

Similarly, $p(w_2|\mathbf{r}_2) \simeq 1$ as well. The relative sizes of the large likelihoods $p(\mathbf{r}_1|w_1)$ and $p(\mathbf{r}_2|w_2)$ does not matter here, as calculations for region 1 do not use any information from region 2 and vice versa. So, focusing on regions, the two words are equally likely to be associated with the image. However, by (6.36),

$$\frac{p(w_1|\mathbf{R})}{p(w_2|\mathbf{R})} = \frac{p(w_1)p(\mathbf{R}|w_1)}{p(w_2)p(\mathbf{R}|w_2)} = \frac{p(\mathbf{r}_1|w_1)p(\mathbf{r}_2|w_1)}{p(\mathbf{r}_1|w_2)p(\mathbf{r}_2|w_2)} \cong \frac{p(\mathbf{r}_1|w_1)}{p(\mathbf{r}_2|w_2)} = C.$$

(6.40)

Hence, if the density for $\mathbf{r}_1$ is ten times that for $\mathbf{r}_2$ (i.e., $C = 10$), then the first word will be estimated as ten times more probable then the second. This is less than ideal, given that the details for computing densities are not particularly stable across training data.

[Aside].   For completeness, let us consider the effect of having K identical copies of region $\mathbf{r}_1$. As before, assume that $p(\mathbf{r}_1|w_2) \cong p(\mathbf{r}_2|w_1)$ is small. Now the region oriented method would declare the first word as being K times more probable, which could be helpful if the estimates are relatively noisy, but biased if the identical regions are due to poor segmentation or from tiles. On the other hand, SML would compute

$$
\begin{aligned}
\frac{p\left(w_1\mid\mathbf{R}\right)}{p\left(w_2\mid\mathbf{R}\right)} &= \frac{p\left(w_1\right)p\left(\mathbf{R}\mid w_1\right)}{p\left(w_2\right)p\left(\mathbf{R}\mid w_2\right)} \\
&= \frac{p\left(\mathbf{r}_1\mid w_1\right)^k p\left(\mathbf{r}_2\mid w_1\right)}{p\left(\mathbf{r}_2\mid w_1\right)^k p\left(\mathbf{r}_2\mid w_2\right)} \\
&\cong \left(\frac{p\left(\mathbf{r}_1\mid w_1\right)}{p\left(\mathbf{r}_1\mid w_2\right)}\right)^{K-1},
\end{aligned}
\tag{6.41}
$$

which is potentially a very large bias.

In summary, the absolute probabilities from both computations can be inaccurate due to the failures of the assumptions made. However, rank ordering as needed by image annotation, can still be adequate.

6.4.6   DISCRIMINATIVE MODELS FOR TRANSLATION

Another translation approach is to train discriminative classifiers that map region feature vectors to words. Most commonly, such classifiers are binary valued, classifying each region into either being in the class associated with word, w, or not. In this case, for a vocabulary of size V, V classifiers are required. The most commonly used classifier is the binary (two-class) support vector machine (SVM) [100, 118, 509, 572]. However, extensions for multiclass classification [150] and exploiting structure within data [566] could be used to an advantage for multimodal translation.

To train discriminative classifiers we typically need labeled data, which in the domain of images regions and keywords would require that we know which word goes with which region. Since much data does not have this property,[25] we would like to train the classier despite the correspondence ambiguity. In the context of building discriminative models, doing so is referred to as multiple instance learning (MIL),[26] which was first systematically applied to drug discovery. As originally developed, the method assumes positive training examples where a *single* label is applicable to at least one instance within a "bag" of instances (the "multiple-instances"), and negative training examples where the label is considered not applicable to any of the instances in the bag. For example, if we have images with the class label "waterfall," and random images that are not labeled "waterfall," then MIL attempts to learn a classifier that associates waterfall regions with the label.

Multiple instance learning methods typically have two components: A core classification method, and a strategy to improve it in face of the ambiguity of the instance labels. Core classification methods studied include SVM and diverse density (DD) which tries to find a point, t,

---

[25]To be fair, some work has considered training classifiers for region labels using region-labeled data. Early work includes the neural network approach of Vivarelli and Williams [582] and the SVM approach of Cusano et al. [154]. These works were limited to a small number of classes, and hence it is not clear if they would scale up to many classes. Some of the increasingly large some localized datasets reviewed in §3.4.1 could be used for this.

[26]There is a fair bit of literature on MIL, beginning with Dietterich [177] and Maron [405]. Alternative approaches and improvements include [36, 37, 648]. Work using MIL for scene classification includes [36, 37, 406, 649].

in the feature space so that which is close to at least one instant per positive training bag, and far from the instances in the negative training bags, with respect to a probabilistic developed measure. The point t can be sought via optimization [405, 406]. Perhaps a more canonical strategy that has been used in conjunction with both DD [648] and SVM [648] is to alternately estimate the relevance of each instance in the training data using the classifier parameters, and then retrain the classifier using the updated estimates for the relevance of each instance.

While the original work on image classification did not consider multiple words, naively extending the method to do so is straightforward. Suppose that some of the waterfall images also had the keyword "forest." We observe that the existence of "forest" does not detract from using the image as a positive example for waterfall images, and further enables it to be used as a positive example for forest images as well. Hence, it is fair to consider MIL as a region labeling method, as well as an image classification method.[27] However, as the vocabulary size increases, MIL training time increases linearly. A more substantive issue is that as the number of binary classifiers—one per word—increases, there will be more false positives. This is due to the result of hard classification where a yes-no decision is made for every word independently. In discriminative frameworks, there is typically no principled way to choose the K best words, although this can often be done heuristically as classification methods generally provide some score as to the robustness of the decision. Indeed, using such scores to rank or weight words can be important for good performance.[28]

Notice that each classifier is built independently without regard to how common the concept is. This can be an advantage for identifying rare items, but is less advantageous when performance is measured by indiscriminant counting of correct predictions, as this favors methods that do well for common cases. If doing well on such a measure is needed, then the output can be biased by the word frequency. This is justified, assuming conditional independence of regions given words and a reasonable representation in the training data, $\mathcal{T}$, by first observing

$$p(w\,|\mathbf{r}, \mathcal{T}) = \frac{p(\mathbf{r}\,|w, \mathcal{T})\,p(w\,|\mathcal{T})}{p(\mathbf{r}\,|w, \mathcal{T})\,p(w\,|\mathcal{T}) + p(\mathbf{r}\,|\bar{w}, \mathcal{T})\,p(\bar{w}\,|\mathcal{T})}$$
$$= \frac{p(\mathbf{r}\,|w)\,p(w\,|\mathcal{T})}{p(\mathbf{r})}, \tag{6.42}$$

where $\bar{w}$ designates the absence of w. Then

$$p(w\,|\mathbf{r}) = \frac{p(\mathbf{r}\,|w)\,p(w)}{p(\mathbf{r})} = \frac{p(w\,|\mathbf{r}, \mathcal{T})\,p(w)}{p(w\,|\mathcal{T})}, \tag{6.43}$$

---

[27]Region-labeling using MIL was first considered by Yang et al. [624], who also considered feature selection. Detailed region labeling results based on treating the words as independent labels are reported in Barnard et al. [63] for the purpose of comparing against other methods.

[28]In one set of experiments [63, (Tables 2–5)], making use of soft scores instead of simply using hard assignments had a significant benefit across a number of variants.

where $p(w|\mathcal{T})$ is typically one half (equal numbers of positive and negative examples), and $p(\mathbf{r}|w,\mathcal{T})$ is estimated either as 0/1 (hard classification) or by the soft score.[29]

6.5   IMAGE CLUSTERING AND INTERDEPENDENCIES AMONG CONCEPTS

The models considered so far assume that the semantic concepts associated with images are independent. Thus, they do not exploit concept co-occurrence. For example, consider an ambiguous red region, which by itself could be connected to the concept "stop-sign" or "rose" (see Figure 1.4). But this dilemma could potentially be resolved by considering the rest of the image—surrounding grass, leaves, and other flowers would suggest the first answer, whereas cars and pavement would suggest the second one. A useful abstraction here is *image category*, or *group*, denoted by *g* in the equations. Note that image category is often implemented as a second latent quantity, and thus category is an abstraction that loosely encodes content that often appears together.

In the rose/stop sign example, the image categories might be garden images and street images. A given image type implies higher probability for some latent concepts and lower probability for others. In addition, image categories also imply aggregate concepts such as the category itself. For example, birthday-party images could be labeled "birthday-party," even though multiple simpler concepts (e.g., "children," "cake," "candles") typically are needed to suggest the type of image.

6.5.1   REGION CONCEPTS WITH IMAGE CATEGORIES (CIRCM)

For models based on multimodal latent factors for concepts, image categories can be implemented by associating them with a distribution over the latent factors. In particular, we can assume that the images are associated with groups of latent factors coming from the distribution for a particular category. A graphical model that extends the image region concept model (IRCM) to include image categories (CIRCM) is shown in Figure 6.3.[30] The joint density is

$$p(g,\mathbf{c},\mathbf{w},\mathbf{R}) = p(g)p(\mathbf{c}|g)\,p(\mathbf{R}|\mathbf{c})\,p(\mathbf{w}|\mathbf{c}), \qquad (6.44)$$

where **c** is now conditioned on the image category variable, *g*. This is a simple extension of (6.8), and the two right most factors are defined as in (6.8). Specifically, $p(\mathbf{R}|\mathbf{c})$ is given by (6.10), and $p(\mathbf{w}|\mathbf{c})$ is given by (6.7).

Since images often contain elements that are very general and common (e.g., "sky") and other which are relatively rare (e.g., "penguin"), we can reduce the number of concepts needed by sharing the common ones. For example, we can arrange the concepts in a binary tree (see

---

[29]In one set of experiments [63, (Tables 2–5)] using $p(\mathbf{r}_i|w)$ alone provided competitive results using the "semantic range" measure, and less competitive result using the "frequency correct" measure. The reverse was found to be true using $p(w|\mathbf{r}_i)$. Both results are as one would expect.

[30]This is essentially model I-2 in [60], which additionally allows for sharing latent factors to encourage better learning of common concepts, and more compact models. The model (6.44) is the special case where there is no sharing.

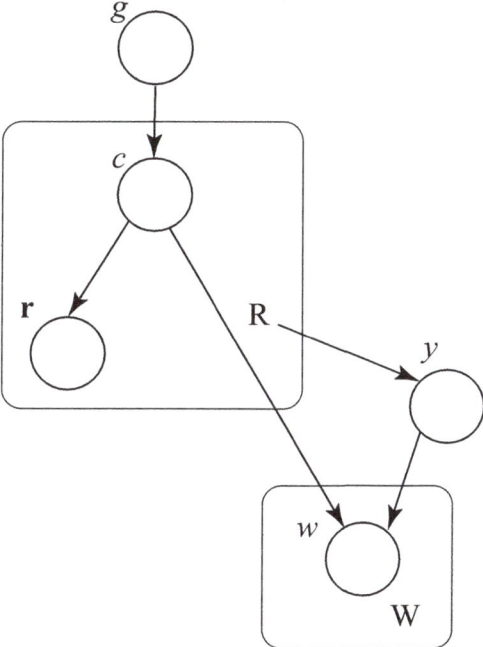

Figure 6.3: The CIRCM graphical model which is the IRCM graphical model (Figure 6.2) extended to include a cluster variable g. Now image regions are sampled by first sampling an image category or type from $p(g)$, which is typically learned from training data. Then all R image concepts are sampled conditioned on a shared sample of g. Hence, concepts now come from $p(c \mid g)$ instead of $p(c)$. Given the concepts, data is generated as in IRCM.

Figure 6.4).[31] Here each distribution $p(\mathbf{c} \mid g)$ is constrained to use only the concepts on the path from the leaf to the root.[32]

In addition to implementing context for our concepts, this kind of model also provides for multimodal image clustering which respects compositional structure in images. Here, images are clustered based both on region features and keywords, in the same way we would train (6.44) for image annotation. A cluster would then consist of concepts that as a group tend to emit words and regions that co-occur. Hence, for example, a cluster of underwater images containing coral will tend not to have images with roses, despite the visual similarity. Conversely, we may have several clusters with ocean themes that are distinctly visually different (see [64, Figures 2–4] and [59]).

---

[31]Sharing parameters of common document elements using a fixed hierarchy was introduced in the context of text document clustering [280]. The method was subsequently adopted into models for words and pictures [59, 60, 64].

[32]Going much further, Li et al. [370] proposed a model focused on extracting such a *semantivisual* hierarchy from large image data sets with tags, and importantly, evaluating such hierarchies.

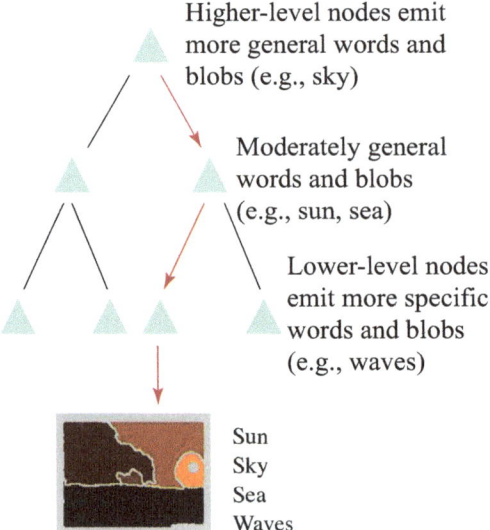

Higher-level nodes emit more general words and blobs (e.g., sky)

Moderately general words and blobs (e.g., sun, sea)

Lower-level nodes emit more specific words and blobs (e.g., waves)

Sun
Sky
Sea
Waves

Figure 6.4: One example of how concepts can be shared across image clusters (groups, categories) in the CIRM model (§6.5.1). Here each cluster is associated with a path from root to leaf, and the concepts used to generate image data for the cluster are drawn from a learned distribution over the concepts. Alternative structures are clearly possible, and alternative models are developed in Barnard et al. [60] which differ by how the words and image regions are sampled from the concepts (nodes). Image is from [64] (reprinted with permission).

Learning the parameters (i.e., $p(g)$, $p(c|g)$, $p(w|c)$, $p(\mathbf{r}|c)$) from image region feature vectors and associated keywords is much like learning parameters for the IRCM, but we have even more corresponding ambiguity as we do not know which image comes from which group. Hence, reliably finding the best model for the data is again intractable. As with many of the models already discussed, one approach to estimate model parameters is the EM algorithm.

6.5.2   LATENT DIRICHLET ALLOCATION (LDA)

An alternative to CIRCM is correspondence latent Dirichlet allocation (CORR-LDA) [89]. In LDA, what we have being referring to as concepts are referred to as topics. Further, I will develop LDA methods using notation consistent with that used for CIRCM. LDA [88] puts a Dirichlet prior over the multinomial distribution over topics. The Dirichlet distribution is the extension of the Beta distribution for the single parameter for a binomial distribution (e.g., the degree of bias of coin flip). Intuitively, a draw from a Dirichlet distribution of dimension C provides the loadings of a C sided die under the influence of the C dimensional parameter $\boldsymbol{\alpha}$. For completeness, the Dirichlet distribution over the multinomial components, c_k, representing, for example, the probability of each of C concepts, is given by

$$Dir(\boldsymbol{\alpha}) = \frac{1}{\beta(\boldsymbol{\alpha})} \prod_{k=1}^{C} c_k^{(\alpha_c-1)}, \text{ where the normalizing constant}$$

$$\beta(\boldsymbol{\alpha}) = \frac{\prod_{k=1}^{C} \Gamma(\alpha_k)}{\Gamma\left(\sum_{k=1}^{C} \alpha_k\right)}, \text{ and } \Gamma(\bullet) \text{ is the gamma function.} \qquad (6.45)$$

The basic notion in LDA is that documents consist of topics, which are associated with conditionally independent distributions over observables such as words and region features. Further, the topics for a document are drawn from a document specific distribution, itself drawn from a corpus specific Dirichlet distribution. The key difference from CIRCM is the source of the distribution over topics. In CIRCM they come deterministically from the cluster via $p(\mathbf{c}|g)$, where both $p(\mathbf{c}|g)$ and $p(g)$ are learned from the corpus. In CORR-LDA the distribution over topics come stochastically from $p(\mathbf{c}|\boldsymbol{\alpha}) \sim Dir(\boldsymbol{\alpha})$, where the C dimensional parameter $\boldsymbol{\alpha}$ is learned from the corpus. In other words, in (CORR-LDA) [89], $p(g)p(\mathbf{c}|g)$ in (6.44) becomes $p(\boldsymbol{\alpha})p(\mathbf{c}|\boldsymbol{\alpha})$, with the nature of $p(\mathbf{c}|g)$ and $p(\mathbf{c}|\boldsymbol{\alpha})$ being quite different.

Replacing learned cluster distributions, $p(\mathbf{c}|g)$, with draws from a distribution allows for additional smoothing over the mix of topics in documents, and potentially better generalization. Further, this is achieved with fewer parameters.[33] Finally, since the Dirichlet distribution is the conjugate prior for the multinomial, the formulation is elegant, and some computations during inference can be done analytically.

On the other hand, if the goal is to cluster documents, additional processes are needed in contrast to CIRCM where the notion of clusters is built in. Also, tying the scope of topic mixing to the number of topics using a specific $\boldsymbol{\alpha}$ might be either too restrictive or too expressive (leading to over-fitting) depending on the corpus and the number of topics, which is set in advance. This could be mitigated by learning the number topics or using a model that allows for any number of topics.[34]

---

[33]If we assume that all atomic data are represented the same (e.g., as double precession floating point numbers, then CIRCM has G*(1+C)+C*D parameters, where G is the number of clusters, C is the number of concepts (topics), and D is the number of parameters needed for a concept which is typically dominated by the vocabulary size V. On the other hand, CORR-LDA has C+C*D parameters, i.e., O(G*C) fewer, which is substantive unless V is much larger than G.

[34]Yakhnenko et al. [618, 619] extended the MoM-LDA model from [60] to enable arbitrary numbers of mixture components. MoM-LDA and their extension MoM-HDP model regions and words being generated independently from a shared distribution over components (also like model I-2 in Barnard et al. [60], in contrast to Corr-LDA, IRCM (§6.3), and CIRCM (§6.5) that condition word generation on the collection of latent factors that generated the regions.

6.5.3 MULTICLASS SUPERVISED LDA (SLDA) WITH ANNOTATIONS

The multiclass supervised LDA method (sLDA) extends the CORR-LDA approach to simultaneously model regions labels and image categories using the same latent space $p(\mathbf{c}|\boldsymbol{\alpha})$ [588]. We have already considered work on assigning a single category label (e.g., "beach") to an image (§6.1), but the sLDA work explores the hypothesis that grouping and annotation can help each other (see also Li and Fei-Fei [367]). Unlike CIRCM (§6.5.1), where groupings are learned, this approach uses fixed set of known categories, which are provided as labels during training. Given the generated region topics, $\mathbf{c}$, annotation occurs just as in CORR-LDA. (Again, I have changed notation from the original work to be consistent with related models considered here). For generating the image category label, g, Wang et al. [588] proposed using a distribution based on the empirical topic frequency distribution for the document given by

$$\bar{\mathbf{c}} = \frac{1}{N_r} \sum_{i=1}^{N_r} c_i.$$ (6.46)

The image class label is generated by the softmax distribution

$$p(g|c) = \exp\left(\boldsymbol{\eta}_c^T \bullet \bar{\mathbf{c}}\right) / \sum_{h=1}^{G} \exp\left(\boldsymbol{\eta}_k^T \bullet \bar{\mathbf{c}}\right),$$ (6.47)

where is G the number of image category labels, and the weights are $\boldsymbol{\eta}_c$ learned during training. Wang et al. [588] reported slightly better annotation and image labeling over comparable models that do only one or the other. In particular, region annotation performance was better than (CORR-LDA) [89], and image classification performance was better than multiclass supervised LDA (sLDA) without annotation.[35]

An alternative latent topic model for the joint modeling of images of scenes and their components employs a switching variable that models two possible ways that words are generated [369]. First, words can be generated from objects (topics) associated with regions, and thus their semantics are relevant to the visual properties of the particular object. Second, leftover words that are less visually relevant can be generated from the scene type itself. This reduces the impact of noisy annotations in training data, and makes the representation more sensible, as many words that might be related to the class will not be associated with visual attributes.

6.6 SEGMENTATION, REGION GROUPING, AND SPATIAL CONTEXT

To further model the semantics of the world underlying images and keywords, we can consider spatial relations among the pieces. For example, in most images with sky and water, sky regions

---

[35]Realistically, the improvements reported were very small. One might expect that with additional refinements and/or different corpora, annotation and categorization might be able to help each other more.

tend to be toward the top of the image, above most other image regions, and similarly water regions tend to be below other image regions. This goes beyond the image clustering just considered (§6.5) which merely encodes the common occurrence of sky and water in images (as commonly found in landscape scenes, or more specifically, beech scenes). From the perspective of inference, spatial arrangement can modify our beliefs of putative image labels. For example, consider an image split horizontally into two regions, where the labels sky and water are equally likely for both based on appearance. Further, during learning, if both "sky" and "water" appear as part of the keyword list, it makes sense to implicitly assume that each of them correspond to at least one image region.[36] Hence, assigning the labels to the regions should be based on their spatial arrangement, which can be done based on the previously learned, or simultaneously learned, quantification of the notion that sky is more often above water than the other way around.

Such spatial relationships reflect the world and the pictures that people take of it. However, when dealing with image regions, there is a second possible semantic relationship between regions, namely that they are different parts of the same entity. An example of this, which we have already used, is regions for the black and white halves of a penguin. These are impossible to merge based on similar color as their colors are very distinct, and difficult to merge based on contour in the typical environments where penguins are photographed. However, if both black and white regions have some association with "penguin," especially during training where this need only be in comparison to other keywords, then a merge can be considered based on label probabilities. Further the familiar configuration of penguin parts can either be exploited, or learned (see §7.1.3 for learning configurations in particular domains).

This suggests a general strategy for simultaneously segmenting and labeling images.[37] We begin with regions that are sufficiently small and/or consistent in appearance that they are likely to have the same label. Then we reason about the labels, balancing the label probability to the appearance of regions (or grouped regions), and the relationships between region labels. Possible choices for the initial regions include single pixels, super-pixels which are very conservatively segmented regions (for example, using strict thresholds) based on color and texture, regions from a general purpose image segmentation algorithm, blocks (patches) from a grid, or overlapping randomly selected patches. In what follows we will refer to all forms of these primitives as regions. Possible spatial relationships among regions include the following.

- Adjacent regions, especially super-pixels, are likely to have the same label. Applying this cue is sometimes referred to as semantic smoothing. Wachsmuth et al. [586] broke this

---

[36]The assumption is that it is beneficial to find a corresponding visual entity for each word is referred to as exclusion reasoning in Barnard and Fan [62] and the exclusion principle in by Siskind [528]. Clearly, the strength of this assumption is relative to the data. In the case of the Corel data set, every key word has a corresponding visual element with high probability. In descriptive captions, this is mitigated by the ability of automated language understanding. In loosely associated text gathered from the web, or noisy text extracted from audio signal in video, the probability that any particular word is visually relevant can be quite low.

[37]In the bulk of methods for including spatial relations, labels are a proxy for semantics. In other words, the methods mentioned in this section are most analogous (or extensions of) region-to-word translation models. Further, spatial relations are typically modeled with respect to 2D image positions, and thus are not completely congruent with the semantics of the underlying 3D world.

situation into three types: Type A (accidental); Type P (parts) where the pieces are seen in various guises, but sometimes a silhouette segmentation occurs; and C (compound) where objects are always segmented into parts (e.g., our Penguin case).

- Region semantics are statistically linked to the semantics of immediate neighbors. For example, sky regions often surround birds, and sailboat regions are often next to water regions.

- Going further, region semantics are statistically linked to the semantics of all image regions, especially in concert. This is related to the clustering context described previously (§6.5), but includes additional information because additional fine-grained dependencies of the entities can be captured compared with (for example) CIRCM where the entities are conditionally independent given the category.

- Some image entities are relatively higher or lower in the image than other regions.[38] The simplest example is sky regions, which are toward the top of the image, and above most regions. Strictly relative relations are more useful, as they encode information about the world that is independent of the image framing (e.g., person above bicycle). Further, absolute position is easily included in the region features, which is common.[39]

Notice the complexities of the joint probability distribution of the labels for all image regions and their features. The labels for each region are potentially influenced by the labels for all regions in the image, and those labels have interdependencies among them. In other words, we have circular dependencies among the random variables. If we want to respect this in our models, we no longer can express the joint probability distribution as directed graphical model as we have used for other models such as IRCM and CIRCM. Instead, the most natural representation of the joint probability distribution are undirected graphical models (Markov random fields (MRFs)) or, more commonly, conditional random fields (CRFs) (both reviewed shortly). The joint distribution is further complicated if we acknowledge that the relationships between labels and features, depend on label groupings. For example, if we build disparate regions into an entity (e.g., a penguin), we would ideally consider these together, both when we consider the likelihood of the visual evidence suggesting "penguin," and for any reasoning about the location of the penguin and other entities in the scene. Various approaches have been developed to exploit spatial relationships with various tradeoffs between model complexity and speed of learning and inference. We summarize some of these efforts next. One distinction that applies across the approaches is whether they assume fully labeled data for learning (training), or whether they attempt to learn region—word correspondence as well as contextual relationships.

---

[38]Symmetrically, we can also consider relative horizontal position as well as relative vertical position, but this is less useful cue in most image data sets, such as generic web photos [234].

[39]Position is encoded in the regions features in most image annotation work that use regions. See, for example [60, 61, 64, 182].

6.6.1   NOTATIONAL PRELIMINARIES (CONTINUING §6.3.1 AND §6.4.1)

To simplify expressions among labels, we will introduce specific notion of words that are associated with regions to distinguish words that are associated with documents and indexed by (i.e., $w_{d,j}$). In particular, we will use $a_{d,i} = v$ to denote that the vocabulary word, v, that is associated with i'th region of document d. The set of all assignments for document d is denoted by $\mathbf{a}_d$. As before, we will often drop the subscript d when referring to a single arbitrary document.

6.6.2   RANDOM FIELDS FOR REPRESENTING IMAGE SEMANTICS

There are many excellent sources of information on Markov random field (MRF) models[40] and the related conditional random field (CRF) models, which are very useful for incorporating interactions between sematic labels in images. For convenience, we will review briefly the basic notions, using the graphs in Figure 6.5 for concrete examples. By convention, circles denote random variables, with shaded nodes indicating the ones that are observed in the given context. Links (undirected) indicate a statistical relationship between variables connected by links. It is conventional to group variables into maximal cliques. (A clique is a set of nodes that are fully connected. A maximal clique is a clique where adding any other node to the set is not a clique.) However, in computer vision it is more common to group the relationships into pairwise interactions, regardless of whether the cliques for each pair of linked variables are maximal. This restricts the possible interactions of variables in larger cliques, but generally simplifies the model without loosing too much power.

Given a set of nodes, $\mathbf{x}$, in a Markov random field, the key property is that given any two nodes $x_i, x_j \in \mathbf{x}$ that are not connected by a link are conditionally independent given the rest of the nodes. Adapting notation from Bishop [87], we have, $x_i \perp x_j \,|\mathbf{x}\backslash \{x_i\, x_j\}$. This property means that given a choice of cliques, $\{X_C\}$, and strictly positive *potential functions* $\Psi(X_C)$ over them, the *Gibbs* distribution over the set of variables, $\mathbf{x}$, is given by:

$$p(\mathbf{x}) = \frac{1}{Z} \prod_C \Psi(X_C). \tag{6.48}$$

Here the *partition function*, Z, normalizes the probability distribution. Specifically,

$$Z = \sum_{\mathbf{x}} \prod_C \Psi(X_C). \tag{6.49}$$

It is also common to express $\Psi(X_C)$ in terms of *energies* given by:

$$E(X_C) = -\log(\Psi(X_C)) \qquad (\text{recall that } \Psi(X_C) > 0). \tag{6.50}$$

---

[40]Markov random field (MRF models) are nicely covered in modern machine learning text books (e.g., [87, 331, 435]) and the early classic reference [320]. Conditional random field (CRF) models were introduced by Lafferty et al. [346], and Kumar and Hebert [340–342] introduced the term discriminative random field (DRF) for CRF models which integrated local discriminative classifiers for some of the potentials.

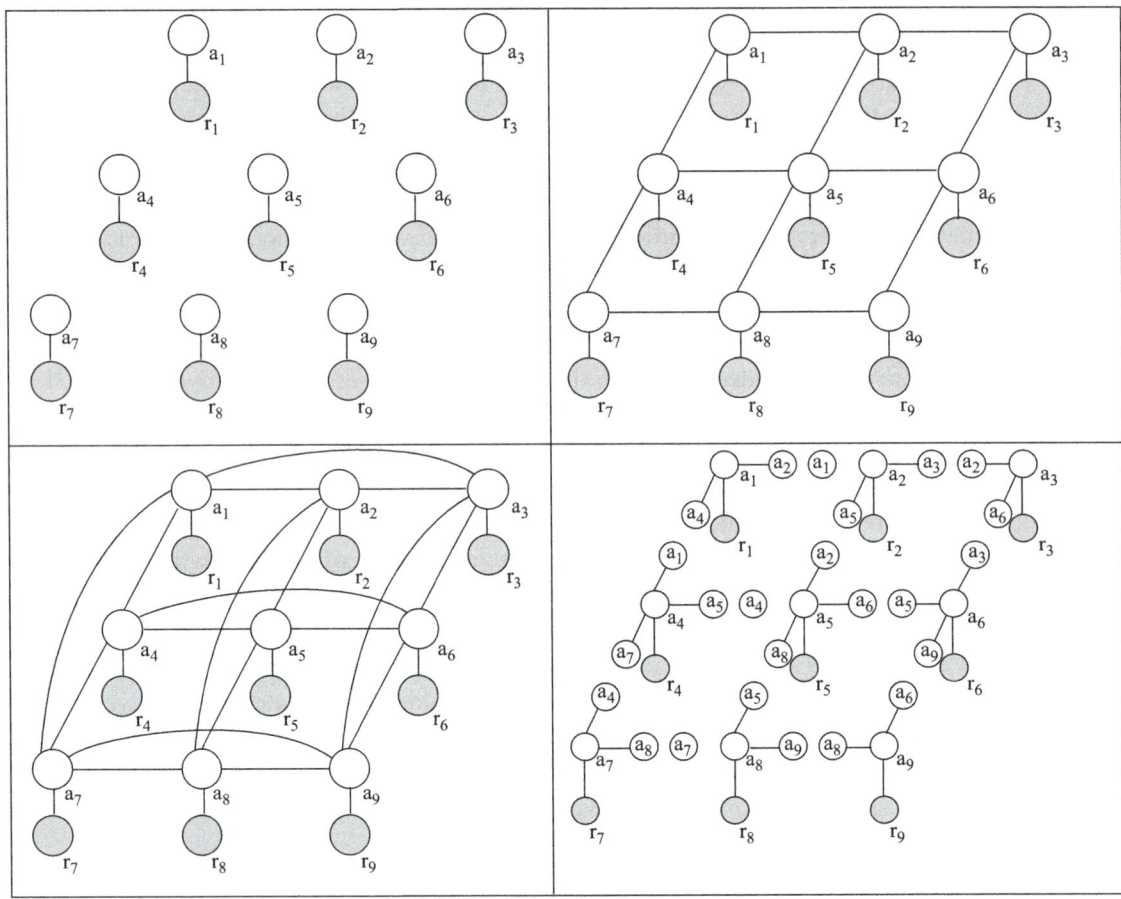

Figure 6.5: Four difference models for an image broken into a 3 × 3 grid. The open circles are labels (words) for each region. The shaded circles are the observed region features. Sub-figure (a) shows a basic translation model where the words are statistically connected to the region data, but there are no region-region interactions. In (b) there are local interactions between the label for a region and that of its left-right and upper-lower neighbors. The model (c) has pairwise interactions between all regions aligned either horizontally or vertically. A fully dense model where any pair of regions can interact would include links across the diagonal (not shown). Finally, (d) shows the pseudo-likelihood approximation for (b) as used by Carbonetto et al. [106].

In general, the set of variables $\mathbf{x}$ will include all model parameters and all observed variables. However, given a prescribed task (e.g., region labeling), it might not make sense to have the model account for the statistics of variables that are always observed.[41] If we allow the potential functions to be a function of observed variables, the MRF is then commonly referred to as a *conditional random field* (CRF). Following Lafferty et al. [346], if we now denote observed data by $\mathbf{x}$, and the labels sought by $\mathbf{y}$, our models is:

$$p\left(\mathbf{y}\,|\mathbf{x}\right) = \frac{1}{Z} \prod_{C} \Psi\left(X_C, \mathbf{x}\right). \tag{6.51}$$

The distinction between the CRF approach and the MRF one is much like the distinction between generative models such as the image region concept model (IRCM), and direct translation models such as RTM. Specifically, if we do not plan to expand the model beyond mapping the observed data to labels, then a model trained to do exactly that has a good chance of working better. In addition, the significant flexibility that we have in choosing the potential functions allows us to integrate the significant technology available for discriminative learning into potential functions—sometimes referred to as discriminative random fields [340–342]. Further, the function of the observed data can incorporate global features (e.g., region information for the entire image) without much computational cost compared of relying on interactions between distant latent variables. On the other hand, one downside to piling heuristics on top of each is that the resulting model becomes increasingly specific to the task and harder to interpret and reason about.

Turning to the examples in Figure 6.5, there are two kinds of pair-wise relationships. The first kind is between labels and region features, which we expect to observe in a translation model. The second kind of relationships is between labels. In the CRF framework, the first kind of potentials is typically a function of a single free variable (unary potentials), as we assume that the region features are observed. We can break up the expressions for the probabilities for the fields in Figure 6.5 into unary and binary potential functions

$$p(\mathbf{a}, \mathbf{r}) = \frac{1}{Z} \prod_{i=1}^{9} \Phi\left(a_i, r_i\right) \prod_{i, i' \in C} \Psi\left(a_i, a_{i'}, \mathbf{r}\right), \tag{6.52}$$

where in the examples shown, $\psi(a_i, a_{i'}, \mathbf{r}) = \psi(a_i, a_{i'})$, and the set of cliques, C, vary from the empty set (Figure 6.5a) to direct horizontal and vertical neighbors (6.5b), to all neighbors in horizontal and vertical directions (6.5c).

6.6.3 JOINT LEARNING OF TRANSLATION AND SPATIAL RELATIONSHIPS

Carbonetto et al. [106] endowed a discrete word translation model with the spatial relationships shown in Figure 6.5b, which I will refer to as the contextual translation model (CTM).[42] For

---

[41]Paraphrasing [435, §19.6].
[42]Again, notation is adjusted from [106] to be more consistent with that used for other models discussed here.

regions, they considered with both grid blocks and segments from a normalized cuts (ncuts) based segmentation method [395, 517, 518], finding similar performance in the two cases. To keep the model simple, they clustered regions into tokens (visual words) using K-means as in the RTM (§6.4.2). In the CTM, the unary potentials are simply the translation probabilities, $t(q, w) = p(q|w)$, where $q = q(\mathbf{r})$ is the region token index found by mapping the region to the nearest cluster center. Then, for a given image, labeling can be achieved by maximizing

$$p(\mathbf{a}|\mathbf{q}, \Theta) \propto \prod_{i=1}^{R} \Phi(q_i, a_i, \Theta) \prod_{(i,i') \in C} \Psi(a_i, a_{i'}, \Theta) \qquad (6.53)$$

with respect to $\mathbf{a} = \{a_i\}$ which is the assignments of words to regions. Here, C denotes the set of cliques representing the pair-wise relationships. Notice that without pairwise terms, we would simply assign each region the word that maximizes the translation. Alternatively, if we replace the pairwise assignments with priors on the words, we would get the same labeling as a discrete version of WTM (§6.4.4). Finally, adding the pairwise assignments provides a prior that combines neighbor label affinities together with the prevalence of each word individually.

Learning the CTM from loosely labeled aata.   In CTM the model parameters Θ are the $K \times W$ translation table encoding $t(q, w) = p(q|w)$ and a symmetric $W \times W$ label affinity table, $\psi(i, i')$. Model parameters can be estimated from training data by maximizing the complete likelihood over all training documents with respect to the unobserved assignments, $\mathbf{a}_d$, and the model parameters Θ. The CTM complete likelihood is given by:

$$p(\{\mathbf{q}_d\}, \{\mathbf{a}_d\}|\{\mathbf{w}_d\}, \Theta) = \prod_{d=1}^{D} \frac{1}{Z_d(\mathbf{a}_d, \mathbf{q}_d, \Theta)} \cdot \prod_{i=1}^{R_d} \Phi(q_{d,i}, a_{d,i}, \Theta)$$
$$\cdot \prod_{(i,i') \in C_d} \Psi(a_{d,i}, a_{d,i'}, \Theta). \qquad (6.54)$$

The left-hand side is a function of the observed $\mathbf{w}_d$ because during training the assignments are constrained to words in the image caption (i.e., $a_{d,i} \in \mathbf{w}_d$). We can encode the role of correspondence more explicitly using the indicator function $\delta(\bullet)$ which is 1 if its argument is true and 0 otherwise, in the following expressions for $\Phi(\bullet)$ and $\Psi(\bullet)$:

$$\Phi(q_{d,i}, a_{d,i}, \mathbf{w}_d, \Theta) = \prod_{v=1}^{V} t(q_{d,i}, v)^{\delta(a_{d,i}=v)}$$
$$\Psi(a_{d,i}, a_{d,i}, \mathbf{w}_d, \Theta) = \prod_{v=1}^{V} \prod_{v'=1}^{V} \psi(u, v)^{\delta(a_{d,i}=v)\delta(a_{d,j}=v')}. \qquad (6.55)$$

Notice that the indicator function selects the appropriate translation probability and spatial linkage for the proposed assignment.

Despite the simplicity of the model, learning is challenging. As in most learning described so far, the proposed method for estimating the maximal value of (6.54) proceeds iteratively with EM. However, both the E step and the M step require approximations. For the E step, the unobserved $\mathbf{a}_d$ are estimated using loopy believe propagation [437]. For the M step, proper estimation of the parameter updates requires estimating the values of the partition function for each document, which is too expensive. To improve matters, Carbonetto et al. [106] approximated the random field (Figure 6.5b) by one for the pseudo-likelihood shown in Figure 6.5d. Estimates for parameters to maximize the expected log likelihood can be obtained by taking derivatives.

A related approach by Verbeek et al. [580] is based on probabilistic latent semantic analysis (PLSA) which is close in spirit to CIRCM (§6.5.1) and LDA (§6.5.2). They augmented a PLSA approach to modeling images with spatial structure encoded in a tree graph (PLSA-TREE) and an MRF with cliques consisting of a node an its eight neighbors (PLSA-MRF).[43] Perhaps most relevant to this discussion, Verbeek et al. [580] compared training their model with pixel labeled data (the MSRC data set [520]), both with the pixel level labels, as well as collating the labels for the image to create loosely labeled data. They found only a modest drop in performance when training with loosely labeled data.[44]

6.6.4   MULTISTAGE LEARNING AND INFERENCE

We can simplify inference over spatial relationships by first estimating region word probabilities, and then revising the estimates using spatial relationship information. While this risks a suboptimal solution for the model parameters, in general we do not expect to learn an optimal model due to the complexity of inference. Conversely, simplifying inference by first learning a local classifier for $p\,(a\,|\mathbf{r})$ can lead to a better solution if the simplification makes exploring the space of relationships more efficient. We expect learning $p\,(a\,|\mathbf{r})$ to be especially effective if we have strong labels (i.e., images with labels for each pixel[45]), and a number of methods have been developed under this assumption as discussed shortly.

Naive label refinement.   An early proposal was to post-process the result of region labeling by merging regions that have similar of word probability distributions[46] for semantic segmentation. Going further, regions merging can be executed based on common shape models [586]. Follow-up work to this is covered in §7.1.3.

---

[43]Additional work on spatially endowed topic models includes Sudderth et al. [536], Wang and Grimson [597], and He et al. [271].

[44]Specifically, training using the pixel labels gave an accuracy of 73.5% (average over all pixels in the test set) on the MSRC data [520], comparable with the state of the art at the time (textonboost [520]), which gave 72.2%. Using weakly labeled data gave an accuracy of 60.6%.

[45]Data with localized labels include the pixel labeled Sowerby [24] and MSRC [520] data sets, and the object bounding box labeled PASCAL [201] and LableMe [494]. Less commonly used pixel labeled data include various subsets of the Corel[TM] data set (e.g., [63, 272]).

[46]This simple mechanism was initially proposed using the dot product of the probability distributions of adjacent regions [61] where it was reported that the proposed merging score correlated with human evaluators.

For context we could consider how the probabilities of words in the surrounding regions (or the entire image) influences the probability of each word. More formally, for region $r_{d,i}$ let $S_{d,i}$ denote the spatial semantic context information implied by surrounding regions (not necessarily only immediate neighbors). Then we can improve the estimate of $p(w \mid r_{d,i}) \propto p(r_{d,i} \mid w) p(w)$, using spatial information $S_{d,i} = S_{d,i}(\mathbf{R}_d \setminus \mathbf{r}_{d,i})$ found in a previous step by

$$p(w \mid r_{d,i}, S_{d,i}) \propto p(w, r_{d,i}, S_{d,i}) = p(w) p(r_{d,i} \mid w) p(S_{d,i} \mid w)$$
$$\propto p(r_{d,i} \mid w) p(w \mid S_{d,i}). \tag{6.56}$$

In this formulation, $p(w \mid S_{d,i})$ can be interpreted as a more informative prior than the previous $p(w)$. Alternatively, we can express this as an update of the labeling from the previous step by:

$$p(w \mid \mathbf{r}_{d,i}, S_{d,i}) \propto p(w \mid \mathbf{r}_{d,i}) \bullet \frac{p(w \mid S_{d,i})}{p(w)}. \tag{6.57}$$

A simple choice for $p(w \mid S_{d,i})$ is the expected value of the co-occurrence probabilities of w with each word over the neighboring regions [62]. Then

$$p(w \mid S_{d,i}) = p(w \mid \mathbf{R}_d \setminus \mathbf{r}_{d,i}) = \frac{1}{|nb(i)|} \sum_{n \in nb(i)} \sum_{v=1}^{V} p(w \mid v) p(v \mid \mathbf{r}_n), \tag{6.58}$$

where $nb(i)$ is the set of neighbors of i and $|nb(i)|$ is the number of neighbors. This can be extended to compute a probability map over words for each $r_{d,i}$ conditioned on all $\mathbf{r}_{d,i'} \in \mathbf{R}_d$ based on the relative location of $r_{d,i'}$ with respect to $r_{d,i}$ as used by Gould et al. [247, §4.1] together with a CRF for smoothing.

CRF models for semantic spatial relationships.   The simple approach (6.56) assumes that context $p(S_{d,i} \mid w)$ applies to each word independently,[47] which is naive and does not promote holistic solutions. This could be mitigated by additional iterations,[48] but a more principled approach is to model the entire set of words together, possibly as a function of the observed data, with a CRF. Notationally, we have

$$p(\mathbf{a} \mid \mathbf{R}) = \prod_{i=1}^{R} p(a_i \mid \mathbf{r}_i) \frac{1}{Z(\theta)} \prod_{(i,i') \in C} \Psi(a_i, a_{i'}, \mathbf{R}, \theta). \tag{6.59}$$

Notice that any method for estimating $p(a \mid \mathbf{r}_i)$ can be used independent from the random field, although one expects that it is best to keep the pairing consistent between learning and testing. Methods for computing $p(a \mid \mathbf{r}_i)$ often use image evidence around the region as well as the region itself, especially when pixels are considered regions, as this is then necessary for texture features. However, since $p(a \mid \mathbf{r}_i)$ is computed independently for each region, we will simply use $p(a \mid \mathbf{r}_i)$.

---

[47]This is similar to the pseudo-likelihood approximation used for the M step of EM by Carbonetto et al. [106] (illustrated in Figure 6.5d). However, the loopy belief propagation in the E step does allow for longer-range influence.

[48]For example, in a related domain, iterating between classification and contextual reasoning has been developed in a boosting framework for learning object detectors [223, 436, 558].

From relationship reasoning to local spatial features.   In what follows we describe additional methods for integrating spatial context for image understanding. All methods that follow are structured around an initial estimate of $p(a|\mathbf{r}_i)$ or hard region classification (i.e., $p(a|\mathbf{r}_i) \in (0,1)$). Most assume that pixel-level labeled data is available for training, and none of them try to handle the correspondence issue simultaneously with spatial relationship parameters. Broadly speaking, the methods can differentiated on the sophistication of the spatial reasoning over label relationships (typically executed using a CRF) vs. the amount of spatial information is integrated into the feature set for computing $p(a|\mathbf{r}_i)$. In what follows, the first three (§6.6.5, §6.6.6, §6.6.7) are on the spatial reasoning end of the spectrum, and the next three (§6.6.8, §6.6.9, §6.6.10) trend in rough order to the local spatial feature end of the spectrum, with the last of the three (§6.6.10) not using CRFs at all, and is entirely classifier based. By contrast, the last method (§6.6.11) is a holistic method based on a CRF that integrates many sources of evidence, but uses the classifier developed for the previous method (§6.6.10) for the unitary potentials for $p(a|\mathbf{r}_i)$. Additional general choices include the following.

- Whether spatial information is simply co-occurrence of labels within an image, or whether it makes use of relative position.

- Whether spatial information is local (neighbors), medium range, dense (every image element is considered), or global but unstructured (essentially scene type, as discussed in §6.5). Several methods integrate several of these.

- Whether spatial information is represented semantically versus using image feature (e.g., (from [519])) whether cows tend to be surrounded by green colored pixels versus cows tend to be surrounded by grass.

- The degree to which images with pixel level labeling is essential for training.

Despite increasing reliance on pixel-labeled data, and powerful but semi-opaque discriminative learning, all methods covered next integrate spatial context for image understanding in ways that can translate images into a localized word representation (e.g., regions with semantic labels). Having done so, one can translate images into simple language descriptions (e.g., "There is a cow surrounded by grass").

As in most technical work discussed in this book, the goal is to provide the basic ideas of some of the approaches that have been pursued. The reader is referred to the original works for more details.

6.6.5   DENSE CRFS FOR GENERAL CONTEXT

A simple but powerful approach to image context was proposed by Rabinovich et al. [476] which considers the co-occurrences of all semantic entities in a scene. This is different from using the type of scene (e.g., birthday party) to provide priors for what is found in the image, which are invariably assumed to be conditionally independent give the scene (e.g., CIRCM (§6.5.1) and

LDA (§6.5.2)). Dividing images into a modest number of scene types might make sense if we restrict our attention to particular data sets, but is not necessarily realistic in general due to the large number of compositions. Consider, for example, an image that has both office elements, and garden elements due to the window, or a playground image that has both a sports activity and a picnic activity.

In more detail, in this model each region is connected to every other region, and the model parameters reflect the joint probability of two labels occurring in the same image. The model for an image labeling is thus:

$$p\left(\mathbf{a}\,|\mathbf{R}\right) = \prod_{i=1}^{R} p\left(a_i\,|\mathbf{r}_i\right) \frac{1}{Z\left(\theta\right)} \exp\left(\sum_{i=1}^{R}\sum_{i'=1}^{R} \phi\left(a_i, a_{i'}, \theta\right)\right), \tag{6.60}$$

where, following Rabinovich et al. [476], we represent the pairwise potentials by their logarithms. The parameters for the pairwise potentials, θ, are simply the entries of a $V \times V$ symmetric matrix that can be estimated from empirical co-occurrences in weakly labeled images (i.e., from image captions). However, choosing between alternatives of these parameters to maximize the training data likelihood requires estimating the partition function, $Z = Z\left(\theta\right)$, which is too computationally expensive to do directly. Instead, Rabinovich et al. [476] estimated it as needed using Monte Carlo integration [485] with importance sampling based on the marginal probability of each word (i.e., more common words were sampled more frequently).

6.6.6   DENSE CRFS FOR MULTIPLE PAIRWISE RELATIONSHIPS

The previous model was extended by Galleguillos et al. [234] to include multiple spatial relationships between each pair of regions. Since computing the relationships now requires region locations, learning the model now requires data that can provide region level labels (Galleguillos et al. used the MSRC [520] and PASCAL [201] data sets). In addition, instead of assuming a fixed set of relationships, Galleguillos et al. [234] clustered vertical and containment representations of relative spatial relations to find four common relations corresponding approximately to above, below, inside, around. Formally, the multiple relation model extends (6.60) to

$$p\left(\mathbf{a}\,|\mathbf{R}\right) = \prod_{i=1}^{R} p\left(a_i\,|\mathbf{r}_i\right) \frac{1}{Z\left(\theta\right)} \exp\left(\sum_{i=1}^{R}\sum_{i'=1}^{R}\sum_{s=1}^{S} \alpha_s \phi_s\left(a_i, a_{i'}, \theta\right)\right), \tag{6.61}$$

where S is the number of spatial relation types (4 in [234]), s indexes them, and α_s is a tradeoff parameter encoding the relative importance of the S cues as learned from training data. Unlike the previous model, the encodings of the context relationships are not symmetric as relationships like "below" are not symmetric.

6.6.7   MULTISCALE CRF (mCRF)

In an early approach, He et al. [272, 273] studied a two-layered scheme for interactions between labels on top of a separately trained neural network classifier for $p(a|\mathbf{r})$. In this work, regions (sites to be labeled) simply correspond to pixels. The middle layer consists of overlapping regions, and the top layer consists of the entire image (although larger regions that do not consume the entire image could be used). Label features capture relationships between objects, such as sky above ground, which is represented by sites in the upper part of a region have a sky label, and the ones below having the ground label (see Figure 6.6). Global feature patterns are handled similarly. Each region is matched with a label pattern that is encoded as a hidden selection variable. This provides a nice framework for learning such expressive labels from data.

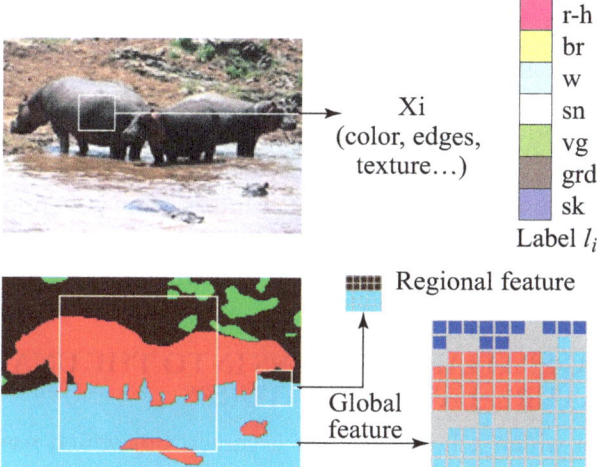

Figure 6.6: Illustration of label features at different scales as used by He et al. [272] (reprinted with permission). Inference involves choosing a label feature for a region such as the ground above sky regions shown.

Labeling an image with mMRF begins by computing $p(a|\mathbf{r})$ for the labeling sites, i, using the neural network. Then the marginal posterior marginals (MPM) are maximized using Gibbs sampling. The marginals provide a good estimate for the label of each site, and thus is a good match for the typically quantitative evaluation of region labeling. However, since each estimate is independent, it is possible that the labeling as whole will be inconsistent and have low probability.

6.6.8   RELATIVE LOCATION PRIOR WITH CRFS

An alternative method to bring the entire spatial context into the two-stage CRF framework is to bring the spatial information into the first stage as a prior to improve the local estimates. Here the spatial information is aggregated into a local feature indicative of the class label at each pixel. The spatial information is encoded along the lines of (6.58) except the sum is now over all regions and relative position is taken into account. In more detail, Gould et al. [247] define a mapping function over normalized image coordinates (i.e., all image dimensions are scaled to a fixed range such as $[0, 1] \times [0, 1]$). Given a pixel at p at (u, v) with a label a and p' at (u', v') with label a', $(\hat{u}, \hat{v}) = (u - u', v - v')$ is the offset (relative location) of p with respect to p' $((\hat{u}, \hat{v}) \in [-1, 1] \times [-1, 1])$. Then they define a map,

$$\mathcal{M}_{a|a'}(\hat{u}, \hat{v}) = p\left(a \,|\, a', \hat{u}, \hat{v}\right), \qquad (6.62)$$

which is learned from labeled training data. Because the distribution is over four variables, one does not expect good representation of each possibility in the training data (i.e., the training examples are sparse), and some sort of smoothing is needed. Gould et al. [247] addressed this with a Dirichlet priors for the counts, and post process the maps with Gaussian blurring.

During labeling, initial labels for regions (here, super-pixels) are combined with the map and aggregated into a relative location feature for each region. This is combined with appearance features for each region to build a logistic regression classifier. At this point, we have a discriminative classification system whose local appearance information is augmented with global context information that relies on an initial labeling. However, going further, Gould et al. [247] improved the method using a CRF with pair-wise interaction potentials for neighboring regions.[49]

6.6.9 ENCODING SPATIAL PATTERNS INTO THE UNARY POTENTIALS WITH TEXTURE-LAYOUT FEATURES

A similar CRF model which achieved similar accuracy, but which was developed for scalable performance, was proposed by Shotton et al. [520, 521]. Again, the sites to be labeled are pixels. Here, one of three unary potentials encodes a relatively large degree of spatial information through *texton* (§4.1.3) maps, which encodes texture in regions around the pixel. To be consistent with other methods discussed here, and to remind us that sites to be labeled need not be pixels, we will continue referring pixels to be labeled by **r**, and use **s** for surrounding regions, which in this method and the next necessarily contain many pixels. Then, texton layout features are defined for a texton-region pair, $(t, \mathbf{r})$, with the value being the percentage of texton t among all the textons extracted from **s**. Good texton layout features are found discriminatively using boosting made possible by training images labeled at the pixel level. This texture layout feature was noted as being significantly more useful than the other two that encode color of the pixel and its location within the image.

---

[49]Gould et al. [247] found that each refinement led to improved performance on three data-sets (Sowerby [24], 7-class Corel™ [272], and MSRC [520]). In particular, the CRF improved over the similar logistic regression model with and without the location prior, and the location prior improved both. However, the method appeared not to perform quite as well as He et al. [272] using a different testing protocol.

In this work the pairwise potentials only depend on the difference in color of neighboring pixels, and whether they have the same label (similar to [489]), specified by

$$\phi\left(a_i, a_{i'}, \mathbf{g}_{i,i'}\left(\mathbf{R}\right), \theta_\phi\right) = -\theta_\phi^T \mathbf{g}_{i,i'}\delta\left(a_i \neq a_{i'}\right), \tag{6.63}$$

where $\phi\left(\bullet\right)$ is in log space, $\mathbf{R}$ is all regions (pixels in this work)—i.e., the image, θ_ϕ is a two dimensional vector of weights for the importance of color contrast and overall bias, $\delta\left(a_i \neq a_{i'}\right)$ is 0 if the two pixel have the same label and 1 if they have different labels, and

$$\mathbf{g}_{i,i'}\left(\mathbf{R}\right) = \left| \begin{array}{c} \exp\left(-\beta\left(\mathbf{R}\right)\bullet\|c\left(\mathbf{r}_i\right) - c\left(\mathbf{r}_{i'}\right)\|^2\right) \\ 1 \end{array} \right|, \tag{6.64}$$

where $c\left(\bullet\right)$ extracts the color vector, the unitary second component of $\mathbf{g}$ is for the bias, and the parameter $\beta\left(\mathbf{R}\right)$ is set automatically for each image by

$$\beta\left(\mathbf{R}\right) = \left(2\bullet\left\langle\|c\left(\mathbf{r}_i\right) - c\left(\mathbf{r}_{i'}\right)\|^2\right\rangle\right)^{-1} \quad \text{using } \langle\bullet\rangle \text{ for average.} \tag{6.65}$$

Hence, the semantic smoothing simply penalizes neighboring pixels that are labeled differently but have similar color. Shotton et al. [520, 521] learned the parameters of each of the four potentials separately (piecewise learning, [540]). After they learned the three unary potentials, they tuned the two parameters for the simple pairwise model based on performance on a validation set.

6.6.10 DISCRIMINATIVE REGION LABELING WITH SPATIAL AND SCENE INFORMATION

The effectiveness of the method just discussed is largely due to the texture layout classifier, which contains most of the contextual information. The CRF component mostly contributes to label smoothing. Rather than increase the semantic power of the label interactions (like He et al. [272, 273]), Shotton et al. [519] added semantic information into the unary potential, and dispensed with the CRF altogether.

The key building block is semantic texton forests, which are collections of randomized decision trees, with decision nodes being binary splits of simple features. During training, decision split criteria are chosen among random proposals based on the largest information gain in the categories if the distribution were to be split with the proposed criterion. Also during training, texton labels counts are deposited at the leafs of the randomly generated trees, thereby encoding a distribution over the labels. During testing textons can then be classified quickly by each of the T trees, and the distributions over labels can be retrieved and aggregated over the trees. The distributions over labels for the textons within a region can then be aggregated. In particular, given a region, $\mathbf{s}$, two quantities can be computed from its textons: (1) the aggregate label probability, $p\left(a\,|\mathbf{s}\right) = \langle p\left(a\,|t\right)\rangle_{t\in\mathbf{s}}$, using $\langle\bullet\rangle$ for average; and (2) a histogram over the nodes used by the textons in the region, including the higher level (non-leaf nodes), which they denote as a semantic texton histogram. These histogram features are analogous to bag-of-words (BoW) features (§4.4), where the tree nodes are playing the role of visual words.

To map these features to labels application to the image taken as a whole, Shotton et al. [519] built a support vector classifier for each class vs. the others using the histogram for the entire image. Here, they used a spatial pyramid matching kernel [248] in order to take advantage of the hierarchal structure of the decision tree nodes. Finally, the role of each node, n, was boosted by $p(a|n)$ computed by aggregating the distributions $p(a|t)$ for the textons in the sub-tree anchored at n. The result is a classifier that can produce multiple labels associated with an image, with all the data from the image potentially helping.

For pixel-level labeling, Shotton et al. [519] created contextual features for the pixel based on regions moderately near the pixel. This is much like the previous method (§6.6.9, i.e., [520, 521]), except that the semantic texton histograms take the place of the texton layout features, and during labeling, the prior $p(a|\mathbf{s}) = \langle p(a|t)\rangle_{t \in \mathbf{s}}$ is included in the distribution $p(a|\mathbf{r})$ for a given region (pixel) to be labeled. Finally, these distributions are combined with an image level prior (ILP), $p(a|\mathbf{r}_i)(p(a|\mathbf{R}))^{\alpha}$, using the tunable parameter α to modulate the contributions of the two somewhat independent factors. The inclusion of the ILP provided a surprising amount of smoothing leading to better looking segmentations, as well as a substantive increase in performance.

6.6.11   HOLISTIC INTEGRATION OF APPEARANCE, OBJECT DETECTION, AND SCENE TYPE

Yao et al. [632] developed an integrative CRF model and associated inference for region class (object or background) labels and scene type that combines information from region appearance, object detectors (see also [166, 345]), scene type classifiers (see also [242, §6.1]), and an approximation of class co-occurrence probabilities. Instead of super-pixels, which is more common, they used relative large regions as computed by the method of Arbelaez et al. [45], which reduces the computational expense. To represent yet larger semantically coherent regions, they used a second level of segmentation that combines smaller segments, using variables for class labels for both segment types. Finally, the representation provided by a standard object detector [211] also provided shape information for the proposed objects. Parameters for the needed unary and binary potentials were learned from held out ground truth using the message passing algorithm developed by Schwing et al. [511]. Yao et al. reported that their holistic approach was able to improve performance on pixel labeling and scene classification compared with using only some of the cues, and that the method is relatively fast.

6.7   IMAGE ANNOTATION WITHOUT LOCALIZATION

There exist many more algorithms for image auto-annotation. The methods considered so far are well suited to region labeling; regardless of whether this was the main motivation during their development. However, for image retrieval, it is often assumed that accurately tagging entire images with semantic labels is sufficient, and thus a number of methods that optimize this task have been developed. Here I describe a modest subset of research with this focus—naturally, many interesting methods had to be excluded.[50] Some of the ideas in the methods that follow could be adapted or extended to provide localization, but this is secondary to the focus of simply providing annotation words in the context of image search by text.

6.7.1 NONPARAMETRIC GENERATIVE MODELS

Parametric generative models such as IRCM, CIRCM, and Corr-LDA, struggle to encode the extreme complexity of the joint distribution of image region features and words. They simplify the statistics of the training data, and if doing so encodes important structure in preference to noise, then they can generalize very well. However, effective representations are hard to find. An alternative is to replace the latent variables with the training data points. An example of such a model is the multiple-Bernoulli relevance model (MBRM).[51] We can see this as a generative process for new data, given the training data, as follows. First, sample a training example, $J \in \mathcal{T}$, from $P(J)$ (typically uniform). Then sample the word occurrences from the image specific multiple-Bernoulli distribution for J. This distribution is based on the occurrences of the words in J, but smoothed by the distribution of words over all training data. Specifically,[52] The Bernoulli component for vocabulary word v is given by

$$P(v \,|\, J) = \frac{\mu \bullet \delta_{v,J} + \sum_{d=1}^{D_{\mathcal{T}}} \delta_{v,d}}{\mu + D_{\mathcal{T}}}, \tag{6.66}$$

where $\delta_{v,J}$ is 1 if v is in J and 0 otherwise, $D_{\mathcal{T}}$ is the number of training documents, $\sum_{d=1}^{D_{\mathcal{T}}} \delta_{v,d}$ counts occurrences of v over the training data, and μ is a smoothing parameter set using held out data. Finally, we sample the features for R regions, using a kernel density function that puts

---

[50]Additional methods for image annotation include the simple latent semantic analysis (LSA) method and probabilistic LSA (pLSA) methods described in Monay et al. [428, 429], matrix factorization methods [457], building boosted classifiers for each keyword based on image level features [576], generative models for keywords and image-level features [69], graph-based approaches [381, 458, 459], extensions to pLSA in Li et al. [374], the nonparametric Bayesian model in Li et al. [366], and optimizing matrix representations of the data in Li et al. [373]. For the analogous problem of annotating video shots based visual features see Velivelli and Huang [575] and Wang et al. [589].

[51]The multiple-Bernoulli relevance model (MBRM) is described in detail in [213]. It builds upon the continuous relevance model (CRM) [294], which in turn builds on the cross-media relevance model (CMRM) [293]. All these models are nicely explained in their respective papers and are relatively easy to implement. The CRM was extended by Feng and Lapata [214] who added using word context to improve ranking of predicted keywords.

[52]The details that follow are from [213], although I have changed the notation somewhat to be consistent with other parts of the book.

a Normal distribution over each of the R_J feature vectors for J. Formally,

$$p(\mathbf{r}|J) = \frac{1}{R_J} \sum_{i=1}^{R_J} \frac{(\mathbf{r} - \mathbf{r}_{J,i})^T \Sigma^{-1} (\mathbf{r} - \mathbf{r}_{J,i})}{\sqrt{(2\pi)^F |\Sigma|}}, \tag{6.67}$$

where F is the number of features (dimension of $\mathbf{r}$). A simple choice for Σ is $\Sigma = \beta I$, where I is the identity matrix of size F, and β is a constant, which can be set using a validation subset of the data.[53]

The joint distribution for a document coming from the same process as J is thus modeled by

$$p(\mathbf{w}, \mathbf{R}|J) = \prod_{i=1}^{R} p(\mathbf{r}_i|J) \prod_{v \in \mathbf{w}} p(v|J) \prod_{v \notin \mathbf{w}} (1 - p(v|J)), \tag{6.68}$$

which is computed using the expressions (6.66) and (6.67). Of course, the appropriate J is not known, and so the overall joint density is the marginal over $\mathcal{T}$:

$$p(\mathbf{w}, \mathbf{R}) = \sum_{d=1}^{D_{\mathcal{T}}} p(J) \, p(\mathbf{w}, \mathbf{R}|J)$$

$$= \frac{1}{D_{\mathcal{T}}} \sum_{d=1}^{D_{\mathcal{T}}} p(\mathbf{w}, \mathbf{R}|J) \qquad \text{(for uniform } p(J)). \tag{6.69}$$

Notice that considering the regions of each training image as group (in (6.67)) means that region feature correlations, perhaps due to image class, are considered. Thus, from the perspective of which cues are exploited, this model is somewhat comparable to the CIRCM and Corr-LDA models applied to the image level annotation task, and less comparable to either IRCM or RTM, where concepts are independent. Empirically, MBRM performs significantly better than a model similar to the RTM for image annotation.[54] On the other hand, while words are assumed to come from regions, the model does not support region labeling.

---

[53]These details are from [213]. Using a single variance bandwidth parameter, β, which is shared by all features, is sensible if the features are comparable scale. One way to arrange this is to map each feature so that their mean is 0 and their variance is 1, across all training data.

[54]Feng et al. [213] compared MBRM to the original translation model [182], which is very close to RTM. There are multiple possible reasons for the large increase in performance, which are best analyzed by considering the MBRM precursors. The CMRM [293] is different from RTM by the nonparametric formulation and that it models region dependencies. With approximately the same regions and features, CMRM did better than the translation model. Going to the continuous formulation (CRM [294]), which can be seen as relaxing the commitment to tokens, yielded improvements over CMRM. MBRM proposed using small tiles compared with large regions, and different features, which also improved CRM. Finally, going from the improved CRM to MBRM by adding in the multiple-Bernoulli formulation gave another (modest) increment in performance.

6.7.2   LABEL PROPAGATION

A surprisingly effective method for image scale annotation is to adopt labels from similar images in a reference database of images with keywords or captions. Doing so has two sub-problems. First, computing image similarity, and second, choosing words from the captions of similar images. Initially, Makadia et al. [393, 394] proposed this approach as baseline for the image annotation task, and explored several relatively simple methods for the two sub-problems. They built image similarity measures from histograms for seven features (three for color, four for texture) for image representation. To compute the differences between histograms of the same type, they evaluated the Kullback-Leibler (KL) divergence[55] and the L_1 norm (Manhattan distance)[56] and chose different distance measures for the various feature types. Then, in their basic JEC method (joint equal contribution), the distance between images is simply the sum of the distances over all the feature types. Given the similarity between the image to be annotated and all images in the database, they assign a pre-specified number of words, n, from database image word list as follows. They first assign words from the word list of the nearest image, in order of their frequency over the entire database. If more words are needed to get n, they proceed to the next closest image, now ordering the words from that image by the product of their frequency and their co-occurrence in the database with the words already chosen. Notice that this selection problem biases word choice toward ones that are likely to be visual, and ones that are likely to co-occur (if more than one image is consulted). This simple method performed better than other methods compared with, including MBRM (§6.7.1, [213]) and SML (§6.4.5, [110]). Other work in label propagation includes Wang et al. [590] who focus on images of objects (e.g., from the PASCAL visual object challenges (VOC) 2007 and 2008 [18, 201]), Wang et al. [598] who focus on near duplicate images in a very large dataset, and TagProp [258, 579] discussed next.

TagProp.   Guillemin, et al. [258, 579] improved upon JEC in their the Tag Propagation (Tag-Prop) method. A key contribution is to use a Bernoulli model (similar to MBRM (§6.7.1, [213]) for the log likelihood, $\mathcal{L}$, of the training data labels as a measure to set the parameters. For example, in one variant (RK), they wish to propagate labels from K nearest numbers, weighted by their ranking (e.g., the nearest neighbor has rank 1). They learn the weights by optimizing $\mathcal{L}$ with respect to them. In a different variant (ML), they assume a fall off in the weights as a function of the distance to each of the nearest neighbors, where the distance is a linear function of a vector of distances, $\mathbf{d}$, with the elements being diverse distance measures (similar to the seven distances used by JEC as described in the previous paragraph). Notationally, for images i and j, $d_{\mathbf{w}}(i, j) = \mathbf{w}^T \bullet \mathbf{d}_{i,j}$. In this case, Guillemin et al. [258, 579] use $\mathcal{L}$ to optimize the weight

---

[55]To compute the KL difference between histograms, we first normalize them to be valid probability distributions. Denoting p_i and q_i to be the value of bin i for histograms p and q then $KL(p||q) = \sum_{\text{bins}} p_i \bullet \log\left(\frac{q_i}{p_i}\right)$. This is not symmetric. If p and q have symmetric roles, it is common to use $KL(p||q) + KL(q||p)$, which is symmetric.

[56]Using the notation from Footnote 55, $L_1 = \sum_{\text{bins}} |p_i - q_i|$.

vector, **w**. Finally, to boost performance on rare words, Guillemin, et al. [258, 579] experimented with learning a word dependent artificial boasting of occurrence. They reported that ML outperformed JEC even without word boosting, and that word boosting increased the performance even further.

CHAPTER 7

Beyond Simple Nouns

Keywords are largely simple nouns (e.g., backgrounds and objects, also referred to as stuff and things [231]). While much of the technology developed for jointly modeling visual and linguistic data has focused on keywords for images, there is much to be gained by going beyond keywords. Images with full text captions are common, and such captions typically contain deeper semantic information than curated keywords or user supplied tags (e.g., Flickr tags). Hence, there is potential for better algorithmic understanding of the underlying scene, which is the key intellectual pursuit considered in this book. Better automated scene understanding will enable opportunities to learn more sophisticated knowledge about the world from huge image collections as being explored by Chen at al. [128] with their Never Ending Image Learner (NEIL) system. Further, the various aspects of semantic knowledge can help disambiguate each other while training auto annotation systems. For example, even if we only care about simple nouns such as "car," captions with adjectives (e.g., "red car") or prepositions (e.g., "the car is on the pavement") can exploited to better learn models for visual properties linked to nouns, and thus lead to better image annotation and region labeling for the purposes of image search by text.

On the flip side, being able to produce more sophisticated textual representations for images and video has many applications, including assisting the visually impaired, information retrieval, and mining aligned visual and linguistic data. Here the emphasis is on producing full sentence captions, rather than exploiting them for understanding. To achieve this goal, knowledge about visual meaning of multiple parts of speech is needed, and various approaches use different combinations of built in knowledge, multiple training modules for different parts of speech, and joint learning of multiple parts of speech. Going beyond producing a list of keywords, or localized simple nouns (e.g., region labeling), these richer representations enabled a finer-grained and more intricate search. As a simple example of a non-keyword search, perhaps someone would like to search for images of red cars surrounded by grass with a person dressed in white in front of the car. As discussed previously (§2.1), the intuition that improvements in this direction would be useful is supported by studies into user needs in the search of multimedia archives in the context of journalism, medical research, and librarianship.[1] This body of work urges building what is needed in contrast with can be easily built.[2] As a second application, it would also be useful to caption images with full sentences so that their content can be translated into natural language spoken

---

[1]In particular, Enser [192] summarized the limitation of simple index terms; see also Jorgenson [304] and Eakins [187, 188]. User needs (in contrast with what people do with a specific search task and retrieval system, e.g., [244, 606]) has been the subject of empirical by several groups for a number of years. For example, see [47, 193, 244, 403, 404, 451–453, 473, 603].

[2]Paraphrasing [192] quoting [304, p. 197].

language and thus available to visually impaired. Alternatively, translating images into sentences (written or spoken) could help language learners.

In this chapter we will intertwine computational approaches relevant to one or both of these two broad goals—specifically, integrating linguistic and visual information for understanding what is in the scene, and more sophisticated tagging and captioning. We will assume that language pre-processing has provided parts of speech tags, and perhaps sense-disambiguated words as described in Chapter 5. We exclude from this chapter various simple ways to use Wordnet (§3.1) to filter noisy words from image annotation words, or map between vocabularies, to the extent that they were previously covered (§5.5).

7.1   REASONING WITH PROPER NOUNS

Proper nouns often indicate specific, identifiable instances of a category, and thus can provide distinctly different information than category nouns. For example, a collection images labeled with the "keyword" people is quite different than the same number of images labeled with names of people. As a second example, proper names for landmarks enable multiple images on the Web to be integrated to provide 3D structure for them [31]. This would not work if the caption simply referred to each such object as a "landmark."

7.1.1   NAMES AND FACES IN THE NEWS

Names and associated faces commonly co-occur in news data. Automatically linking names and faces was first addressed in the case of broadcast news by Sato and Kanade [508]. Their "name-it" system aligned faces represented by a vector in a low-dimensional sub-space of the raw pixel space (eigenfaces [568]) with proper nouns extracted from closed captioning data. Given a face (or name), the appropriate corresponding name (or face) can be estimated using temporal co-occurrence, computed using a relative co-occurrence function. Using a relative measure makes sense because the anchorperson's face co-occurs with most proper names. Hence, an absolute co-occurrence measure is not appropriate for this task.

Edwards et al. [189] showed that the analogous task with respect to news photos (stills) with captions can be studied on a large scale. In particular, they reported collecting from 800 to 1500 news photos with captions every day from Associated Press and Reuters. The photographs largely contain people, and standard frontal face detection software can find the bulk of them. Most of the images are of a few famous people, but a very large number of people appear only in a few images, i.e., the distribution of people vs. number of occurrences has a very long tail. The image captions are similarly mostly about the people in the image, but often some of the proper nouns are not people, e.g., "Winter Olympics," or people not in the image. In addition, not all people mentioned in the caption are necessarily in the image (see Figure 7.1). Thus, we have the a familiar situation of matching words to localized image regions (here face detector boxes around faces) and vice versa, with each modality often having elements with no match (represented by associating the name with a "NULL" for face, and vice versa).

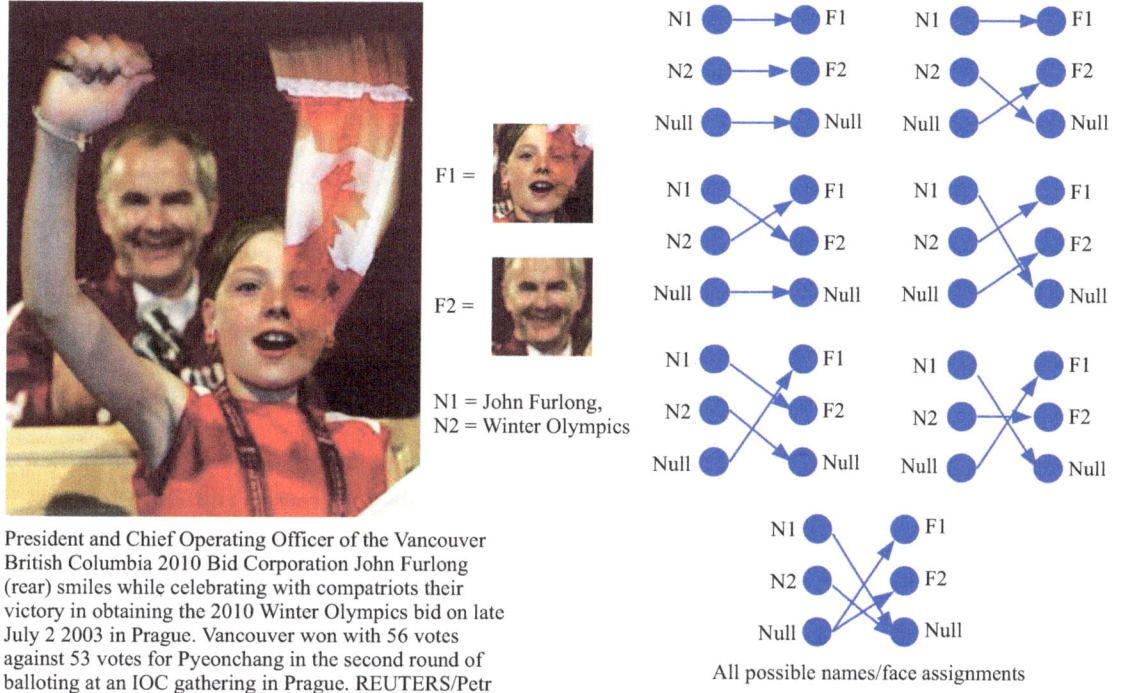

F1 =

F2 =

N1 = John Furlong,
N2 = Winter Olympics

President and Chief Operating Officer of the Vancouver British Columbia 2010 Bid Corporation John Furlong (rear) smiles while celebrating with compatriots their victory in obtaining the 2010 Winter Olympics bid on late July 2 2003 in Prague. Vancouver won with 56 votes against 53 votes for Pyeonchang in the second round of balloting at an IOC gathering in Prague. REUTERS/Petr Josek.

All possible names/face assignments

Figure 7.1: Correspondence ambiguity between detected faces and proper nouns in the captions. Given language processing and relatively reliable face finding, the number of possible matches is relatively small, and for this photo they are listed to the right. Notice that the most prominent face is not named in the caption. The possibility that either a names or a face does not have a match is represented using "Null." This is Figure 1 in Berg et al. [84], reprinted with permission.

Language models. The relatively structured captions in news photos enable relatively robust extraction of proper nouns. For example, Edwards et al. [189] and Berg et al. [85] reported reasonable performance by simply looking for strings of one or more capitalized words followed by a present tense verb. This was improved [84] by a language model that includes additional language context features, $C_1, C_2, \cdots, C_n$. The parameters for whether a word depicts something in the image, $p\left(\text{pictured} \mid C_1, C_2, \cdots, C_n\right)$, are learned using EM. More specifically, the learning algorithm alternates between computing the correspondences, and the parameters for the language model as well as the parameters for $p\left(\text{face} \mid \text{name}\right)$ over all potential names. Because the number of people in the photos studied is relatively small, it is possible to compute the likelihood for each possible correspondence, with the constraint that faces link to at most one non-null name, and vice versa. From these likelihoods, either the maximal one, or their weighted average (i.e., the expectation), can be used as the current hard or soft assignments for that iteration. Berg et al. [84] reported better results using the maximal assignment. Perhaps more relevant here, the stronger, learned language model [84], gives significantly better performance than the simple word filter studied initially [85].

Vision helping language—learning synonyms.   In news data sets people are often referred to in different ways at a given time. For example [85], *Colin Powell* vs. *Secretary of State*. However, given a joint appearance model learned over many faces, there is strong evidence that these faces are of the same person, and hence the two face clusters can merged. Berg et al. [85] report being able to do so with some success. Note that the temporal nature of this assignment of denotations such as *Secretary of State* is interesting in its own right, as it points to different levels of description that could potentially be discovered from data.

Vision helping language—learning about captioning.   The language model learned by Berg et al. [84] implicitly learns a classifier for a proper noun being "pictured," at least for news photo captions. Reported good cues for being pictured include whether the noun occurs near the beginning of the caption, is followed by a present tense verb, and is near the abbreviations "(L)," "(R)," and "(C)." From a general standpoint, what is being learned is some understanding of the visualness of fragments of text, which is related to learning the visual nature (or lack thereof) of basic adjectives, comparison adjectives, and action verbs are as discussed shortly (§7.2, §7.3, §7.1.2, respectively). Finally, in the context of news photos with captions, Deschacht and Moens [174, 175] also considered visualness of WordNet synsets of caption words as part of their method for determining if the corresponding entities are actually in the image [174], which they also use for searching for images that have the best depiction of an entity [175].

7.1.2   LINKING ACTION VERBS TO POSE–WHO IS DOING WHAT?

The ideas described in §7.1.1 for learning models for faces based on news image captions have been extended by Jie et al. [301] to link action verbs with people's poses (see Figure 7.2). While action might be better understood in general using video, as noted by Edwards et al. [189], photo journalists provide images that are richly suited for communication. One way that this manifests is that actors performing actions relevant to the topic are generally in recognizable and distinct poses. Hence, pose becomes the key part of still-image visual representation of action.

Jie et al. [301] exploited the consistency of the occurrence of pose and action verbs to better disambiguate names and faces, as well as learn pose recognizers from the loosely labeled data inherent in captioned news photos. Because better-labeled faces and better-labeled pose help each other, pose models and face models are modeled jointly in a generative fashion, and learned simultaneously. Jie et al. [301] reported that names are better learned when pose linking is included. This is intuitive because the pose of the body (which is connected to the face) can be linked to the verb that is connected to subject (and hence the face). In short, the two sources of information are largely complementary.

 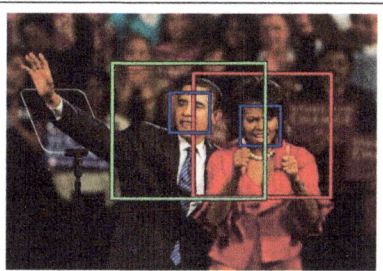

(a) *Four sets ...Roger Federer prepares to hit a backhand in a quarter-final match with* **Andy Roddick** *at the U.S. Open.*

(a) *U.S. Democratic presidential candidate Senator Barak Obama waves to supporters together with his wife Michelle Obama standing beside him at his North Carolina and Indiana primary election night rally in Raleigh.*

Figure 7.2: Examples of news photos and captions which can be better understood if the link between human pose and action verbs can be understood [301]. As in names and faces in the news (§7.1.1, [84, 85, 189]), doing so relies on face detections (blue boxes). However, the people's upper bodies are also considered (bigger boxes) to extract regions and features relevant to pose. These become part of a joint model for names, faces, action verbs, and pose, with the appearance models for faces given a name, and pose given a verb, being learned simultaneously. This is Figure 1 in Jie at al. [301], reprinted with permission.

7.1.3   LEARNING STRUCTURED APPEARANCE FOR NAMED OBJECTS

While the names and faces work relied on being able to detect faces, it is also possible to learn appearance models from loosely labeled data where patterns are repeated in multiple images, which often co-occur with words in their captions. For example, Jamieson et al. [292] were able to learn relatively complex models for the visual appearance of hockey team emblems from collections of hockey images where the captions were likely to include the team name / city (combined to be equivalent in a preprocessing step). For example, "Florida's Olli Jokinen gets bumped by Alexei Ponikarovsky of the Maple Leafs" captions an image that shows the players named, and where the corresponding team emblems are visible on the players. While this work used only minimal language pre-processing (more could be done), it is well suited to, and only tested on, proper names (team names and landmarks) or labels that play the role of a proper noun in the dataset (e.g., in the TOYS dataset, "horse" is a specific toy horse). Given commonly occurring names (e.g., hockey team names) and visual patterns (emblems), the patterns can be learned despite deformations and occlusions. Very roughly, the fact that the prevalent words that are leaned are proper nouns means that the variance is due to viewpoint and deformation rather than object category variance.

Similar to methods that use single-word web searches followed by modeling visual appearance to extract relevant exemplars (e.g., [218, 368, 621, 622]), Jamieson et al. [292] developed an appearance model for each common caption word in turn, independently. They showed it was possible to do this despite significant visual noise (e.g., background clutter) and occlusion in the images. While emblems were typically learned as the most distinctive pattern co-occurring with team names, other parts of uniforms such as shoulder patches or sock patterns where found as a distinctive pattern instead. Finally, for a few teams, non-distinctive patterns (e.g., hockey net) were learned instead.

Models for the appearance for entities such as hockey emblems need to be sufficiently flexible to detect them despite deformations, occlusions, and viewpoint. This was managed by representing the appearance by a collection of SIFT keypoint [387] with approximate spatial relations developed by Carneiro et al. [110]. In addition to allowing some deformation, the model provides a penalty term for missing keypoint detections due to occlusion and noise. This is a sensible model for the objects studied (e.g., emblems in hockey pictures), but modeling an object from multiple parts creates further correspondence ambiguity while learning. The strategy used by Jamieson et al. [292] was to grow promising seed part models by tentatively adding additional spatially nearby points, and keeping those that improve confidence in detecting instances of the pattern. The appearance model was further improved by using multiple diverse parts for an object [291], which allowed models to cover a more significant fraction of objects. Finally, the overall strategy was adopted to learn contour models for shape for object categories [359], going beyond specific objects.

7.2   LEARNING AND USING ADJECTIVES AND ATTRIBUTES

Early work in learning the visual characteristics of attribute words considered color and texture within regions [621] (see Figure 7.3a), as well as patterns over smaller segments encoded by the geometry of pairs of segments [220] (see Figure 7.3b). Models for such visual attributes can be learned by gathering images from the Web using keyword search to provide positive training examples for each attribute word of interest. Each attribute word is also assigned negative examples. A key assumption for the approach is that there will be one or more foreground regions in the positive examples that have a consistent appearance, with the background of the positive examples being statistically more similar to the negative examples. Hence, in this approach we need to determine foreground versus background in the training examples, as well a model for each attribute word and a generic model for the background. These may be generative models [621], or, alternatively, we could use a discriminative model to distinguish between the visual characteristics of the attribute and generic background [220].

Since we do not know which parts of the image are relevant to the attribute, we have the usual correspondence problem, which can be tackled by alternating between estimating the model and the correspondences. One way to re-compute the assignments of regions to foreground is to consider entropy reduction of the foreground set [621], but likelihood of the data in a clustering approach such as probabilistic latent semantic analysis (PLSA) as used by Weijer et al. [601] is a

Figure 7.3: Early attempts at learning visual attributes using web image search. (a) Images with the five highest probably yellow regions after one iteration of a method that alternates between (1) modeling yellow and non-yellow (background), and (2) assigning regions to yellow and non-yellow. At this point, much of the ambiguity inherent in images found using the search word "yellow" remains. This is the top row of Figure 1 in Yanai and Barnard [621]. (b) Images with the five highest probably yellow regions after five iterations from Figure 2 in [621]. (c) Two examples of addressing texture patterns from Ferrari and Zisserman [220, Figure 6]. The left pair shows an example image found by searching for "stripes" with the resulting heat map result showing the probability that each pixel is in stripy region in according to the learned model (warmer colors are higher probability). The right pair is for "dots."

fair alternative. Yanai et al. [621] chose to define the "visualness" of a word based on the entropy of regions classified as being associated with the word with respect to visual features such as color and texture. If the distribution over those features is narrow (small entropy), then the word is declared as relatively visual. Given the feature distribution of a visual word (e.g., "red"), and parts of speech analysis on simple phrases (e.g., "red car"), such learned visual meanings could be used to help disambiguate which nouns correspond to which regions [67, Figure 1].

7.2.1   LEARNING VISUAL ATTRIBUTES FOR COLOR NAMES

Weijer et al. [601] argued that for retrieval applications it makes sense to use the well-known fact that color names are indeed visual, and that features other than color ones are immaterial and even possibly a source of noise. In this context they developed a PLSA approach limited to color name data and color features, gamma correcting their data and experimenting with multiple color spaces. They tested the resulting understanding of color name used in Internet images using 440 eBay images. More specifically, the data was gathered based on the conjunction of one of 10 object names and one of 11 color names (e.g., "blue car"). The parts of the image relevant to that color were manually segmented to provide a mask for that color. This allows for the evaluation of the color labeling of each pixel in those regions. Weijer et al. [601] first verified the assumption that the perceptual L*a*b color space would give the best performance on pixel labeling. They then showed that their model trained on real internet images lead to significantly better performance than an approach based on standard color chip naming data from Benavente et al. [77].

7.2.2   LEARNING COMPLEX VISUAL ATTRIBUTES FOR SPECIFIC DOMAINS

Berg et al. [83] used images collected from the web to learn complex visual attributes in specific domains—e.g., the attributes "dress sandal," "stiletto heel," and "synthetic mesh" for shoes. They also consider handbags, earrings, and ties. The data generally came from merchandising websites, and hence the images were generally free of clutter. On the other hand, the descriptions of the objects were free form and very noisy by comparison—in some sense, this is the opposite case of images with keywords. They comment that many words to describe such consumer items have meanings that depend very much on the context. For example, the meaning of "stiletto" as an attribute of a shoe (or more precisely of the heel) is distinct from its meaning as a kind of knife. They also observe different attribute phrases, which are visually synonymous with respect to their method, and construct visual synsets for their domains. For example, one of the synset for shoe attributes that they found was: <"stiletto," "stiletto heel," "sexy," "traction," "fabulous," "styling">.[3]

To learn visual representations from loosely labeled data, Berg et al. [83] used a boosted multiple instance learning method to associate sufficiently common descriptive phrases (more than 200 occurrences) to visual data. Features were grouped into shape, color, and texture, which allowed grouping the learned attributed phrases into corresponding types. Like Yanai and Barnard [621] they also gauged the "visualness" of their attributes, but with a different mechanism. In addition, they introduced the notion of "localizable" as a characteristic of their attributes which measures the extent that the visual features for the attribute are associated with a smaller part of the object (e.g., the heel of a shoe) versus the entire object.

7.2.3   INFERRING EMOTIONAL ATTRIBUTES FOR IMAGES

There is significant interest in attaching appropriate affective attributes to images, and in particular many researchers have focused on labels meant to reflect emotional responses to images. We consider this task as relevant to language much in the same way that the overall scene (e.g., beach scene) influences possible linguistic representations. More specifically, the use of language

---

[3]Clearly, to the extent that some of these visual synonyms reflect reality (as opposed to limitations of the system), they are very dependent on culture. For example, the notion of "traction" as part of this synset is particularly curious.

associated with, or to be generated for, an image or a video can be a function of how people feel in response to the visual data.

In general, as subjective notions, there is the possibility for large variance due to the individual and their context, and early efforts to address this are discussed in §7.2.7. However, most efforts so far assume that there is sufficient commonality to proceed. Under this assumption, the common technical strategies tend to be similar to learning visual attributes from images of objects without backgrounds as just discussed (§7.2.2), or scene (e.g., sunset or birthday party for an image (§6.1) without regard to details of objects within the scene). This is because the affect label is generally assumed to pertain to the image as whole. More specifically, given a labeled training set of images, one extracts features that have some chance of being indicative of the labels, and trains a classifier to distinguish among the labels. Alternatively, as introduced in §2.3.1, emotion can also be represented as points in continuous 3D emotion space (e.g., valance-arousal-control (VAC). Commonly, the third dimension (control) is dropped as the most of the action is captured in valence and arousal. It is also common to simply consider valence (negative to positive affect).

If we assume that the goal is to infer induced emotion in the viewer, a reasonable choice of data sets are those used by psychologists for this purpose, with the best known example being the International Affective Picture System (IAPS) [10, 349, 418] (see also the Geneva affective picture database (GAPED) [157, 158]). There have been a number of machine learning based efforts for predicting emotion labels for the IAPS images. A significant fraction of the collective effort has focused on representations of low and mid-level features that can be linked to characterizations of emotion. Features and representations studied include distributions over localized color and texture [628]; color features inspired by art theory and/or image composition based on artistic principles [382, 652] and together with face and skin detection [392]; SIFT features (§4.1.4) [372]; concatenation of local color descriptors [383]; visual context [364]; shape as represented by the edge structure of images [389]; and characterization based on models of visual perception in the human brain [482].

There have also been efforts on inferring affect from images in more specific domains. For example, Li et al. [362, 363] considered detecting horror in web images in the context of applications for filtering unsuitable content for children. Here the data was simply collected from the web and labeled by Ph.D. students into three classes (non-horror, a little horror, horror). They also identified the most salient area of the image with respect to horror, in contrast to most work in affective image analysis, which ignores localization. This makes sense for their data—many of the images are disturbing because of particular disturbing things within them.[4] They defined emotional salience for image pixels based on color, and combine this with color and texture features to characterize image patches. They then clustered these patch features to create visual words that were aggregated into histograms for horror and non-horror patches. They then trained a support vector machine (SVM) to classify images into horror categories based on their histograms.

---

[4]More graphically, their example images contain people with serious injuries where the color of blood is obviously a useful feature.

Other forays into labeling affect based on low-level features include labeling outdoor scenes with one of five emotion words (sad, happy, disgust, fear, surprise) [168], labeling affect induced by portraits [176], and inferring affect words for images of art (e.g., [392, 506, 600, 628, 652]).

7.2.4   INFERRING EMOTIONAL ATTRIBUTES FOR VIDEO CLIPS

Inferring induced emotion from video has similarly caught the attention of computational researchers. Video provides additional capabilities to induce emotion, and additional cues for inferring it. Most salient are the temporal component, and the commonly available audio channel. The audio channel provides sound qualities such as voice pitch, as well as mood sounds and music. Text information can be extracted from the sound, or reliably extracted from closed captioning when available.

Despite the large range of videos available, most work on inferring induced emotion has focused on movies where artistic talent is often applied to create emotional experience for the watcher. Thus, it makes sense that someone might want to search for a video based on induced emotion. However, other domains such as news video or YouTube videos might also create such a need (see Jiang et al. [299] for work on user-generated videos).

Often, short clips are considered under the assumption that the emotional content is roughly constant. For example, Wang and Cheong [592] trained affect classifiers on audio-visual features on scenes extracted from popular films and tested them on held out examples (see also [134, 310, 537]). Alternatively, some temporal structure over the shots in short video clips can be integrated using a Hidden Markov Model (HMM) [548]. The temporal structure of movies as a whole has also been considered in several ways. First, emotional content has been proposed as a natural criteria for breaking videos into chunks for searching or browsing (video segmentation) [46]. Second, induced emotion has been posited to tend toward certain temporal patterns (e.g., some are more likely to follow a particular one than others), leading to hidden Markov models (HMMs) [309] or conditional random fields (CRFs) [615] to learn and exploit temporal context. Finally, others have considered that users searching for movies might be interested in ones that have a particular signature over time for emotional content [103, 263].

7.2.5   SENTIMENT ANALYSIS IN CONSUMER PHOTOGRAPHS AND VIDEOS

Flickr images with tags provide a context to address affective image properties on a large scale. For example, Jia et al. [296] built a system to predict one of 16 affect categories from a large set of images pulled from Flickr using one of those categories as a tag. Siersdorfer et al. [522] filter and enrich affective Flickr tags using the lexical resource SentiWordNet [51, 198, 199] which provides sentiment valence (negative, neutral, positive) for the WordNet senses (§3.1). They then train a classifier to link image features to the sentiments. Borth et al. [91] similarly used SentiWordNet as well as the SentiStrength tool [549–552] which provides finer grained valences for short texts. Borth et al. ([91]; see also [126, 129]) proposed using adjective-noun-pairs (ANP) to make use of the connection between the noun-context and the meaning of an affective adjective. For example, "cute dog" and "disgusting food" are reasonable, perhaps even common, pairings. Notice that the variance of the visual instantiation of the affective adjective is much reduced when conditioned on the noun. Borth et al. [91] provide 3,000 ANPs, and detectors for 1,200 of them online [28]. To infer more general sentiment categories for images (e.g., 8 emotion categories from Plutchik [470]), the ANP detector output were used as mid-level feature input for a second classifier.

An alternative for mid level features is generic attributes [295, 644]. The intuition for this approach is that animal attributes such as "small," "white," and "tail," might link to the subjective notion of "cute." Yuan et al. [644] integrated general mid-level attributes learned from the SUN dataset [26, 611, 613] with emotion detection in faces to improve sentiment classification in a different dataset limited to faces. For predicting sentiment for pictures of animals, Jeong and Lee [295] collected affect data (10 categories) for the images in the "animals with attributes" data set [347, 348]. Different than Yuan et al. [644], the prediction of affect was through a hidden network layer for the estimated animal class, rather than directly through the attributes. In other words, the extent to which an image was believed to be a Chihuahua (due to attributes) feeds into the degree to which the system thinks that Chihuahuas are cute. Taking an alternative stance, You et al. [637] argued against predefined attributes, and instead learn a convolutional neural network with multiple stages that can go from image features to affect words [637].

In a different domain, Morency et al. [431] developed a multimodal approach to inferring opinions expressed in YouTube videos. Here, they used transcribed text, facial expression, and audio features (specifically, the percentage of time the speaker was silent, and the standard deviation of pitch) to infer whether the expressed opinion was positive, neutral, or negative.

7.2.6   EXTRACTING AESTHETIC ATTRIBUTES FOR IMAGES

Peer ratings of photographs are available on-line from various websites serving amateur photographers (e.g., [5, 21]), and collections of the data for research have been constructed (e.g., [439]). Early work on such data attempted to link aesthetic judgment to images based on low-level image features and computable heuristics (e.g., "rule of thirds," or limited depth of field) [161, 402]. Going a bit further, Yeh et al. [636] proposed using relative features as defined from groups of images of the same landmark, and correlated with quality as measured by aggregating opinions of five or more participants. Others have considered image content as being a factor in the perceptions of aesthetics from such features, and have proposed developing different classifiers for different image categories (e.g., landscape, plant, animal, night, human, static) [391]. However, this does not address the assumed subjectivity of the task, as the aesthetic ratings were free of user context.

In general, the features used by these machine learning approaches are relatively low level, with a few global features based on photography principles. It seems tractable to produce a classifier which can rule out many poor compositions, and helping inexperienced photographers in real time has been noted as a plausible application of such work [161]. It also seems reasonable for a system to learn to rank one's own photos from one's own feedback [285, 635]. However, picking out real innovative gems from the web at large seems much harder, and the choices are likely a function of the viewer, reflecting the subjective nature of the task.

7.2.7 ADDRESSING SUBJECTIVITY

While it is widely acknowledged that predicting subjective words will be limited by individual differences,[5] only a relatively small portion of the research addresses this computationally. One kind of data that supports doing so is ratings of photographs from photo sharing websites by relatively large numbers of peer raters [401, 609]. While many of the distributions are close to Gaussian, there are many interesting cases with diverse ratings [401, 439], which provide an interesting handle into subjective differences. Taking a different tactic, Lovato et al. [385] showed that the features of images that someone prefers can be used to distinguish them from other participants.

Given variation for preferences, a reasonable approach for improving affective image and video retrieval is to develop user profiles or models. This can be done on an individual basis, where a model of what someone chose in the past can inform new choices, as investigated by Canini et al. in the case of movies [102] (see also [650]). Going further, profiles can be constructed for multiple participating users, which supports selecting content based on what others with similar profiles have preferred in the past [41]. We are all familiar with such *collaborative filtering recommender* systems [101, 274], as they are a common component of on-line shopping. One way to construct a recommender system for image or video retrieval is simply to use metadata tags [555], which reduces the problem to using tags in recommender systems in general (see Milicevic et al. [423] for a survey). Going further, Tkalcic et al. [556] investigated user modeling for recommendation in an experiment with 52 participants who rated IAPS images [10, 349, 418] while being captured on video. They studied the effectiveness of user profiles based on genre and looking time, solicited ratings for the images as wallpaper images, and facial expression from captured video (see also [42, 43]).

7.3 NOUN-NOUN RELATIONSHIPS–SPATIAL PREPOSITIONS AND COMPARATIVE ADJECTIVES

We have already considered how the relative locations of regions can provide helpful context for learning visual representations for objects and backgrounds associated with nouns (§6.6). In some cases (e.g., §6.6.6) learned arrangements were noted to correspond to common concepts such as

---

[5]As already discussed (§2.3.1) there are a number of studies addressing the extent of individual variation in emotional response to the IAPS images [10, 349, 418] (e.g., [33, 71, 455, 609]). In addition, Odic et al. [446] reported variation in emotion induction from movies which correlate with whether people watch alone or as a group, as well as self-reported personality measures.

above, below, inside, and around. However, these efforts did not consider learning or exploiting preposition used in captions.

A computational approach for integrating preposition use in captions into image understanding was introduced by Gupta et al. [259] who assumed captions could provide relationships between nouns such as "below(birds, sun)" and "brighter(sun, sea)" (examples from [259, Figure 5(a)]). Intuitively, such assertions can reduce the usual correspondence ambiguity that we have between words and image entities. Going further, Gupta et al. [259] set out to learn the meanings of the noun-noun relationships from loosely labeled data. In particular, they jointly learned: (1) the parameters of the noun-noun relations; (2) the noun appearance models; and (3) the prior probability of each relation occurring with each noun pair for the arguments. The learning algorithm was a variant of expectation-maximization (EM), which, similar to many methods already studied, alternates between computing expectation of correspondences (E step) and model parameters (M step).

When the learned models are applied to images without captions, the learned noun-noun relationships and their priors are helpful for region labeling in the same way that this kind of information is helpful in models that make use of visual context (§6.6). A key difference here is that learning the contextual models can take advantage of the loosely labeled relationships. A second difference worth emphasizing is that Gupta et al. [259] showed how spatial relationships and comparative adjectives (e.g., brighter than) can be handled in the same framework. Finally, the approach learns the linking between visual appearance and noun-noun relationships, which can be used for annotating images with those relationships.

7.3.1   LEARNING ABOUT PREPOSITION USE IN NATURAL LANGUAGE

Dawson et al. [163] also investigated learning spatial prepositions. In particular, they developed a generative model for word sequences for abstract perceptual representations of spatial arrangements. They developed their method in the context of rendered scenes of distinctively colored objects (e.g., orange blocks) resting on a table. Participants from Amazon Mechanical Turk were asked to complete sentences about the scene to describe objects identified in the scene by numbers (see Figure 7.4). Other than this prompting, the system allowed the format of the sentences to be unconstrained. The sentences were processed using parts of speech tagging using the Charniak PCFG parser [123], and further manipulated using the Tsurgeon tool [361].

Preposition use was grounded by *applicability* functions, which were specified in advance (specifically, "ON," "NEAR-TO," "FAR-FROM," "LEFT-OF," RIGHT-OF," "FRONT-OF," and "BEHIND"). These functions expressed spatial relationships between a landmark object and an object being described. The analytic forms of these functions were provided, but the specific parameters where learned from data, as the researchers were interested in how these concepts are applied in practice. Importantly, the representation included the notion of relative applicability, which modeled the selection of the relationship to be expressed. In other words, while multiple of the relationships might be technically true, humans will judge some of them as more salient, and this will be reflected in their descriptions. This will in turn shape the applicability functions that are learned. In addition to relative applicability, the distance between the object being described and the landmark object contributed to the probability that the concept in the applicability function was expressed.

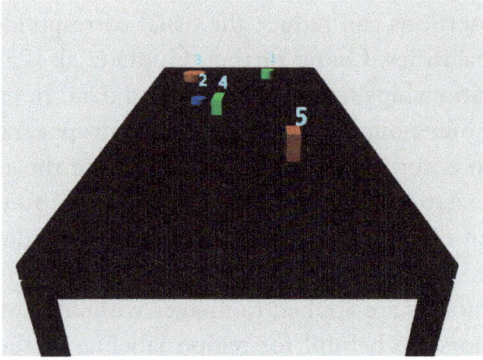

Complete the sentence to describe object 5 in the scene above:
Object 5 is an orange rectangle
Complete the sentence to describe the position of object 5 in the scene above:
an orange rectangle is in the middle of the table

Figure 7.4: A user interface for collecting natural sentences that are guided toward the purpose at hand. Participants are asked to complete sentences regarding the identity and appearance of a specified objected, as well as sentences that localize the object. This is Figure 5 in Dawson et al. [163], reprinted with permission.

Notably, during learning, Dawson et al. [163] simultaneously estimate the production probabilities for their context free grammar (CFG) and the parameters of the applicability functions. They also developed an algorithm to infer the referent of a sentence, given these parameters. They were able to determine the correct referent in held out sentences about 50% of the time, which is substantively better than chance (20% in this data set).

7.4 LINKING VISUAL DATA TO VERBS

Since we have now considered computational approaches to linking visual data to most parts of speech other than verbs, it seems natural to consider verbs next. Verbs are potentially the most challenging word category to link to visual data. Consider, for example, the difference between chase, follow, flee, or race, or the differences between police chasing suspects, children chasing each other while playing, soccer players chasing a ball, or boats racing. Such reflection reveals that verb understanding requires significant temporal context, and often reasoning about the intent of the actors, which might only be revealed in subtle ways. Hence, it is very attractive to consider learning how verb use links to visual representations from more complete natural sentences, which we discuss in the next chapter (specifically §8.1.4). More generally, much relevant work on verbs has been driven by the task of generating sentences for videos, which we also consider in §8.1.4. Here we consider discuss extracting verbs from videos as a partial step of such video captioning work.

Inferring verbs generally means inferring the actors. In other words, we are interested in who is doing what to whom. Thus, inferring verbs often means understanding one or more semantic elements within the temporal scene. Notice that this is somewhat analogous to inferring appropriate prepositions where, for example, inferring "above" means inferring what is above what. Because verbs typically speak to elements within the scene, they tend not be a property of entire temporal scenes. Hence, for our discussion on verb understanding, I exclude the extensive body of work aimed at classifying video clips into activity categories (e.g., [314, 526]), although such efforts could be leveraged for this task much like knowing scene type (e.g., "beach") can help identify objects within.

A common strategy for inferring verbs from video is to first find the tracks of the objects (usually people) within (e.g., [57, 261]). Then the bounding box of each person in each frame provides evidence for the action specific to that person. Similarly, tracks themselves, or relations among tracks (think "chase") could provide evidence for verbs. An alternative to object tracks is extracting descriptors from lower-level motion trajectories such as the dense trajectories from Wang et al. [591]. Regardless, often the goal is restricted to determining a dominant subject-verb-object (SVO) triplet for the video clip (e.g., [256, 335, 553]), which has similarities to activity classification, but training labels are typically verbs that are expected to be bound to subjects and verbs.

Considering context.   Most work on inferring verbs generally exploits the fact that there is great variation on how common SVO triplets are. For example, person-rides-horse is common, but horse-rides-person is not. The prevalence of SVO is often implicit in the training data (e.g., [204]), but language sources can be mined for a different estimate [256, 335, 553]. Further, training data scope can be extended by applying what is learned to other verbs that are semantically close [204, 256, 335, 553], as often done for nouns (e.g., [166]). In addition, a learned temporal logic for certain activities such as baseball can further help choose the correct verb (§8.1.3, [261]). For example, in a baseball play, the batter hits before the batter runs. Finally, the overall scene can provide useful context [553].

7.5   VISION HELPING LANGUAGE UNDERSTANDING

As discussed in detail in Chapter 1, visual and linguistic information can be complementary. That is, analyzing them together is helpful. Again, this is different than using them together only in training, which focuses on learning representations for redundant information. Here we consider methods where visual information helps understand language where it is otherwise ambiguous. In particular, image information has been recruited to help with two classic natural language processing problems, namely word sense disambiguation and coreference resolution.

7.5.1   USING VISION TO IMPROVE WORD SENSE DISAMBIGUATION

We previously considered one method to use visual information in word sense disambiguation (§1.4.3) as an example of cross-modal disambiguation. That method required sense disambiguated image captions for learning, which are not readily available. To create such data, Barnard et al. [66, 67] by matched sentences from a sense-disambiguated language corpus (SemCor [22, 424]) to an image dataset. However, the supervised nature of the approach does not scale. Instead, May et al. [411] proposed an unsupervised approach based on Yarowsky method [634]. That method iteratively labels senses based on collocated words, beginning with a high confidence seed set of collocated words (e.g., from WordNet) which is expanded as the process repeats. May et al. [411] simply add visual words (§4.3) to the mix, and reported that including the visual information improved sense disambiguation. For their experiments, they used a selection of ImageNet, and acquired captions for them using Amazon Mechanical Turk.

7.5.2   USING VISION TO IMPROVE COREFERENCE RESOLUTION

In natural language multiple words can refer to the same thing. The most common examples are pronouns. In complex sentences it can be difficult (even for humans) to determine who or what "she" or "he" or "it" is actually referring to, and there is a long history in natural language processing on developing methods to infer what is being referred to. In the case of image or video captions, the writer is often referring to elements in the image in similarly ambiguous ways. Since the two modalities are meant to be understood together, it is reasonable that joint inference with the visual and linguistic data is helpful. This is exactly what was found by Ramanathan et al. [479] in the case of people in TV videos with scripts, and Kong et al. [333] in the case of captions for indoor scenes.

7.5.3   DISCOVERING VISUAL-SEMANTIC SENSES

We previously considered that different senses of words typically have different visual attributes has introduced above (§3.2) in the context of constructing datasets for large scale recognition as explored by Saenko and Darrel [496, 497]. As they largely exploit language to do so, this is an example of language helping vision. A somewhat different task is to mine web data to discover visual-semantic concepts similar to those discussed in the context of graphical models for words and pictures (§6.3). For this task, Chen et al. [127] developed a co-clustering approach which emphasizes that document text can depict a traditional word sense (e.g., the fruit meaning of "apple"), but relevant visual data can induce sub-clusters (e.g., "red apple" vs. "green apple"). Here, visual information helps create finer grained semantic categories grounded in appearance.

7.6   USING ASSOCIATED TEXT TO IMPROVE VISUAL UNDERSTANDING

The opposite scenario from those discussed in the previous sub-section is considering how associated text (e.g., keywords, captions), can improve computer vision systems. We have already considered the example of the query on rose (Figure 1.4), where having the keyword rose excludes the image with the red stop sign, which, given the blob representation, matches the features of a rose image. As also previously discussed (§1.4.2), we can cast associated text as a way to disambiguate the choices of a noisy vision system. Not surprisingly, region labeling is more effective if labels are biased toward keywords [62, 67]. This idea can naturally be extended to making use of images captions, which have more hints as to the content than keywords, as discussed next.

7.6.1   USING CAPTIONS TO IMPROVE SEMANTIC IMAGE PARSING (CARDINALITY AND PREPOSITIONS)

Fidler et al. [222] integrated textual information into their CRF model for semantic scene parsing (§6.6.11 [632]). Like others, they used modern natural language tools (§5.3) to distill captions into a more usable format.[6] To extend the previous model to a joint model for scenes and captions, they added potentials for: (1) the existence of each class (recall that in the MSR data set there are twenty classes) based on the presence of the class name and synonyms for the class name in the text; (2) the cardinality of each object, based either on the cardinality as provided explicitly by language processing, or through heuristic operations that estimate a lower bound for the cardinality which, again, account for synonyms for the object name; (3) spatial relations through the spatial prepositions; and (4) scene type as a learned function of class labels. Similar to the model without text (§6.6.11, [632]), learning and inference is again based on the message passing algorithm developed by Schwing et al. [511]. The authors found that the additional information provided by the text has very helpful for both scene type classification and semantic parsing of the scenes, as verified by comparing to their previous model without caption text.

7.7   USING WORLD KNOWLEDGE FROM TEXT SOURCES FOR VISUAL UNDERSTANDING

Large text corpora can implicitly provide knowledge about the world that can be exploited to improve inferring what is going on from visual data. This makes sense because the ability of the human vision system to do its job is partly due to our vast knowledge about the world and what we expect to see. One kind of world knowledge already considered in detail is context information (§6.5, §6.6). However, recall that which items co-occur with others or within scene types was largely learned from image data. Alternatively such information can be mined from text corpora. In this section we address methods developed for using world knowledge to improve visual un-

---

[6]Specifically, the authors of report using [562] for parts of speech, [325] syntactic parsing, and [165] for type dependencies. These are critical for extracting relationships. All these tools are available as part of the Stanford core NLP suite [25].

derstanding. This endeavor can be motivated by the commonly held assumption that one reason why the human vision system is effective is because we use a great deal of knowledge about the world and what we expect to see.

7.7.1   SEEING WHAT CANNOT BE SEEN?

Imagine watching a video of someone, say a criminal, being chased by the police. If you are asked about the mental state of the person being chased, "scared" might be an appropriate response. Of course, one does not have access to others' true mental states, but nonetheless, people behave as though they do, and it seems to be helpful to us. One way that we come up with answers to such a question is by imagining ourselves in that situation, and responding how we would feel in that situation. To address this computationally, one could mine text sources that implicitly encode content such as being chased is associated with fear, and the presence of police is associated with negative emotion.

This general idea has been implemented by Tran et al. [564] to infer mental states of people in chase videos ranging from police chases to children playing to sports. They reduced the visual content of videos to one or more activity-actor pairs such as (chase, police).[7] While the method theoretically supports arbitrary sized tuples, they simplified matters by having additional actors simply leading to additional pairs. They then constructed a set of 160 mental state words gathered from several resources and extended using WordNet synsets. They experimented with several ways to measure similarity between the activity-actor pairs based on the Gigaword 5th Edition corpus [462] which is derived from newspaper texts. This large corpus encodes relevant world knowledge through co-occurrence of mental state words, and the pairs.

One mechanism to compute the similarity was to first encode the corpus using the recurrent neural network language model (RNNLM) from Mikolov et al. [420]. As discussed previously, (§5.5.2), this provides a mapping, $vec(\bullet)$, from words to points in a relatively high dimensional space (they used 600). To map pairs they simply summed the vectors for each of the two words. They then computed the cosine similarity between the vector for the tuple and the vector for each mental state word to estimate the mental states.[8] In a second method they estimated the probability of seeing the mental state word with each the tuple directly from the corpus. And in the third method they used deeper analysis of the text in the corpus around the event (e.g., "chase") to infer possible mental states of the participants in the corpus. If actors in the corpus match the actor in the observed pair from the video, then the mental state distribution from that portion of the video is added to the mental state distribution for the video clip being analyzed.

---

[7]In the published study [564] they used ground truth detections. In a subsequent study [563, § 7.4] they degraded detection accuracy to state of the art performance.

[8]The method also used "back-off," which combines the estimates from single elements in the tuple with estimates from pairs.

7.7.2 WORLD KNOWLEDGE FOR TRAINING LARGE-SCALE FINE-GRAINED VISUAL MODELS

In their learning everything (visual) about anything (LEVAN) system, Divvala et al. [178] make use of world knowledge for learning visual classifiers. They observe that given sufficient training data, building finer-grained classifiers (e.g., one for "horse rearing") can be easier than coarser grained ones (e.g., "horse" or "rearing"), for the simple reason that the variation over visual representations of the former is much smaller than the later. But how does one know that "horse rearing" is a concept, or that "rearing" often applies to horses, but not sheep? Here Divvala et al. [178] use the Google Books Ngrams data [414] to develop a vocabulary of finer-grained concepts. These are then exploited to get many visual examples from the Web, and train classifiers for them.

CHAPTER 8

Sequential Structure

While the previous chapter considered many aspect of language use, the computational methods largely handled one aspect in isolation. Further, while language pre-processing might have been used to extract language components, the subsequent integration of vision and language described largely ignored the ordering of language data. However, order matters in written text, much as spatial arrangement matters in visual data. Further, in video, narrative also matters. Recent research has begun to consider sequential aspects in several ways including (1) taking advantage of the information within ordering; (2) producing sequential output (e.g., image and video captioning); and (3) interpreting more complex queries for image search and visual question and answering. Some of these efforts are covered in this chapter.

8.1 AUTOMATED IMAGE AND VIDEO CAPTIONING

Recently, there has been a flurry of activity in the next obvious step in image and video annotation, specifically generating natural language captions that tell much fuller stories about the scene. One approach to producing reasonable sentences that overlap in content with images or video is to recycle existing image captions (§8.1.1). Alternatively, one can create captions from scratch. Perhaps the simplest and most obvious approach for producing grammatical sentences is to use templates (§8.1.2). However, doing so leads to limited and uninspiring captions. These two methods dodge the challenges with automated language generation, but recent substantive progress on learning to do so from corpora has led to approaches that do not rely on templates or existing sentences (§8.1.4).

8.1.1 CAPTIONING BY REUSING EXISTING SENTENCES AND FRAGMENTS

Captioning an image or video clip tends to proceed in two steps. First, the image or video is analyzed to extract a simplified symbolic representation of the key semantics. Using the terminology of Farhadi et al. [204], these representations live in a *meaning space*. This process of deciding what is where, and doing what, is often referred to as the *content planning* stage. Second, the symbolic representation is used to generate captions, which is often referred to as the *surface realization* stage. In the case of captioning by ranking, this is implemented by scoring the meaning against available image captions, and choosing the best one. Notice that this can be run in reverse—from caption to highly ranked meanings to images with those meanings—to find images for sentences as well. In the case of Farhadi et al. [204], meaning is represented by < object, action, scene >

triplets inferred for images using a Markov random field model whose potentials are trained discriminatively using a method for structure learning [547]. Scoring matches between meanings and sentences is executed as follows. First, sentences are parsed to generate < object, action > pairs and scene word candidates. Then the extracted tokens are compared with the meaning tokens using a WordNet similarity method (specifically, Lin similarity [376]). A second two-step method was proposed by Ordonez et al. [450] who scaled up captioning by ranking by several orders of magnitude to the one million images in their SBU captioned photo database [449]. They provided results for increasingly large subsets of their data set, and, as one might hope, the bigger the dataset the better the results, as a larger data set is more likely to include similar images with a good caption. Other work using the two-step strategy includes Socher et al. [532]. Finally, instead of an explicit two-step approach, Hodosh et al. [243, 278, 279] consider various approaches based on learning a common sub-space for joint visual and linguistic data.

Some of the issues with recycling whole sentences can be overcome by reusing parts of existing sentences accompanying images that have some aspects in common with the image being captioned. This process better reflects the compositionality of both images and text. It has been implemented based on n-grams [371] and parse tree fragments [343, 344].

A different interpretation of the image captioning task is to produce a single, head-line like sentence that conveys the story behind the image [215]. This makes sense in the context of images that were chosen to illustrate news stories. Here, Feng and Lapata [215] made use of both the longer story, and the image, to automatically produce such captions. These were evaluated against the human generated captions available for BBC news images.

8.1.2 CAPTIONING USING TEMPLATES, SCHEMAS, OR SIMPLE GRAMMARS

In BabyTalk, Kulkarni et al. [338, 339] integrated evidence from detectors for objects, detectors for attributes of objects, and spatial reasoning into a CRF model for scene content. Inferred content then forms the basis of a sentence with nouns, adjectives, and prepositions. They experiment with three approaches for language generation, and report that a simple template approach provided the most fluent captions (see Figure 1.6d for example results). Less fluent, but possibly more creative captions arose from building captions using n-grams mined from the Web (see also [371]). Alternatively, grammatical sentences can be achieved by using a simple grammar (e.g., as done by Yao et al. [631] on semi-supervised image parses). Yang et al. [627] provided a simple HMM model for an underlying semantic structure for relatively constrained sentences. The HMM has factors for the emission of detections for possible objects and scenes. The HMM predicts a verb from the nouns (using learned conditional probabilities), and similarly, compatible scene label from the verb and nouns. The structure is then used to compose simple sentences. Other work using template filling for image captioning include Elliot and Keller [191] and Gupta and Mannem [260].

Improving object noun choices.   A potential issue with using simple word models is that optimal word choice depends on several factors, and the methods described so far will choose them based on labels used for training. For object nouns, Ordonez et al. [448] suggested using the entry level category words that most people would use to name the object (e.g., "dolphin" instead of "grampus griseus," despite the later being more specific). Ordonez et al. showed how to mine web data such as their SBU captioned photo database [449] to determine the entry level category words. To implement this for annotation, one could choose to train classifiers for only those words. Instead, Ordonez et al. [448] (see also [173]) developed an approach for based on building classifiers for leaf nodes in ImageNet [9, 172], and then predicting the entry level category. While this work was developed in the context of simply annotating ImageNet images with a single category label, the issue is particularly relevant to captioning because we implicitly assume that people might actually read captions. For image search by keyword, semantic similarity measures could mitigate the difference between training class and entry-level categories, although (for example) we would lose the notion that "grampus griseus" might be the canonical dolphin. The same research group also provide data about what people describe in images, and how this relates to content [82] and eye tracking behavior [645].

Captioning video clips.   In the case of videos, Kojima et al. [330] demonstrated generating simple sentences for surveillance video. In this early work on captioning, the number of objects and actions (and the relation between objects and actions) were relatively constrained (e.g., they assumed only one human in the scene). More recently, Barbu et al. [56] developed a comprehensive system for creating simple sentences from templates for video clips. The system crafts together the output of a variety of detectors to fill in predefined templates. The system was extensively tested on the Mind's eye year one dataset [15].

Krishnamoorthy et al. [335] developed a video captioning system that adopts the two-step paradigm introduced in §8.1.1. They identify the most likely subject, verb, and object for a video clip as an intermediate representation, and then generate candidate sentences with respect to a predefined template. These candidates are ranked using a language model trained on the GoogleNgram corpus [241]. Part of the innovation of the work is a set of pragmatic mechanisms for determining reasonable subject-word-object triples. Thomason et al. [553] extended this work to more formally use prior knowledge mined from the web for the occurrence of subject-verb-object triplets. In addition, they integrated scene information, which had previously been considered in images, but not in video. These two systems were tested on the Microsoft research video description corpus [124, 125]. Other work on providing captions for videos (often of people cooking) that is based on semantic modeling followed by constructing sentences from templates include Das et al. [159, 160], Rohrbach et al. [488], Senina et al. [513], and Xu et al. [616, 617]. Issues addressed by these efforts include moving to generating multiple consistent sentences, and more jointly modeling videos and language.

8.1.3   CAPTIONING VIDEO USING STORYLINE MODELS

Gupta et al. [261] developed an approach to learn storyline models for baseball plays from simple language descriptions of them. Here they implicitly exploited that what might happen at a high level of abstraction is quite constrained by rules of the game. For example, the pitch of the ball must precede the hit of the ball. They proposed to model the semantics of baseball with an AND-OR graph, with the details being learned from videos of plays with simple English captions. An AND-OR graph is a directed graph with two node types, with each OR node representing a choice among its children, and each AND node representing that all of its children are active/true/used. In this particular use of AND-OR graphs, the directed arrows indicate causality. Thus, the OR node for "pitch-by-pitcher" connects to two AND nodes, one for "hit-by-batter" and the other for "miss-by-batter." In other words, pitching causes one of two things to happen. Further, the AND node for "hit-by-batter" has two necessary consequences: the batter runs and a fielder runs. Hence, one can see that baseball plays can be nicely (but approximately) encoded using this mechanism, which provides for the composition of possible things that can happen. Much like many of the graphical models developed in the previous chapter, the nodes also link to both visual and textual evidence. Importantly, Gupta et al. [261] were able to learn the compositional model from data. Having done so, they showed that the model can generate captions. This amounts to using the data to infer the particular instance of the semantics of the play from video, and then using the participating nodes to generate the caption. The directed graph inherently provides for correct ordering, although, as there is choice in which branch of AND nodes with more than one child is used first, the ordering might seem odd for human readers.

8.1.4   CAPTIONING WITH LEARNED SENTENCE GENERATORS

Recently, there has been great interest in learning language generators for creating captions for images and video clips using neural networks. For example, Kiros et al. [321] proposed a network that predicts successive words in sentences from a context window of preceding words together with image features which either bias the input from the words, or gates nodes in the hidden layer between input words and the output. Images are represented by the output of a convolutional neural network (CNN), whose weights can be learned simultaneously with the language generator. They tested the approach on three corpora with images and captions (IAPR TC-12, attribute discovery [83], and SBU [449]).

Donahue et al. [179, 577, 578] implemented an alternative system that uses recurrent neural network (RNN) modules for sequence representation for activity recognition in videos, and, more germane to this discussion, caption generation (see Figure 8.1b). RNNs are invariant in time (or sequence position) which function by consuming an input, updating their hidden state, and producing an output. Sequences are generated by using word n as the input to generate word $n + 1$. Of course, this process can also be influenced by a representation of the visual data (again, invariably a CNN). While RNNs have been around for a long time, difficulties with learning and using them when dependencies between distant sequence positions are important have only

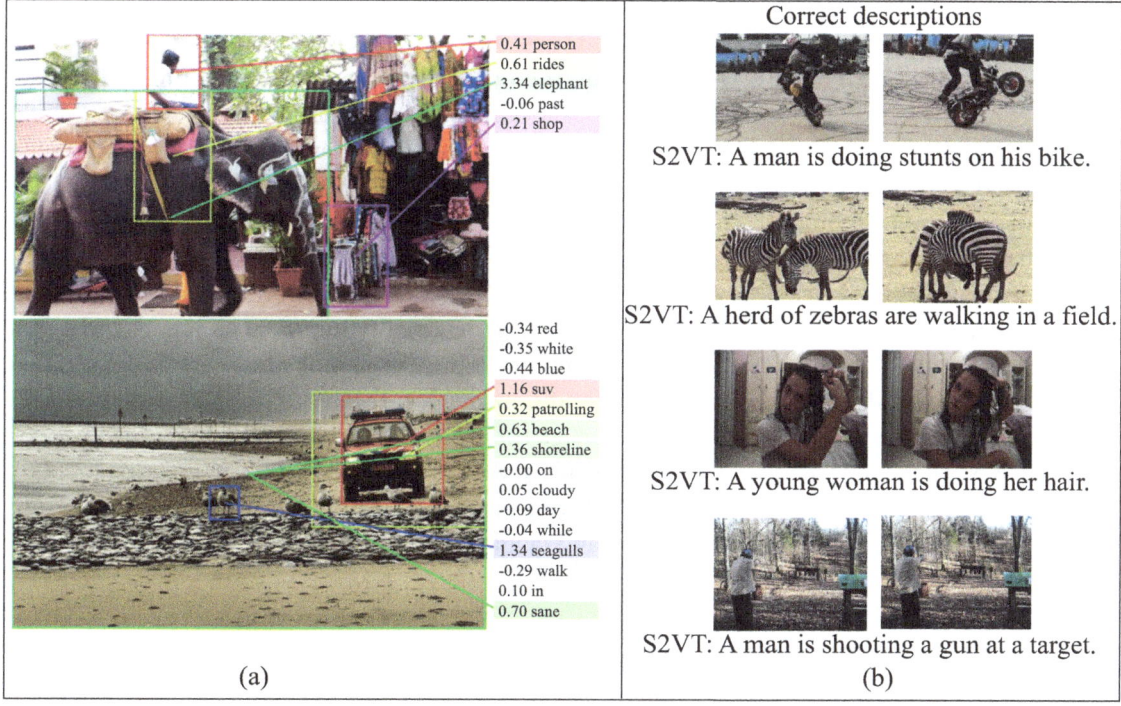

Figure 8.1: Selected good captioning results for images (a) and video clips (b) using learned language models. The left-hand panel (a) is from Figure 5 of Karpathy and Fei Fei [312], reprinted with permission. The inferred sentence is aligned with pieces of the image with the confidence of each word indicated. The right-hand panel (b) is Figure 3(a) from Venugopalan et al. [577], reprinted with permission. The sentences inferred by their S2VT model are shown beneath two representative frames from the corresponding video clips.

been resolved relatively recently. In particular, Donahue et al. [179, 577, 578] make use of long short-term memory (LSTM) blocks [277], which enable hidden states to be remain unchanged, be updated, or be reset. In particular, they make use of recent extensions and improvements to the long short-term memory approach [133, 539, 646]. They refer to their combined architecture as long-term recurrent convolutional networks (LRCNs). Since they are jointly trained on images (or video) and captions (like Kiros et al. [321]), the output is both likely to be relevant and reasonably grammatical and natural. They implemented their LRCNs for various task (activity recognition, image description, video description), in the Caffe open source framework for deep learning [297]. Similar systems that exploit CNNs for learned image representations, and LSTMs or other RNNs for caption generation include Kiros et al. [322], Vinyals et al. [581], and Mao et al. [400].

For the captioning methods discussed so far, localization is either a means to an end, or ignored completely. Further, the target output is usually a single sentence or caption for the entire image. Karpathy and Fei Fei [312, 313] took the next step of generating multiple phrases that correspond to parts of images (i.e., language is localized)—see Figure 8.1a. To achieve this they first learn a joint space for image elements (here, bounding boxes) and words, whose representation includes some context words, using a bidirectional recurrent neural network (BRNN) [510]. Then they infer an alignment between word groups and image elements, using an objective function that encourages nearby words to correspond to the same image elements as well as being good matches with the element with respect to an MRF model. Finally, they build a RNN model for text generation that includes input from the image representation. For training data they used either images and their captions, or image elements and their caption fragment, which were inferred as just described. Like others, they condition the RNN on the image representation. To generate text for an image or a region, the image (or region) is fed through the learned network, and the RNN generates the caption using the initial word "The," followed by generating successive words and updating its state until the END token is generated. In summary, researchers interested in computationally integrating vision and language best become expert in modern network methods.

8.2   ALIGNING SENTENCES WITH IMAGES AND VIDEO

As discussed previously in the context of images with keywords (§1.4.2 §1.4.3), jointly considering visual and textual information can improve both, largely through disambiguation. Further, the resulting aligned visual-text corpus supports data-set building, information retrieval, and multi-modal data mining. Far richer alignments are possible in the sequential domain, where we can consider narrative as being multi-modal, and inferring the alignment has the same benefits on a larger scale.

Recall that we have already discussed simple alignments of caption words with broadcast video that used minimal sequential structure (§6.4.3). Cour et al. [145] extended the degree of sequential reasoning, especially with respect to the closed-captioned text. This work was motivated largely by the task of semi-automatic data-set construction. However, the work also applies to retrieval. For example, they observed that pronouns occur in closed-captioned text relatively often compared with the corresponding proper nouns (e.g., character names). Hence, automated co-reference resolution on the text side improves searching for scenes based on character name, and of course, alignment in general is helpful for accurate search. In particular, as already noted (§6.4.3), the narrative often mentions people who are not visible in the corresponding video segment.

Different than most alignment efforts, rather than work with closed-captioned text, Tapaswi et al. [546] worked with on-line plot summaries. This supports queries about the plot, which are generally at a higher level of abstraction than closed-captioned text. In a related project [545], they explored aligning book chapters with movie scenes taken from novel-to-movie adaptations. Here they found it important that the alignment was necessarily sequential. This work supports the additional application of inferring which parts of the novel were not in the movie and vice versa. Going further, Zhu et al. [655] tackled aligning entire novels with movies. Their approach encodes movies into a suitable neural network space developed for video captioning [322] as mentioned in §8.1.4. This system was trained on video clips and associated descriptions provided by Rohrbach et al. [487]. They encode the book text using representations from sentence-level encoder trained on predicting nearby sentences in a large corpus (skip-thought vectors, [323]). Finally, they use a neural network approach to align the two that takes into account the broader context of the representations to be aligned.

Alignment for natural language queries.   Several of the methods just described could be used to find visual information based on natural language queries. Once trained, rather than align additional sentences with visual data, one can compute which visual data aligns best with a new query sentence. Along similar lines, Dahua et al. [155] developed a system for finding RGBD video clips in the context of driving. They distill query sentences into a simpler form that retains the parts of the sentence that are likely to be visually evident, and then formulate the search as a graph-matching problem.

8.3   AUTOMATIC ILLUSTRATION OF TEXT DOCUMENTS

While much of this book addresses mapping visual representations to linguistic ones, the reverse task, sometimes referred to as *auto-illustration* [64], has many applications such as semi-automated web page building, language learning, interfaces for people with language and/or cognitive deficits, and cross-lingual communication tools and interfaces [569]. Auto-illustration can often be divided into two parts: text analysis followed by choosing images. For many applications, the sequential aspects of the text matter, both at the level of sentences, and at the level of the overall narrative. Hence, we consider auto-illustration in this chapter, even though much of the work so far distills text documents into a bag of keywords, or assumes that the narrative is provided symbolically through a user interface. In the later case, sequential structure is sometimes used, but it is not inferred from data. Providing images given the text can either be prescriptive by mapping semantics to graphics constructs (e.g., [149, 332]), or labeled icons or clipart elements (e.g., [657]), or using semantics inferred from the text to search for images within datasets or the web (e.g., [140, 305, 306]).

Early work on auto-illustration as image search [59] reduced a paragraph of text to keywords, using parts-of-speech tagging to consider only nouns (the text "analysis") to query a data set of images represented by a probabilistic model (similar to CIRCM (§6.5.1)) for both visual and text information. Feng at al. [216] developed a similar approach using topic models and tested it more extensively. Joshi et al. [305, 306] simply used the keywords as search terms, but further processed extracted nouns to give proper nouns more importance, disregard nouns with high polysemy (as these have too many potential meanings). They then ranked the resulting images using mutual reinforcement—similar images contributed more to each other's rank than dissimilar ones—for which they computed a combined visual and keyword similarity. Coelho [140] developed a comprehensive system that is similar in spirit, but applied it on a large scale (see also [141]). Jiang et al. [298] developed a system along the general lines of these methods to endow chat systems with visual content.

Illustrating sentences.   Much of the recent work in understanding sentences, either as applied to captioning or search (e.g., [155]) could be applied to illustrating them. Zitnick et al. [657] test their method for learning semantics of sentences both in captioning and on illustration, using their clip-art based paradigm [656] that abstracts visual meaning. Their probabilistic model trained on captioned examples is able to generate new abstract scenes for test sentences. Since the representation is with respect to the clip-art primitives, the scenes can be can be completely novel.

Storytelling.   Delgado et al. [167] illustrated news articles by finding candidate images for sentences by word matching, but then also considered sentence-to-sentence consistency, which begins to address the sequential structure that is important for most applications. Huang et al. [283] decomposed fairy tales into themes, and then extract words for themes with contexts. They then retrieve pictures for each story elements from the web using keyword search, which also includes words for the fairy tale as a whole. Kolomiyets and Moens [332] extracted more details about the activities in their system for providing animations of narrative. Using quite a different paradigm, Kim et al. [319] took a learning approach to produce image images sequences for sequences of paragraphs, in the context of Flickr photo streams, blog posts, and reviews on TripAdvisor and YELP. Finally, several researchers have studied extracting sentiment from text in order to enhance graphic representations [240, 266].

8.4 VISUAL QUESTION AND ANSWERING

Answering arbitrary questions about an image has recently emerged as a new task for demonstrating the extent that computational systems understand visual information. The analogous task for language has been an active topic of research for a long time. This paradigm is partly inspired by the famous Turing test for intelligence. The bar for the AI community is that an interrogator can ask the computational system as many questions as they like, and still be unsure if the answers are coming from a computer or a human. A handful of methods for implementing image-question answering with a computational system have been developed recently. Tu et al. [567] described a method for joint parsing of images and associated text. The image parse is encoded as an AND-OR graph (see §8.1.3). Once parameters are set through training, the system can then simultaneously parse an image and a query about it, leading to an alignment that can answer simple questions, which are necessarily directly about the visual content.

Malinowski and Fritz [396] derived predicates ("facts") about the image from visual processing. The predicate formulation allows them to answer questions matching pre-defined templates. They allowed for uncertainty by considering multiple processing results such as assigning labels to segments, and marginalize over the results to answer the questions.

Most other methods target increasingly open ended questions, and are typically based on neural network encodings for both visual data and language. For example, Malinowski and Fritz [398], distinct from their previous work just described, represented images with a CNN network, and encode language with a long short-term memory LSTM network, which is fed a concatenation of questions and answers during training. During testing, LSTM is fed the question and the answer words generated so far, until a stop symbol is generated. Their system is trained end-to-end on the ability to predict training set answers. In a somewhat similar system, Gao et al. [235] chose to handle questions and answers with separate LSTMs, but with some weights being shared between them. In a third neural network approach, Ren et al. [483] implemented question answering as classification, and focus on generating single word answers. They also use an LSTM to encode question text, but different than others, they use the CNN representation of the image as the first word in the query. Finally, Antol et al. [40] developed a data set for open-ended visual question answering having both real images and abstract images constructed from clip-art designed to enables researchers to focus on the high level aspects of the problem if they choose. They provided several naïve baseline results on their data set, as well as results from a system similar to Malinowski and Fritz's neural network [398].

APPENDIX A

Additional Definitions and Derivations

A.1 BASIC DEFINITIONS FROM PROBABILITY AND INFORMATION THEORY

Variables x and y are *independent* (denoted by $x \perp y$) if and only if $p(x|y) = p(x)$ or $p(x) = 0$ (equivalently, $p(y|x) = p(y)$ or $p(y) = 0$). This is equivalent to $p(x, y) = p(x) p(y)$. In addition, variables x and y are *conditionally* independent given a third variable z (denoted by $x \perp y|z$) if and only if $p(x|y, z) = p(x|z)$ or $p(y, z) = 0$ (equivalently, $p(y|x, z) = p(y|z)$ or $p(x, z) = 0$). This is equivalent to $p(x, y|z) = p(x|z) p(y|z)$.

Second, the *entropy* of the discrete distribution $p(x)$ is defined by[1]

$$H[x] = -\sum_x p(x)\log_2(p(x)), \tag{A.1}$$

which generalizes to the joint distribution $p(x, y)$ as

$$H[x, y] = -\sum_{x,y} p(x, y)\log_2(p(x, y)). \tag{A.2}$$

The entropy measures the number of bits needed to efficiently encode the distribution. It also measures the uncertainty represented by the distribution. The entropy is maximal when distribution is flat, and generally decreases as the distribution becomes more peaked.

Now, with respect to the discrete distribution $p(x, y)$, if we know x, then the uncertainty in y is given by the conditional entropy, defined by

$$H[y|x] = \sum_{x,y} p(x, y)\log_2(p(y|x)) = H[x, y] - H[x]. \tag{A.3}$$

Finally, the *mutual information* is the reduction in entropy in one of $p(x)$ or $p(y)$ given the other, which is computed by

$$I[x, y] = -\sum_{x,y} p(x, y)\log_2\left(\frac{p(x) p(y)}{p(x, y)}\right) \geq 0. \tag{A.4}$$

---

[1]As is common, I will use base two logs for information theory quantities. Using a different base simply scales the quantities by a constant factor. Using natural logarithms instead, the units for entropy are often referred to as *nats*.

Alternatively,

$$I\,[x, y] = H\,[x] - H\,[x\,|y] = H\,[y] - H\,[y\,|x]. \tag{A.5}$$

The mutual information is zero when x and y are independent, and increases as x and y become better surrogates for each other.

A.2   ADDITIONAL CONSIDERATIONS FOR MULTIMODAL EVIDENCE FOR A CONCEPT

In §1.1.2 it was claimed that if two observables A and B are both independent, and conditionally independent given a concept variable, c, then it is still possible that both can be informative about c. Without loss of generality, we consider the case where A is known, and learning B is helpful. Formally, we have the properties $A \perp B$, $A \perp B\,|c$, and $c \not\perp B\,|A$ (i.e., $p\,(c\,|A, B) \neq p\,(c\,|A)$ in general). To construct a counter example we can replace $c \not\perp B\,|A$ with $c \not\perp B$ because given the other two properties, one of them implies the other. For completeness:

$$p\,(c\,|A, B) = \frac{p\,(A\,|c)\,p\,(B\,|c)\,p\,(c)}{p\,(A)\,p\,(B)} = \frac{p\,(c\,|A)\,p\,(B\,|c)}{p\,(B)} \tag{A.6}$$

$$p\,(c\,|A, B) = p\,(c\,|A) \Leftrightarrow p\,(B\,|c) = p\,(B).$$

In what follows we will work with $c \perp B$.

Interestingly, we cannot construct a counter example fulfilling the three properties from discrete binary variables (see below). However, a simple example where A and B are binary but c has four possible values is:

$$p\left(A, B, c^0\right) = \begin{vmatrix} \frac{1}{8} & 0 \\ \frac{1}{8} & 0 \end{vmatrix} \quad p\left(A, B, c^1\right) = \begin{vmatrix} 0 & \frac{1}{8} \\ 0 & \frac{1}{8} \end{vmatrix}$$

$$p\left(A, B, c^2\right) = \begin{vmatrix} \frac{1}{8} & \frac{1}{8} \\ 0 & 0 \end{vmatrix} \quad p\left(A, B, c^3\right) = \begin{vmatrix} 0 & 0 \\ \frac{1}{8} & \frac{1}{8} \end{vmatrix}.$$

To endow this abstract example with meaning, suppose that A measures color (red = 0 or blue = 1) and B measures texture (smooth = 0 or rough = 1), c^0 is rough, c^1 is smooth, c^2 is red, c^3 is blue, and that all distributions are uniform. Intuitively, A and B are informative about c differently. It is also easy to check that $A \perp B\,|c$. Formally, we can compute tables for $p\,(A, B)$, $p\,(A, c)$, and $p\,(B, c)$:

$$p(A,B) = \begin{vmatrix} \frac{1}{4} & \frac{1}{4} \\ \frac{1}{4} & \frac{1}{4} \end{vmatrix}$$

$$p(A) = \begin{vmatrix} \frac{1}{2} \\ \frac{1}{2} \end{vmatrix} \text{ and } p(B) = \begin{vmatrix} \frac{1}{2} \\ \frac{1}{2} \end{vmatrix}^T$$

and $p(A)\,p(B) = p(A,B)$

$$p(A,c) = \begin{vmatrix} \frac{1}{8} & \frac{1}{8} & 0 & \frac{1}{4} \\ \frac{1}{8} & \frac{1}{8} & \frac{1}{4} & 0 \end{vmatrix}$$

$$p(A) = \begin{vmatrix} \frac{1}{2} \\ \frac{1}{2} \end{vmatrix} \text{ and } p(c) = \begin{vmatrix} \frac{1}{4} \\ \frac{1}{4} \\ \frac{1}{4} \\ \frac{1}{4} \end{vmatrix}^T$$

and $p(A)\,p(c) \neq p(A,c)$ in general.

$$p(B,c) = \begin{vmatrix} 0 & \frac{1}{4} & \frac{1}{8} & \frac{1}{8} \\ \frac{1}{4} & 0 & \frac{1}{8} & \frac{1}{8} \end{vmatrix} \qquad p(B) = \begin{vmatrix} \frac{1}{2} \\ \frac{1}{2} \end{vmatrix} \text{ and } p(c) = \begin{vmatrix} \frac{1}{4} \\ \frac{1}{4} \\ \frac{1}{4} \\ \frac{1}{4} \end{vmatrix}^T$$

and $p(B)\,p(c) \neq p(B,c)$ in general.

We have $p(B)\,p(c) \neq p(B,c)$, and thus $c \not\perp B$, and from (A.6) $c \not\perp B \,|\, A$. Thus, B can be informative of c even when A is known, and $A \perp B$, and $A \perp B \,|\, c$. Since we also have $p(A)\,p(c) \neq p(A,c)$, this counter-example works symmetrically for the case that we assume we know B and are asking whether A is helpful.

In the case of binary variables, which are more constrained, we have

$$A \perp B \,|\, c \text{ and } A \perp B \;\Rightarrow\; A \perp c \text{ or } B \perp c, \tag{A.7}$$

which we verify next for completeness. We index binary outcomes for A by a^0 and a^1, for B by b^0 and b^1, and for c by c^0 and c^1. Under the two assumptions $A \perp B$ and $A \perp B \,|\, c$:

$$
\begin{aligned}
p(a^0)\,p(b^0) &= p(a^0,b^0) \\
&= p(a^0,b^0,c^0) + p(a^0,b^0,c^1) \\
&= p(a^0,b^0\,|\,c^0)\,p(c^0) + p(a^0,b^0\,|\,c^1)\,p(c^1) \\
&= p(a^0\,|\,c^0)\,p(b^0\,|\,c^0)\,p(c^0) + p(a^0\,|\,c^1)\,p(b^0\,|\,c^1)\,p(c^1) \\
&= \frac{p(a^0,c^0)\,p(b^0,c^0)}{p(c^0)} + \frac{p(a^0,c^1)\,p(b^0,c)}{p(c^1)} \\
&= \frac{p(a^0,c^0)\,p(b^0,c^0)}{p(c^0)} + \frac{\left(p(a^0) - p(a^0,c^0)\right)\left(p(b^0) - p(b^0,c^1)\right)}{\left(1 - p(c^0)\right)}.
\end{aligned}
\tag{A.8}
$$

Multiplying both sides by $p(c^0)(1 - p(c^0))$ gives

$$
\begin{aligned}
(a^0)p(b^0)p(s^0)(1 - p(s^0)) =\;& p(a^0,s^0)p(b^0,s^0)(1 - p(s^0)) \\
& + p(s^0)(p(a^0) - p(a^0,s^0))(p(b^0) - p(b^0,s^1)),
\end{aligned}
\tag{A.9}
$$

and moving all terms to the right-hand side gives

$$
\begin{aligned}
0 =& p\left(a^{0}\right) p\left(b^{0}\right) p\left(c^{0}\right)-p\left(a^{0}\right) p\left(b^{0}\right) p\left(c^{0}\right) p\left(c^{0}\right) \\
&+ p\left(a^{0}, c^{0}\right) p\left(b^{0}, c^{0}\right)-p\left(a^{0}, c^{0}\right) p\left(b^{0}, c^{0}\right) p\left(c^{0}\right) \\
&+ p\left(a^{0}\right) p\left(b^{0}\right) p\left(c^{0}\right)-p\left(a^{0}\right) p\left(b^{0}, c^{0}\right) p\left(c^{0}\right) \\
&- p\left(a^{0}, c^{0}\right) p\left(b^{0}\right) p\left(c^{0}\right)+p\left(a^{0}, c^{0}\right) p\left(b^{0}, c^{0}\right) p\left(c^{0}\right) \\
=& p\left(a^{0}\right) p\left(b^{0}\right) p\left(c^{0}\right) p\left(c^{0}\right)+p\left(a^{0}, c^{0}\right) p\left(b^{0}, c^{0}\right) \\
&- p\left(a^{0}\right) p\left(b^{0}, c^{0}\right) p\left(c^{0}\right)-p\left(a^{0}, c^{0}\right) p\left(b^{0}\right) p\left(c^{0}\right)
\end{aligned}
\tag{A.10}
$$

after cancelling terms. Now let $\kappa_a = \frac{p(a^{0},c^{0})}{p(a^{0})p(c^{0})}$ and $\kappa_b = \frac{p(b^{0},c^{0})}{p(b^{0})p(c^{0})}$. Then (A.10) becomes

$$
0 = 1 + \kappa_a \kappa_b - \kappa_a - \kappa_b = (1 - \kappa_a)(1 - \kappa_b).
\tag{A.11}
$$

Hence, at least one of κ_a or κ_b must be one. Without loss of generality, suppose that $\kappa_a = 1$. Since A and c are binary variables, this also means that they are independent. To verify, we can show that $p(a, c) = p(a) p(c)$ in the four cases.

$$
\begin{aligned}
\text{Case 1:}\quad & p(a^{0}, c^{0}) = p(a^{0})p(c^{0}) \text{ because } \kappa_a = 1 \\
\text{Case 2:}\quad & p(a^{0}, c^{1}) = p(a^{0}) - p(a^{0}, c^{0}) = p(a^{0}) - p(a^{0})p(c^{0}) \\
& \qquad = p(a^{0})(1 - p(c^{0})) = p(a^{0})p(c^{1}) \\
\text{Case 3:}\quad & p(a^{1}, c^{0}) = p(c^{0}) - p(a^{0}, c^{0}) = p(c^{0}) - p(a^{0})p(c^{0}) \\
& \qquad = (1 - p(a^{0}))p(c^{0}) = p(a^{1})p(c^{0}) \\
\text{Case 4:}\quad & p(a^{1}, c^{1}) = p(a^{1}) - p(a^{1}, c^{0}) = p(a^{1}) - p(a^{1})p(c^{0}) \\
& \qquad = p(a^{1})(1 - p(c^{0})) = p(a^{1})p(c^{1}).
\end{aligned}
\tag{A.12}
$$

In summary, assuming $A \perp B | c$, if A and B are not informative about each other, then neither are A and c (nor are B and c). Note that we have one independence relation but we cannot (in general) comment about the other. For example, if $A \perp c$, we cannot say anything about the relationship between B and c—they could be independent, or, at the other extreme, B and c could be duplicates of each other (fully dependent).

A.3   LOOSELY LABELED VS. STRONGLY LABELED DATA

In §1.5.1, we briefly introduced the notion that there can be a tradeoff between having more data that is ambiguous (increasingly loosely labeled data) versus less data that is unambiguous (strongly labeled data). The tradeoff partially depends on the correlations between the entities. For example, if a region-word pair always co-occurs with another (e.g., horses are always standing on grass, with image labels "horse" and "grass"), we are not able to disambiguate them. On the other extreme, if there is a degree of independence between region-word pairs, then the correspondence ambiguity can be resolved, and it is even possible that images with more regions is more informative than a single labeled region, despite the increased ambiguity in the region label. We explore this further here by examining a very idealized scenario for the task of learning to translate regions to words given loosely labeled data as developed algorithmically in §6.4.2.

Let us suppose there are T region tokens that are reliably extracted from images and which always map to one of V words. Conceptually, we can imagine that each word is associated with m tokens, and therefore $T = m \bullet V$, but for what follows we simply require that the distributions are the same (i.e., m need not be integral). In the spirit of the learning region-to-word dictionary problem (§6.4.2), we will allow region tokens to occur multiple times in an image, but if words corresponding to regions are repeated, they are only reported once. For simplicity, we will assume that there are always R regions and up to R different corresponding words. Further, we make the very strong assumption that all probability distributions are uniform.

Now consider the probability $p_{\text{infer}}(n)$ of being able to learn the word corresponding to an arbitrary token, t^*, for particular values for T, V, and R, having been given n data points. We consider three ways that we can learn the word for t^*. First, if there is only a single word for a data point (all tokens map to the same word), then the word is trivially known (this case is subscripted as *single*). This is the only relevant way when $R = 1$. Second, if we see t^* multiple (say k) times, then there will be at least one word common to all k observations. This can be identified as the word for t^* if no other word occurs in all k observations (*common*). To verify that this is sufficient, consider entertaining the possibility that t^* corresponds to some word other than the common word, $w_{\text{not\_common}}$. Since that word does not occur in all k examples with t^*, there must be an example that has t^* but does not have $w_{\text{not\_common}}$. But this contradicts $w_{\text{not\_common}}$ being the word for t^* because it would otherwise be present because t^* is. Third, if we observe t^*, we can choose the correct word if we know the words for the companion regions (exclusion reasoning, subscripted as *exclusion*). Because of symmetry, the chance that we know the word for a companion region is $p_{\text{infer}}(n)$.

Given these three inference strategies, we develop an expression for $p_{\text{infer}}(n)$. To do so we marginalize over the number of occurrences, k, of t^*, which are distributed as the binomial $Bin(k, n, b)$ where b is the probability that t^* is one of the non-exclusive choices for a data point. In particular, b is given by:

$$b = 1 - \left(\frac{T-1}{T}\right)^R. \tag{A.13}$$

Marginalizing over k we get:

$$p_{\text{infer}}(n) = \sum_{k=1}^{n} bin(k, n, b) \bullet p_{\text{infer\_2}}(n, k), \tag{A.14}$$

where

$$p_{\text{infer\_2}}(n,k) = p_{\text{single}}(k) + \left(1 - p_{\text{single}}(k)\right)\left\{p_{\text{common}}(k) + \left(1 - p_{\text{common}}(k)\right)p_{\text{exclusion}}(n,k)\right\}. \tag{A.15}$$

The probability, $p_{\text{single}(k)}$, that one of the k occurrences of images with t^* has only one word (i.e., all words for the region tokens are the same) is given by:

$$p_{\text{single}}(k) = 1 - \left(1 - (1/v)^{(R-1)}\right)^k. \tag{A.16}$$

Notice that $p_{\text{single}}(k) = 1$ when $R = 1$.

Due to the structure of (A.15), in what follows we are now restricted to the case that the words are not all the same. We make the additional simplifying assumption that they are in fact all different (no duplications). To compute $p_{\text{common}}(k)$ our criterion is that, excluding the common word, none of the remaining words appear in all k observations. If any of them did, then they would appear in the first observation. Hence, we can reason about at least one of those words appearing in the remaining $k - 1$ observations, or more directly to our criterion, the probability that this is not the case for the $R - 1$ words other than the common word in the first observation. This suggests that

$$p_{\text{common}}(k) \simeq \left(1 - \left(\frac{1}{(V-1)^{(k-1)}}\right)\right)^{(R-1)}, \tag{A.17}$$

which is not an exact equality because the outer product is over events that are not precisely independent.

Finally, we compute an estimate for $p_{\text{exclusion}}(k)$. An exact computation would require both relaxing the assumption that there are no duplicate words within each observation, and further consider duplicate words across the k observations. Here we simply consider the simplest and most common case that neither of these occurs. Then we compute the probability that all of the $R - 1$ words have been determined for any of the k observations containing t^*. This yields

$$p_{\text{exclusion}}(n,k) = 1 - \left(1 - (1 - p_{\text{infer}}(n))^{(R-1)}\right)^k. \tag{A.18}$$

Now that the parts of (A.14) have been instantiated, we see that $p_{\text{infer}}(n,k)$ ends up depending on itself. Rather than solve for $p_{\text{infer}}(n,k)$ directly, we can proceed iteratively by first setting $p_{\text{infer}}(n,k)$ to zero, and then repeatedly updating (A.14) until convergence.

To illustrate what the analysis shows, we plot $p_{\text{infer}}(n)$ as a function of n for two different choices of T and V with several choices of R in Figure A.1. Interestingly, under the strong assumption of uniform distributions, resolving correspondence ambiguity is quite effective, and, within reason, larger R is better.

Entropy reduction view.   For an alternative formal look at loosely vs. strongly labeled data, we consider the reduction in entropy due to observing the first data point in the two cases of $R = 1$

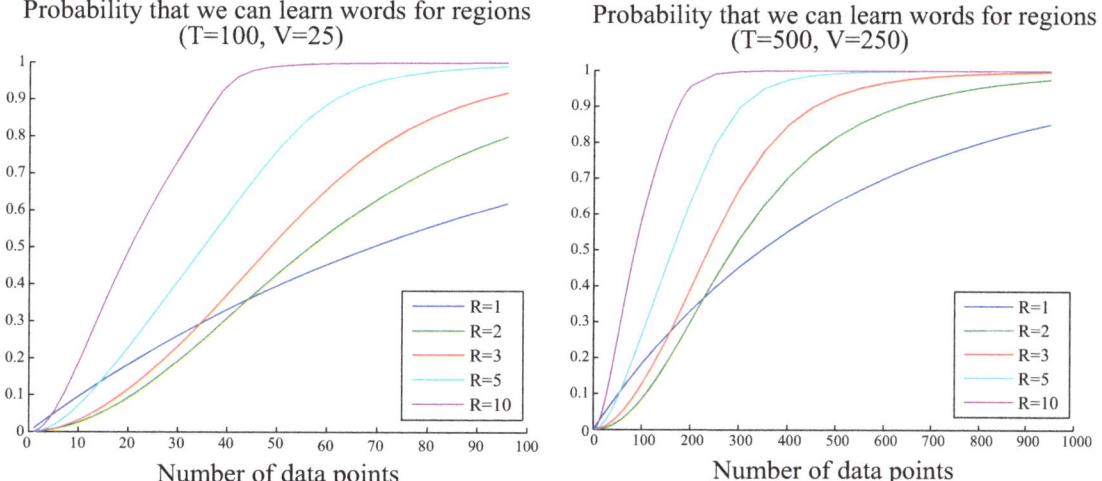

Figure A.1: The probability that we can learn words for regions in an idealized setting with two different values for the numbers of region tokens (T) and vocabulary size (V). We plot the ability to learn words as a function of the number of training examples for differing numbers of observed regions (R). $R = 1$ corresponds to data points with a single strongly labeled region. As R increases we get increasingly ambiguous data for an increasing number of regions. The strongly labeled data has the early lead (most noticeable in comparison to $R = 2$), but as the amount of data at our disposal accumulates, the chances that we observe a region in such a way that we can unambiguously choose a label for it increases. This is amplified by exclusion reasoning. In short, we leverage other images to help understand the images that have the token under study. This is in contrast to the strongly labeled data case where the observations can be considered independent as all information is already exposed.

and $R = 2$. Because of symmetries and our assumption of uniform distributions in all cases, the entropy is simply the log of the number of accessible (valid) states. Without any observed data, this is the number of ways to assign each word to m different tokens. One can imagine each permutation of the tokens overlaid on V successive bins of size m. Noting that orderings within each bin does not matter, we have:

$$H(\emptyset) = \log_2 \left(\frac{T!}{(m!)^V} \right). \tag{A.19}$$

After observing one strongly labeled data point ($R = 1$), we have:

$$H(n = 1, R = 1) = \log_2 \left(\frac{(T-1)!}{(m!)^{(V-1)} ((m-1)!)} \right), \tag{A.20}$$

and the reduction of entropy is given by:

$$H(\emptyset) - H(n = 1, R = 1) = \log_2\left(\frac{T}{m}\right). \tag{A.21}$$

On the other hand, observing the loosely labeled data point with two different region tokens and two different words (the most common outcome for $R = 2$), we have two symmetric alternatives as the first token either links to the first or second word, with the second token necessarily linking to the excluded word. These two alternatives combine with all states where two tokens and two words are excluded to yield:

$$H(n = 1, R = 2) = \log_2\left(\frac{2(T-2)!}{(m!)^{(V-2)}((m-1)!)^2}\right), \tag{A.22}$$

and the reduction of entropy is given by:

$$H(\emptyset) - H(n = 1, R = 2) = \log_2\left(\frac{T \bullet (T-1)}{2m^2}\right). \tag{A.23}$$

Hence, for typical ranges of T and m, the entropy is reduced more in the loosely labeled case. Less formally, depending on the task, learning about two tokens with 50% uncertainty can be better than learning about one token without any uncertainty.

Summary. These analyses are not meant to argue that either loosely or strongly labeled data is better in general, as one will typically take advantage of whatever data is available and helpful for a given task. Further, the assumption of uniform distributions is very strong. However, the analyses give some insight into the subtleties about the information carried by loosely labeled data. First as the number of entities per data point increases, the number of entities that we can learn about also increases. Of course, the amount of information per entity decreases as the ambiguity also increases. Second, multiple data points considered jointly tell us more than if we consider them independently, which is why making use of loosely labeled data can work. By contrast, with strongly labeled data this is immaterial as there is no ambiguity to be resolved by looking at other data. In particular, we developed two examples where loosely labeled data converged to solving the problem of learning region token labels faster with respect to the number of examples as compared with strongly labeled data (Figure A.1). Finally, directly addressing correspondence ambiguity algorithmically, somewhat along the lines of the first analysis, is addressed in Barnard and Fan [62].

A.4 PEDANTIC DERIVATION OF EQUATION (6.13)

In §6.3.3 we developed the IRCM generative model illustrated by Figure 6.2 based on the factorization (6.8) repeated here,

$$p(\mathbf{c}, \mathbf{w}, \mathbf{R}) = p(\mathbf{c})\, p(\mathbf{w}\,|\mathbf{c})\, p(\mathbf{R}\,|\mathbf{c}), \tag{A.24}$$

together with the assumption that regions are emitted from the R concepts in turn, and that words are emitted independently from the same group of concepts considered together as specified by (6.6) repeated here:

$$p(w|\mathbf{c}) = \sum_{i=1}^{R} p(w|c_i)p(c_i) = \frac{1}{R}\sum_{i=1}^{R} p(w|c_i) \text{ as } c \sim \mathcal{U}(1, R). \quad (A.25)$$

We further developed an image annotation model using some intuitive interpretations of the model.

Here we derive image annotation from the joint distribution for a single word by directly marginalizing out all concept assignments. We begin by incorporating the choice (A.25) into the more general formula (A.24) by introducing concept assignment indicator variables for the word, $\mathbf{y}$, which is a binary vector of length R such that y_i is zero except for a single element that is set to one indicating that the word comes from the ith concept. In the generative process, the non-zero element of $\mathbf{y}$ is chosen uniformly at random, and hence $p(y_i) = 1/R$ Notice that this is consistent with the graphical model in Figure 6.2. We can express the full joint distribution by:

$$p(\mathbf{y}, \mathbf{c}, w, \mathbf{R}) = p(\mathbf{y})\, p(\mathbf{c})\, p(w|\mathbf{y}, \mathbf{c})\, p(\mathbf{R}|\mathbf{c}). \quad (A.26)$$

For image annotation we are interested in the word set conditioned on regions, summing over all possible combinations within $\mathbf{y}$ and $\mathbf{c}$. Noting that $p(\mathbf{c})\, p(\mathbf{R}|\mathbf{c}) = p(\mathbf{c}|\mathbf{R})\, p(\mathbf{R})$ by Bayes rule, we get

$$p(w|\mathbf{R}) = \sum_{\mathbf{y}}\sum_{\mathbf{c}} p(\mathbf{y})\, p(\mathbf{c}|\mathbf{R})\, p(w|\mathbf{y}, \mathbf{c}). \quad (A.27)$$

Being more explicit about the two outside sums and bringing the constant $p(y_i) = 1/R$ to the front,

$$p(w|\mathbf{R}) = \frac{1}{R}\sum_{i=1}^{R}\sum_{k_1=1}^{C}\sum_{k_2=1}^{C}\cdots\sum_{k_R=1}^{C}\prod_{i'=1}^{R}\left(p\left(c_{k_{i'}}|\mathbf{r}_{i'}\right) p\left(w|c_{k_{i'}}\right)^{y_i}\right). \quad (A.28)$$

Exchanging sums and products[2] for the inner group we get:

$$p(w|\mathbf{R}) = \frac{1}{R}\sum_{i=1}^{R}\prod_{i'=1}^{R}\sum_{k_{i'}=1}^{C}\left(p\left(c_{k_{i'}}|\mathbf{r}_{i'}\right) p\left(w|c_{k_{i'}}\right)^{y_i}\right). \quad (A.29)$$

Inspecting the inner sum over concepts, we see that if y_i is zero, then the sum is over $p\left(c_{k_{i'}}|\mathbf{r}_{i'}\right)$ alone, which evaluates to 1. On the other hand, if y_i is 1, then the marginalization yields $p(w|\mathbf{r}_{i'})$.

---

[2]Exchanging sums and products is an algebraic manipulation based on the distributive rule. It is the general form of the following example for two indexed variables: $\left(\sum_{i=1}^{N} a_i\right)\left(\sum_{j=1}^{M} b_j\right) = \prod_{i=1}^{N}\prod_{j=1}^{M} a_i b_j.$

Hence,

$$p\left(w\left|\mathbf{R}\right.\right) = \frac{1}{R}\sum_{i=1}^{R}\prod_{i'=1}^{R}p\left(w\left|\mathbf{r}_{i'}\right.\right)^{y_i}. \tag{A.30}$$

Finally, since the factors in the product are one except when $i' = i$, we get

$$p\left(w\left|\mathbf{R}\right.\right) = \frac{1}{R}\sum_{i=1}^{R}p\left(w\left|\mathbf{r}_i\right.\right), \tag{A.31}$$

which is same the expression (6.13) derived less formally in the text.

A.5   DERIVATION OF THE EM EQUATIONS FOR THE IMAGE REGION CONCEPT MODEL (IRCM)

The EM formulism finds a local optimum for a combined space of observed data, X, and unobserved (missing) data, Z. X and Z together is referred to as the complete data, with X being referred to as the incomplete data. In the case of the basic image concept model, X is the observed region features and keywords for each document (image), and Z is the unknown correspondences between regions and concepts and words and concepts, shared with one of the regions. The EM method assumes that computing the maximum likelihood estimate of the parameters given the complete data,

$$\underset{\theta}{\operatorname{argmax}}\{\log\{(Z, X|\theta)\}\}, \tag{A.32}$$

is relatively easy. Here we express the objective function in terms of logs, but the optimum value of the parameters is the same as $\log(\bullet)$ is a monotonic function. The expectation, or E step, is to evaluate

$$p\left(Z\left|X, \theta^{(s)}\right.\right), \tag{A.33}$$

where s indexes the step (we used "old" instead of s in the text). For the basic image concept model we already derived this as expressions for $p\left(c_k\left|\mathbf{r}_{d,i}, \Theta^{(old)}\right.\right)$ in (6.21) and $p\left(c_k\left|w_j, \mathbf{R}_d, \Theta^{(old)}\right.\right)$ in (6.23).

The M step is formally derived by solving for $\operatorname{argmax}_{\theta}\{Q(\theta^{(s+1)}, \theta^{(s)})\}$ where

$$Q\left(\theta^{(s+1)}, \theta^{(s)}\right) = \sum_{Z}p\left(Z\left|X, \theta^{(s)}\right.\right)\log\left(p\left(X, Z\left|\theta^{(s+1)}\right.\right),\right), \tag{A.34}$$

subject to constraints that ensure probabilities sum to one where appropriate. We encode $Z = \{\mathbf{Y}_d, \mathbf{D}_d\}$ where $\mathbf{D}_d = \{\mathbf{d}_{d,i}\}$ with $\mathbf{d}_{d,i}$ encoding $\mathbf{c}_d$ by $d_{d,i,k}$ being set to 1 when $c_{d,i} = k$, and 0 otherwise. Similarly, $\mathbf{Y}_d = \{\mathbf{y}_{d,j}\}$ with $\mathbf{y}_{d,j}$ encoding which of the R_d concepts associated with a region are responsible for emitting w_j. Specifically, $\mathbf{y}_{d,j,i}$ is set to 1 when that region is i, and 0 otherwise. The Q function then becomes,

$$Q\left(\theta^{(s+1)}, \theta^{(s)}\right) = E_{p(Z|\bullet)}\left(\log\left(p\left(X, Z\left|\theta^{(s+1)}\right.\right)\right)\right), \tag{A.35}$$

or, more pedantically,

$$Q\left(\theta^{(s+1)}, \theta^{(s)}\right) = \sum_{d=1}^{D}\sum_{j=1}^{W_d}\sum_{i=1}^{R_d}\sum_{k=1}^{C} p\left(y_{d,j,i}\right) p\left(d_{d,i,k}\right) \log\left(p\left(X, Z \big| \theta^{(s+1)}\right)\right). \qquad (A.36)$$

Using (6.16) and (A.26) we can write

$$
\begin{aligned}
p\left(X, Z \big| \theta^{(s+1)}\right) &= \prod_{d=1}^{D}\prod_{j=1}^{W_d} p\left(\mathbf{y}_{d,j}, \mathbf{D}_d, \mathbf{R}_d, w_{d,j} \big| \theta^{(s+1)}\right) \\
&= \prod_{d=1}^{D}\prod_{j=1}^{W_d} p\left(\mathbf{y}_{d,j}\right) p\left(w_{d,j} \big| \mathbf{y}_{d,j}, \mathbf{D}_d, \theta^{(s+1)}\right) p\left(\mathbf{D}_d \big| \theta^{(s+1)}\right) \\
&\qquad\qquad p\left(\mathbf{R}_d \big| \mathbf{D}_d, \theta^{(s+1)}\right) \\
&= \prod_{d=1}^{D}\prod_{j=1}^{W_d}\left(\frac{1}{R_d}\right)\prod_{i=1}^{R_d}\prod_{k=1}^{C}\left\{ p\left(w_{d,j} \big| c_k, \theta^{(s+1)}\right)^{y_{d,j,i}} p\left(c_k \big| \theta^{(s+1)}\right) \right. \\
&\qquad\qquad \left. p\left(\mathbf{r}_{d,i} \big| c_k, \theta^{(s+1)}\right)\right\}^{d_{d,i,k}},
\end{aligned}
\qquad (A.37)
$$

and, ignoring the constants, R_d,

$$
\begin{aligned}
\log\left(p\left(X, Z \big| \theta^{(s+1)}\right)\right) &= \sum_{d=1}^{D}\sum_{j=1}^{W_d}\sum_{i=1}^{R_d}\sum_{k=1}^{C} d_{d,i,k} \bullet y_{d,j,i} \bullet \log\left(p\left(w_{d,j} \big| c_k, \theta^{(s+1)}\right)\right) \\
&+ \sum_{d=1}^{D}\sum_{j=1}^{W_d}\sum_{i=1}^{R_d}\sum_{k=1}^{C} d_{d,i,k} \bullet \log\left(p\left(c_k \big| \theta^{(s+1)}\right)\right) \\
&+ \sum_{d=1}^{D}\sum_{j=1}^{W_d}\sum_{i=1}^{R_d}\sum_{k=1}^{C} d_{d,i,k} \bullet \log\left(p\left(\mathbf{r}_{d,i} \big| c_k, \theta^{(s+1)}\right)\right).
\end{aligned}
\qquad (A.38)
$$

Taking the expectation over Z of (A.38), and using the independence of the documents for the three terms, as well as the independence of words with respect to the parameters of the second and third terms, we get

$$
\begin{aligned}
Q\left(\theta^{(s+1)}, \theta^{(s)}\right) &= \mathbb{E}_{p(Z|\bullet)}\left(\log\left(p\left(X, Z \,\middle|\, \theta^{(s+1)}\right)\right)\right) \\
&= \underbrace{\sum_{d=1}^{D} \mathbb{E}_{p(Z_i|\bullet)}\left(\sum_{j=1}^{W_d}\sum_{i=1}^{R_d}\sum_{k=1}^{C} d_{d,i,k} \bullet y_{d,j,i} \bullet \log\left(p\left(w_{d,j} \,\middle|\, c_k, \theta^{(s+1)}\right)\right)\right)}_{Q_1\left(\theta^{(s+1)}, \theta^{(s)}\right)} \\
&+ \underbrace{\sum_{d=1}^{D} \mathbb{E}_{p(Z_i|\bullet)}\left(\sum_{i=1}^{R_d}\sum_{k=1}^{C} d_{d,i,k} \bullet \log\left(p\left(c_k \,\middle|\, \theta^{(s+1)}\right)\right)\right)}_{Q_2\left(\theta^{(s+1)}, \theta^{(s)}\right)} \\
&+ \underbrace{\sum_{d=1}^{D} \mathbb{E}_{p(Z_i|\bullet)}\left(\sum_{i=1}^{R_d}\sum_{k=1}^{C} d_{d,i,k} \bullet \log\left(p\left(\mathbf{r}_{d,i} \,\middle|\, c_k, \theta^{(s+1)}\right)\right)\right)}_{Q_3\left(\theta^{(s+1)}, \theta^{(s)}\right)} .
\end{aligned}
\tag{A.39}
$$

Focusing on the first term, $Q_1\left(\theta^{(s+1)}, \theta^{(s)}\right)$ for a particular document, d,

$$
\begin{aligned}
&\mathbb{E}_{p(Z_d|\bullet)}\left(\sum_{j=1}^{W_d}\sum_{i=1}^{R_d}\sum_{k=1}^{C} d_{d,i,k} \bullet y_{d,j,i} \bullet \log\left(p\left(w_{d,j} \,\middle|\, c_k, \theta^{(s+1)}\right)\right)\right) \\
&= \sum_{j=1}^{W_d}\sum_{i=1}^{R_d}\sum_{k=1}^{C} p\left(d_{d,i,k} \bullet y_{d,j,i}\right) \bullet \log\left(p\left(w_{d,j} \,\middle|\, c_k, \theta^{(s+1)}\right)\right) \\
&= \sum_{j=1}^{W_d}\sum_{i=1}^{R_d}\sum_{k=1}^{C} p\left(c_k \,\middle|\, w_{d,j}, \mathbf{R}_d, \theta^{(s)}\right) \bullet \log\left(p\left(w_{d,j} \,\middle|\, c_k, \theta^{(s+1)}\right)\right) .
\end{aligned}
\tag{A.40}
$$

To solve for $p\left(w_v \,\middle|\, c_k, \theta^{(s+1)}\right)$ we can ignore Q_2 and Q_3 in (A.39), as differentiating with respect to $p\left(w_v \,\middle|\, c_k, \theta^{(s+1)}\right)$ will annihilate them. However, we need to account for the constraints that $\sum_{v=1}^{V} p\left(w_v | c_k\right) = 1, \forall k$, which we achieve by introducing a Lagrange multiplier for each c_k. Q_1 then becomes

$$
Q_1^{\dagger} = Q_1 + \sum_{k=1}^{C} \lambda_k \left(1 - \sum_{v=1}^{V} p\left(w_v \,\middle|\, c_k, \Theta^{(s+1)}\right)\right) .
\tag{A.41}
$$

We get

$$
\frac{\partial}{\partial p\left(w_v | c_k\right)} Q_1^\dagger \left(\theta^{(s+1)}, \theta^{(s)}\right) = \sum_{d=1}^{D} \sum_{i=1}^{R_d} \sum_{j=1}^{W_d} \delta\left(w_v = w_{d,j}\right) \frac{p\left(c_k | w_v, \mathbf{R}_d, \theta^{(s)}\right)}{p\left(w_v | c_k, \theta^{(s+1)}\right)} - \lambda_k. \quad \text{(A.42)}
$$

Setting this to zero, putting λ_k on the right-hand side, and multiplying by $p\left(w_v | c_k, \theta^{(s+1)}\right)$, gives

$$
\sum_{d=1}^{D} \sum_{i=1}^{R_d} \sum_{j=1}^{W_d} \delta\left(w_v = w_{d,j}\right) p\left(c_k | w_v, \mathbf{R}_d, \theta^{(s)}\right) = \lambda_k p\left(w_v | c_k, \theta^{(s+1)}\right). \quad \text{(A.43)}
$$

Summing over v removes the $\delta\left(w_v = w_{d,j}\right)$ giving

$$
\sum_{d=1}^{D} \sum_{i=1}^{R_d} \sum_{j=1}^{W_d} p\left(c_k | w_v, \mathbf{R}_d, \theta^{(s)}\right) = \lambda_k. \quad \text{(A.44)}
$$

Using λ_k in (A.43), gives

$$
p\left(w_v | c_k, \theta^{(s+1)}\right) = \frac{\displaystyle\sum_{d=1}^{D} \sum_{i=1}^{R_d} \sum_{j=1}^{W_d} \delta\left(w_v = w_{d,j}\right) p\left(c_k | w_{d,j}, \mathbf{R}_d, \theta^{(s)}\right)}{\displaystyle\sum_{d=1}^{D} \sum_{i=1}^{R_d} \sum_{j=1}^{W_d} p\left(c_k | w_{d,j}, \mathbf{R}_d, \theta^{(s)}\right)}. \quad \text{(A.45)}
$$

This is equivalent to (6.26). To solve for the remaining parameters $p\left(\mu_f | c_k, \theta^{(s+1)}\right)$, $p\left(\sigma_f^2 | c_k, \theta^{(s+1)}\right)$, and $p\left(c_k | \theta^{(s+1)}\right)$, we can apply similar strategies. However, since differentiating with regards to any of these parameters will annihilate terms from $Q_1(\theta^{s+1}, \theta^s)$, we get exactly the same equations as in the case of the Gaussian Mixture Model (GMM). Hence, we omit the rest of the derivation.[3]

---

[3]See [87, §9.2] for details on EM for GMM.

Bibliography

[1] Available from https://code.google.com/archive/p/word2vec/. 61

[2] Aligned Hansards of the 36th Parliament of Canada; http://www.isi.edu/natural-language/download/hansard/. 78

[3] Amazon Mechanical Turk; https://www.mturk.com/mturk/. 22, 32, 37, 38, 41

[4] CMU Sphinx; http://cmusphinx.sourceforge.net/. 56, 81

[5] DP challenge: A digital photography challenge; http://www.dpchallenge.com/. 121

[6] Flickr; https://www.flickr.com/. 39

[7] Flickr services API; https://www.flickr.com/services/api/. 39

[8] GATE: General architecture for text engineering; https://gate.ac.uk/. 57

[9] ImageNet; http://www.image-net.org. 36, 37, 133

[10] International Affective Picture System (IAPS); http://csea.phhp.ufl.edu/media.html. 38, 119, 122

[11] LabelMe; http://people.csail.mit.edu/brussell/research/LabelMe/intro.html. 39, 41, 51

[12] LHI Large-scale Groundtruth Image Database; http://www.imageparsing.com/. 41

[13] Microsoft COCO: Comon objects in context; http://mscoco.org/. 40, 42, 43

[14] Microsoft research image understanding; http://research.microsoft.com/en-us/projects/objectclassrecognition/. 41

[15] Mind's eye videos (year 1); http://www.visint.org/datasets. 37, 74, 133

[16] MIR Flickr; http://press.liacs.nl/mirflickr/. 39

[17] MIR Flickr 25000; http://press.liacs.nl/mirflickr/. 39

[18] The PASCAL Object Recognition Database Collection; http://www.pascal-network.org/challenges/VOC/. 39, 64, 109

[19] PASCAL-Context Dataset; http://www.cs.stanford.edu/~{}roozbeh/pascal-context/. 41

[20] Peekaboom dataset; http://hunch.net/~{}learning/peekaboom.tar.bz2. 40

[21] Photo Net; www.photo.net. 121

[22] SemCor; http://web.eecs.umich.edu/~{}mihalcea/downloads.html#semcor. 126

[23] Small ESP Game Dataset; http://server251.theory.cs.cmu.edu/ESPGame100k.tar.gz. 39

[24] Sowerby Image Database. 40, 99, 104

[25] Stanford NLP Software; http://nlp.stanford.edu/software/. 57, 127

[26] SUN database; http://groups.csail.mit.edu/vision/SUN/. 37, 41, 121

[27] VisA: Dataset with Visual Attributes for Concepts; http://homepages.inf.ed.ac.uk/s1151656/resources.html. 37

[28] Visual Sentiment Ontology; http://www.ee.columbia.edu/ln/dvmm/vso/download/vso.html. 38, 121

[29] "Multimedia systems and equipment—Colour measurement and management—Part 2–1: Colour management—Default RGB colour space—sRGB," International Electrotechnical Commission, 1999. 47

[30] WordNet—a Lexical Database for English; http://wordnet.princeton.edu. 8, 35

[31] S. Agarwal, Y. Furukawa, N. Snavely, I. Simon, B. Curless, S. M. Seitz, and R. Szeliski, "Building Rome in a day," *Communications of the ACM*, vol. 54, pp. 105–112, 2011. DOI: 10.1145/2001269.2001293. 112

[32] E. Agirre and G. Rigau, "Word sense disambiguation using conceptual density," *Proc. 16th Conference on Computational Linguistics*, Copenhagen, Denmark, pp. 16–22, 1996. DOI: 10.3115/992628.992635. 58

[33] A. Aluja, A. Blanch, E. Blanco, and F. Balada, "Affective modulation of the startle reflex and the reinforcement sensitivity theory of personality: The role of sensitivity to reward," *Physiology and Behavior*, vol. 138, pp. 332–339, 2015. DOI: 10.1016/j.physbeh.2014.09.009. 33, 122

[34] J. Amores, "Multiple instance classification: Review, taxonomy and comparative study," *Artificial Intelligence*, vol. 201, pp. 81–105, 2013. DOI: 10.1016/j.artint.2013.06.003. 64

[35] M. Anderson, R. Motta, S. Chandrasekar, and M. Stokes, "Proposal for a standard default color space for the internet,Äîsrgb," *Proc. Color and Imaging Conference*, pp. 238–245, 1996. 47

[36] S. Andrews, T. Hofmann, and I. Tsochantaridis, "Multiple instance learning with generalized support vector machines," *Proc. AAAI*, 2002. 86

[37] S. Andrews, I. Tsochantaridis, and T. Hofmann, "Support vector machines for multiple-instance learning," *Proc. Advances in Neural Information Processing Systems*, 15, Vancouver, BC, 2002. 86

[38] C. Andrieu, N. d. Freitas, A. Doucet, and M. I. Jordan., "An introduction to MCMC for machine learning," *Machine Learning*, vol. 50, pp. 5–43, 2003. DOI: 10.1023/A:1020281327116. 77

[39] S. Antol, A. Agrawal, J. Lu, M. Mitchell, D. Batra, C. L. Zitnick, and D. Parikh, Visual Question Answering dataset; http://www.visualqa.org/. 43

[40] S. Antol, A. Agrawal, J. Lu, M. Mitchell, D. Batra, C. L. Zitnick, and D. Parikh, "VQA: Visual question answering," *Proc. ICCV*, 2015. 43, 52, 139

[41] I. Arapakis, K. Athanasakos, and J. M. Jose, "A comparison of general vs. personalised affective models for the prediction of topical relevance," *Proc. 33rd International ACM SIGIR Conference on Research and Development in Information Retrieval*, pp. 371–378, 2010. DOI: 10.1145/1835449.1835512. 122

[42] I. Arapakis, I. Konstas, and J. M. Jose, "Using facial expressions and peripheral physiological signals as implicit indicators of topical relevance," *Proc. of the 17th ACM International Conference on Multimedia*, pp. 461–470, 2009. DOI: 10.1145/1631272.1631336. 122

[43] I. Arapakis, Y. Moshfeghi, H. Joho, R. Ren, D. Hannah, and J. M. Jose, "Integrating facial expressions into user profiling for the improvement of a multimodal recommender system," *Proc. International Conference on Multimedia and Expo*, pp. 1440–1443, 2009. DOI: 10.1109/icme.2009.5202773. 122

[44] P. Arbelaez, M. Maire, C. Fowlkes, and J. Malik, "From contours to regions: An empirical evaluation," *Proc. IEEE Conference on Computer Vision and Pattern Recognition*, pp. 2294–2301, 2009. DOI: 10.1109/cvpr.2009.5206707. 50

[45] P. Arbelaez, M. Maire, C. Fowlkes, and J. Malik, "Contour detection and hierarchical image segmentation," *IEEE Transactions on Pattern Analysis and Machine Intelligence*, vol. 33, pp. 898–916, 2011. DOI: 10.1109/tpami.2010.161. 50, 106

[46] S. Arifin and P. Y. Cheung, "A Computation method for video segmentation utilizing the pleasure-arousal-dominance emotional information," *Proc. International Conference on Multimedia*, pp. 68–77, 2007. DOI: 10.1145/1291233.1291251. 120

[47] L. H. Armitage and P. G. B. Enser, "Analysis of user need in image archives," *Journal of Information Science*, vol. 23, pp. 287–299, 1997. DOI: 10.1177/016555159702300403. 28, 111

[48] Y. Aytar, M. Shah, and J. Luo, "Utilizing semantic word similarity measures for video retrieval," *Proc. Computer Vision and Pattern Recognition*, 2008. DOI: 10.1109/cvpr.2008.4587822. 59, 60

[49] G. Baatz, O. Saurer, K. Koser, and M. Pollefeys, "Large scale visual geo-localization of images in mountainous terrain," *Proc. ECCV*, pp. 517–530, 2012. DOI: 10.1007/978-3-642-33709-3_37. 28

[50] L. Baboud, M. Cadik, E. Eisemann, and H.-P. Seidel, "Automatic photo-to-terrain alignment for the annotation of mountain pictures," *Proc. Computer Vision and Pattern Recognition*, pp. 41–48, 2011. DOI: 10.1109/cvpr.2011.5995727. 28

[51] S. Baccianella, A. Esuli, and F. Sebastiani, "SentiWordNet 3.0: An enhanced lexical resource for sentiment analysis and opinion mining," *Proc. LREC*, pp. 2200–2204, 2010. 36, 120

[52] F. Balada, A. Blanch, and A. Aluja, "Arousal and habituation effects (excitability) on startle responses to the International Affective Picture Systems (IAPS)," *Journal of Psychophysiology*, vol. 28, pp. 233, 2014. DOI: 10.1027/0269-8803/a000115. 38

[53] L. Ballan, T. Uricchio, L. Seidenari, and A. D. Bimbo, "A cross-media model for automatic image annotation," *Proc. of International Conference on Multimedia Retrieval*, Glasgow, United Kingdom, pp. 73–80, 2014. DOI: 10.1145/2578726.2578728. 60

[54] D. H. Ballard and C. Yu, "A multimodal learning interface for word acquisition," *Proc. IEEE International Conference on Acoustics, Speech, and Signal Processing*, pp. V-784–7 vol. 5, 2003. DOI: 10.1109/icassp.2003.1200088. 78

[55] H. Bannour and C. Hudelot, "Building Semantic Hierarchies Faithful to Image Semantics," in *Advances in Multimedia Modeling, Series, Building Semantic Hierarchies Faithful to Image Semantics*, K. Schoeffmann, B. Merialdo, A. Hauptmann, C.-W. Ngo, Y. Andreopoulos, and C. Breiteneder, Eds., Springer Berlin Heidelberg, pp. 4–15, 2012. DOI: 10.1007/978-3-642-27355-1_4. 60

[56] A. Barbu, A. Bridge, Z. Burchill, D. Coroian, S. Dickinson, S. Fidler, A. Michaux, S. Mussman, S. Narayanaswamy, and D. Salvi, "Video in sentences out," in *arXiv preprint arXiv:1204.2742*, 2012. 133

[57] A. Barbu, A. Bridge, Z. Burchill, D. Coroian, S. Dickinson, S. Fidler, A. Michaux, S. Mussman, N. Siddharth, D. Salvi, L. Schmidt, J. Shangguan, S. J.M., J. Waggoner, S. Wang, J. Wei, Y. Yin, and Z. Zhang, "Video in sentences out," *Proc. 28th Conference on Uncertainty in Artificial Intelligence*, Catalina, CA, pp. 102–112, 2012. 125

[58] K. Barnard, V. Cardei, and B. Funt, "A comparison of computational colour constancy algorithms. Part one. Methodology and experiments with synthesized data," *IEEE Transactions on Image Processing*, vol. 11, pp. 972–984, 2002. DOI: 10.1109/tip.2002.802531. 47

[59] K. Barnard, P. Duygulu, and D. Forsyth, "Clustering art," *Proc. IEEE Conference on Computer Vision and Pattern Recognition*, Hawaii, pp. II:434–441, 2001. DOI: 10.1109/CVPR.2001.990994. 58, 89, 137

[60] K. Barnard, P. Duygulu, N. d. Freitas, D. Forsyth, D. Blei, and M. I. Jordan, "Matching words and pictures," *Journal of Machine Learning Research*, vol. 3, pp. 1107–1135, 2003. 39, 48, 68, 72, 77, 88, 89, 90, 91, 94

[61] K. Barnard, P. Duygulu, K. G. Raghavendra, P. Gabbur, and D. Forsyth, "The effects of segmentation and feature choice in a translation model of object recognition," *Proc. IEEE Conference on Computer Vision and Pattern Recognition*, Madison, WI, pp. II-675–682, 2003. DOI: 10.1109/cvpr.2003.1211532. 48, 69, 72, 94, 99

[62] K. Barnard and Q. Fan, "Reducing correspondence ambiguity in loosely labeled training data," *Proc. IEEE Computer Society Conference in Computer Vision*, 2007. DOI: 10.1109/cvpr.2007.383224. 23, 93, 100, 127, 148

[63] K. Barnard, Q. Fan, R. Swaminathan, A. Hoogs, R. Collins, P. Rondot, and J. Kaufhold, "Evaluation of localized semantics: data, methodology, and experiments," *International Journal of Computer Vision (IJCV)*, vol. 77, pp. 199–217, 2008. DOI: 10.1007/s11263-007-0068-6. 40, 41, 59, 68, 69, 72, 78, 87, 88, 99

[64] K. Barnard and D. Forsyth, "Learning the semantics of words and pictures," *Proc. International Conference on Computer Vision*, pp. II-408–415, 2001. DOI: 10.1109/iccv.2001.937654. 48, 77, 89, 90, 94, 137

[65] K. Barnard, L. Martin, A. Coath, and B. Funt, "A comparison of computational colour constancy algorithms. Part two. experiments on image data," *IEEE Transactions on Image Processing*, vol. 11, pp. 985–996, 2002. DOI: 10.1109/tip.2002.802529. 47

[66] K. Barnard and Matthew Johnson, "Word sense disambiguation with pictures," *Artificial Intelligence*, vol. 167, pp. 13–30, 2005. DOI: 10.1016/j.artint.2005.04.009. 17, 21, 126

[67] K. Barnard, K. Yanai, M. Johnson, and P. Gabbur, "Cross modal disambiguation," in *Towards Category-Level Object Recognition, Series, Cross Modal Disambiguation*, J. Ponce,

M. Hebert, C. Schmid, and A. Zisserman, Eds., Springer, pp. 225–244, 2006. DOI: 10.1007/11957959_13. 17, 21, 117, 126, 127

[68] M. Baroni, G. Dinu, and G. Kruszewski, "Don't Count, Predict! a systematic comparison of context-counting vs. context-predicting semantic vectors," *Proc. Annual Meeting of the Association for Computational Linguistics*, pp. 238–247, 2014. DOI: 10.3115/v1/p14-1023. 61

[69] S. Barrat and S. Tabbone, "Modeling, classifying and annotating weakly annotated images using Bayesian network," *Journal of Visual Communication and Image Representation*, vol. 21, pp. 1201–1205, 2009. DOI: 10.1016/j.jvcir.2010.02.010. 64, 107

[70] A. Barriuso and A. Torralba, "Notes on image annotation," in *arXiv preprint arXiv:1210.3448*, 2012. 41

[71] R. Baur, A. Conzelmann, M. J. Wieser, and P. Pauli, "Spontaneous emotion regulation: Differential effects on evoked brain potentials and facial muscle activity," *International Journal of Psychophysiology*, vol. 96, pp. 38–48, 2015. DOI: 10.1016/j.ijpsycho.2015.02.022. 33, 38, 122

[72] Y. Baveye, J.-N. Bettinelli, E. Dellandrea, L. Chen, and C. Chamaret, LIRIS-ACCEDE; http://liris-accede.ec-lyon.fr/. 32, 38

[73] Y. Baveye, J.-N. Bettinelli, E. Dellandrea, L. Chen, and C. Chamaret, "A large video database for computational models of induced emotion," *Proc. Affective Computing and Intelligent Interaction*, pp. 13–18, 2013. DOI: 10.1109/acii.2013.9.

[74] Y. Baveye, E. Dellandrea, C. Chamaret, and C. Liming, "LIRIS-ACCEDE: A video database for affective content analysis," *IEEE Transactions on Affective Computing*, vol. 6, pp. 43–55, 2015. DOI: 10.1109/taffc.2015.2396531. 32, 38

[75] S. Belongie, C. Carson, H. Greenspan, and J. Malik, "Color-and texture-based image segmentation using the expectation-maximization algorithm and its application to content-based image retrieval," *Proc. International Conference on Computer Vision*, 1998. DOI: 10.1109/iccv.1998.710790. 28

[76] S. J. Belongie, J. Malik, and J. Puzicha, "Shape matching and object recognition using shape contexts," *IEEE Transactions on Pattern Analysis and Machine Intelligence*, vol. 24, pp. 509–522, 2002. DOI: 10.1109/34.993558. 51

[77] R. Benavente, M. Vanrell, and R. Baldrich, "A data set for fuzzy colour naming," *Color Research and Application*, vol. 31, pp. 48–56, 2006. DOI: 10.1002/col.20172. 118

[78] Y. Bengio, "Learning deep architectures for AI," *Foundations and Trends in Machine Learning*, vol. 2, pp. 1–127, 2009. DOI: 10.1561/2200000006. 51

[79] Y. Bengio, A. Courville, and P. Vincent, "Representation learning: A review and new perspectives," *IEEE Transactions on Pattern Analysis and Machine Intelligence*, vol. 35, pp. 1798–1828, 2013. DOI: 10.1109/tpami.2013.50. 51

[80] A. Benitez and S.-F. Chang, "Automatic multimedia knowledge discovery, summarization and evaluation," *IEEE Transactions on Multimedia*, vol. 21, 2003. 59

[81] A. B. Benitez and S.-F. Chang, "Image classification using multimedia knowledge networks," *Proc. ICIP*, 2003. DOI: 10.1109/icip.2003.1247319. 59, 64

[82] A. C. Berg, T. L. Berg, H. Daume, J. Dodge, A. Goyal, X. Han, A. Mensch, M. Mitchell, A. Sood, and K. Stratos, "Understanding and predicting importance in images," *Proc. IEEE Conference on Computer Vision and Pattern Recognition*, pp. 3562–3569, 2012. DOI: 10.1109/cvpr.2012.6248100. 36, 60, 133

[83] T. Berg, A. Berg, and J. Shih, "Automatic attribute discovery and characterization from noisy web data," *Proc. ECCV*, pp. 663–676, 2010. DOI: 10.1007/978-3-642-15549-9_48. 118, 134

[84] T. L. Berg, A. C. Berg, J. Edwards, and D. A. Forsyth, "Who's in the picture," *Proc. NIPS*, 2004. 113, 114, 115

[85] T. L. Berg, A. C. Berg, J. Edwards, M. Maire, R. White, Y. W. Teh, E. Learned-Miller, and D. A. Forsyth, "Names and faces in the news," *Proc. Computer Vision and Pattern Recognition (CVPR)*, Washington D.C, pp. 848–854, 2004. DOI: 10.1109/CVPR.2004.175. 113, 114, 115

[86] A. Bhatia, Dipanjan, C. D. Das, J. Eisenstein, J. Flanigan, K. Gimpel, M. Heilman, L. Kong, D. Mills, B. O'Connor, O. Owoputi, N. Schneider, N. Smith, S. Swayamdipta, and D. Yogatama, Tweet NLP; http://www.ark.cs.cmu.edu/TweetNLP/. 57

[87] C. M. Bishop, *Pattern Recognition and Machine Learning*, Springer, 2006. 4, 18, 51, 66, 68, 77, 95, 153

[88] D. Blei, A. Ng, and M. Jordan, "Latent Dirichlet allocation," *Journal of Machine Learning Research*, vol. 3, pp. 993–1022, 2003. 90

[89] D. M. Blei and M. I. Jordan, "Modeling annotated data," *Proc. 26th International Conference on Research and Development in Information Retrieval (SIGIR)*, 2003. DOI: 10.1145/860435.860460 . 90, 91, 92

[90] E. Boiy, K. Deschacht, and M.-f. Moens, "Learning visual entities and their visual attributes from text corpora," *Proc. DEXA Workshops*, pp. 48–53, 2008. DOI: 10.1109/dexa.2008.59. 60

[91] D. Borth, R. Ji, T. Chen, T. Breuel, and S.-F. Chang, "Large-scale visual sentiment ontology and detectors using adjective noun pairs," *Proc. ACM International Conference on Multimedia*, pp. 223–232, 2013. DOI: 10.1145/2502081.2502282. 38, 120, 121

[92] A. Bosch, A. Zisserman, and X. Munoz, "Image classification using random forests and ferns," *Proc. ICCV*, 2007. DOI: 10.1109/iccv.2007.4409066. 64

[93] A. Bosch, A. Zisserman, and X. Munoz, "Scene classification using a hybrid generative/discriminative approach," *IEEE Transactions on Pattern Analysis and Machine Intelligence*, 2008. DOI: 10.1109/tpami.2007.70716. 64

[94] M. M. Bradley and P. J. Lang, "Measuring emotion: The self-assessment manikin and the semantic differential," *Journal of Behavior Therapy and Experimental Psychiatry*, vol. 25, pp. 49–59, 1994. DOI: 10.1016/0005-7916(94)90063-9. 32, 38

[95] E. Brill, "A simple rule-based part of speech tagger," *Proc. 3rd Conference on Applied Natural Language Processing*, 1992. DOI: 10.3115/974499.974526. 81

[96] E. Brill, "Transformation-based error-driven learning and natural language processing: A case study in part-of-speech tagging," *Computational Linguistics*, vol. 21, pp. 543–565, 1995. 57

[97] P. F. Brown, J. Cocke, S. A. D. Pietra, V. J. D. Pietra, F. Jelinek, J. D. Lafferty, R. L. Mercer, and P. S. Roossin, "A statistical approach to machine translation," *Computational Linguistics*, vol. 16, pp. 79–85, 1990. DOI: 10.3115/991635.991651. 78

[98] P. F. Brown, S. A. D. Pietra, V. J. D. Pietra, and R. L. Mercer, "The mathematics of machine translation: parameter estimation," *Computational Linguistics*, vol. 19, pp. 263–311, 1993. 78, 81

[99] A. Budanitsky and G. Hirst, "Evaluating wordnet-based measures of lexical semantic relatedness," *Computational Linguistics*, vol. 32, pp. 13–47, 2006. DOI: 10.1162/coli.2006.32.1.13. 59

[100] C. J. C. Burges, "A tutorial on support vector machines for pattern recognition," *Data Mining and Knowledge Discovery*, vol. 2, pp. 121–167, 1998. DOI: 10.1023/A:1009715923555. 86

[101] L. Candillier, F. Meyer, and M. Boulle, "Comparing state-of-the-art collaborative filtering systems," in *Machine Learning and Data Mining in Pattern Recognition, Series, Comparing State-of-the-Art Collaborative Filtering Systems*, Springer, pp. 548–562, 2007. DOI: 10.1007/978-3-540-73499-4_41. 122

[102] L. Canini, S. Benini, and R. Leonardi, "Affective recommendation of movies based on selected connotative features," *IEEE Transactions on Circuits and Systems for Video Technology*, vol. 23, pp. 636–647, 2013. DOI: 10.1109/tcsvt.2012.2211935. 122

[103] L. Canini, S. Benini, P. Migliorati, and R. Leonardi, "Emotional identity of movies," *Proc. IEEE International Conference on Image Processing*, pp. 1821–1824, 2009. DOI: 10.1109/ICIP.2009.5413556. 120

[104] J. Canny, "A computational approach to edge detection," *IEEE Transactions on Pattern Analysis and Machine Intelligence*, vol. 8, pp. 679–698, 1986. DOI: 10.1109/tpami.1986.4767851. 47

[105] L. Cao and L. Fei-Fei, "Spatially coherent latent topic model for concurrent object segmentation and classification," *Proc. IEEE International Conference in Computer Vision*, 2007. DOI: 10.1109/iccv.2007.4408965. 51

[106] P. Carbonetto, N. d. Freitas, and K. Barnard, "A statistical model for general contextual object recognition," *Proc. Eighth European Conference on Computer Vision*, pp. 350–362, 2004. DOI: 10.1007/978-3-540-24670-1_27. 83, 96, 97, 99, 100

[107] P. Carbonetto, N. d. Freitas, P. Gustafson, and N. Thompson, "Bayesian Feature Weighting for Unsupervised Learning, with Application to Object Recognition," UBC, 2002; http://www.cs.ubc.ca/~{}nando/papers/shrinkage.pdf. 50

[108] P. Carbonetto, N. d. Freitas, P. Gustafson, and N. Thompson, "Bayesian feature weighting for unsupervised learning, with application to object recognition," *Proc. Workshop on Artificial Intelligence and Statistics*, 2003. 82, 83

[109] G. Carneiro, A. B. Chan, P. J. Moreno, and N. Vasconcelos, "Supervised learning of semantic classes for image annotation and retrieval," *IEEE Transactions on Pattern Analysis and Machine Intelligence*, vol. 29, pp. 394–410, 2007. DOI: 10.1109/tpami.2007.61. 82, 84

[110] G. Carneiro and A. D. Jepson, "Flexible spatial configuration of local image features," *IEEE Transactions on Pattern Analysis and Machine Intelligence*, vol. 29, pp. 2089–2104, 2007. DOI: 10.1109/tpami.2007.1126. 109, 116

[111] C. Carson, S. Belongie, H. Greenspan, and J. Malik, "Blobworld: color and texture-based image segmentation using EM and its application to image querying and classification," *IEEE Transactions on Pattern Analysis and Machine Intelligence*, vol. 24, pp. 1026–1038, 2002. 26, 28, 68, 83

[112] C. Carson, M. Thomas, S. Belongie, J. M. Hellerstein, and J. Malik, "Blobworld: image segmentation using expectation-maximization and its application to image querying," *Proc. 3rd International Conference on Visual Information Systems*, 1999. DOI: 10.1109/tpami.2002.1023800. 28, 50

[113] G. Celeux, S. Chretien, F. Forbes, and A. Mkhadri, "A component-wise EM algorithm for mixtures," *Journal of Computational and Graphical Statistics*, vol. 10, pp. 697–712, 2001. DOI: 10.1198/106186001317243403. 26

[114] A. Chang, M. Savva, and C. Manning, "Interactive learning of spatial knowledge for text to 3D scene generation," *Proc. Workshop on Interactive Language Learning, Visualization, and Interfaces*, pp. 14–21, 2014. DOI: 10.3115/v1/w14-3102. 60, 61

[115] A. Chang, M. Savva, and C. Manning, " Semantic parsing for text to 3D scene generation," *Proc. ACL 2014 Workshop on Semantic Parsing (SP14)*, 2014. DOI: 10.3115/v1/w14-2404. 60, 61

[116] A. X. Chang and C. D. Manning, "Sutime: A library for recognizing and normalizing time expressions," *Proc. Language Resources and Evaluation Conference*, pp. 3735–3740, 2012. 57

[117] A. X. Chang, M. Savva, and C. D. Manning, "Learning spatial knowledge for text to 3D scene generation," *Proc. Empirical Methods in Natural Language Processing*, 2014. DOI: 10.3115/v1/d14-1217. 60, 61

[118] C.-C. Chang and C.-J. Lin, LIBSVM—A Library for Support Vector Machines; http://www.csie.ntu.edu.tw/~{}cjlin/libsvm/. 86

[119] E. Y. Chang, S. Tong, K.-S. Goh, and C.-W. Chang, "Support vector machine concept-dependent active learning for image retrieval," *IEEE Transactions on Multimedia*, 2005. 29

[120] S.-F. Chang, R. Manmatha, and T.-S. Chua, "Combining text and audio-visual features in video indexing," *Proc. IEEE International Conference on Acoustics, Speech, and Signal Processing*, vol. 5, pp. v/1005–1008, 2005. DOI: 10.1109/icassp.2005.1416476. 56

[121] O. Chapelle, P. Haffner, and V. Vapnik, "SVMs for histogram based image classification," *IEEE Transactions on Neural Networks*, vol. 9, 1999. 64

[122] A. Chardin and P. Pérez, "Unsupervised image classification with a hierarchical EM algorithm," *Proc. International Conference on Computer Vision*, pp. 969–974, 1999. DOI: 10.1109/iccv.1999.790353. 26

[123] E. Charniak, "A Maximum-entropy-inspired parser," *Proc. 1st North American Chapter of the Association for Computational Linguistics Conference*, pp. 132–139, 2000. 123

[124] D. L. Chen and W. B. Dolan, Microsoft research video description corpus; http://research.microsoft.com/en-us/downloads/38cf15fd-b8df-477e-a4e4-a4680caa75af/. 42, 133

[125] D. L. Chen and W. B. Dolan, "Collecting highly parallel data for paraphrase evaluation," *Proc. 49th Annual Meeting of the Association for Computational Linguistics: Human Language Technologies*, vol 1, pp. 190–200, 2011. 42, 133

[126] T. Chen, F. X. Yu, J. Chen, Y. Cui, Y.-Y. Chen, and S.-F. Chang, "Object-based visual sentiment concept analysis and application," *Proc. ACM International Conference on Multimedia*, pp. 367–376, 2014. DOI: 10.1145/2647868.2654935. 120

[127] X. Chen, A. Ritter, A. Gupta, and T. Mitchell, "Sense discovery via co-clustering on images and text," *Proc. IEEE Conference on Computer Vision and Pattern Recognition*, 2015. DOI: 10.1109/cvpr.2015.7299167. 126

[128] X. Chen, A. Shrivastava, and A. Gupta, "NEIL: extracting visual knowledge from web data," *Proc. ICCV*, pp. 1409–1416, 2013. DOI: 10.1109/iccv.2013.178. 111

[129] X. Chen, X. Yuan, S. Yan, J. Tang, Y. Rui, and T.-S. Chua, "Towards multi-semantic image annotation with graph regularized exclusive group lasso," *Proc. ACM International Conference on Multimedia*, pp. 263–272, 2011. DOI: 10.1145/2072298.2072334. 120

[130] X. Chen and A. L. Yuille, "Detecting and reading text in natural scenes," *Proc. IEEE Computer Society Conference on Computer Vision and Pattern Recognition*, vol. 2, pp. II-366–373, 2004. DOI: 10.1109/cvpr.2004.1315187. 57

[131] Y. Chen, J. Bi, and J. Z. Wang, "MILES: multiple-instance learning via embedded instance selection," *IEEE Transactions on Pattern Analysis and Machine Intelligence*, vol. 28, pp. 1931–1947, 2006. DOI: 10.1109/tpami.2006.248. 64

[132] Y. Chen and J. Z. Wang, "Image categorization by learning and reasoning with regions," *Journal of Machine Learning Research*, vol. 5, pp. 913–239, 2004. 64

[133] K. Cho, B. van Merrienboer, D. Bahdanau, and Y. Bengio, "On the properties of neural machine translation: Encoder-decoder approaches," in *arXiv preprint arXiv:1409.1259*, 2014. DOI: 10.3115/v1/w14-4012. 135

[134] W. Choe, H.-S. Chun, J. Noh, S.-D. Lee, and B.-T. Zhang, "Estimating multiple evoked emotions from videos," *Proc. Annual Meeting of the Cognitive Science Society*, pp. 2046–2051, 2013. 120

[135] W.-T. Chu and C.-H. Chen, "Color CENTRIST: a color descriptor for scene categorization," *Proc. of the 2nd ACM International Conference on Multimedia Retrieval*, Hong Kong, pp. 1–8, 2012. DOI: 10.1145/2324796.2324837. 64

[136] T.-s. Chua, J. Tang, R. Hong, H. Li, Z. Luo, and Y. Zheng, "NUS-WIDE: a real-world web image database from national university of Singapore," *Proc. Conference on Image and Video Retrieval*, pp. 1–9, 2009. DOI: 10.1145/1646396.1646452. 39

[137] M. Ciaramita, T. Hofmann, and M. Johnson, "Hierarchical semantic classification: word sense disambiguation with world knowledge," *Proc. 18th International Joint Conference on Artificial Intelligence (IJCAI)*, 2003. 58

[138] G. Ciocca and R. Schettini, "Multimedia search engine with relevance feedback," *Proc. Internet Imaging III*, San Jose, pp. 243–251, 2002. DOI: 10.1117/12.452678. 29

[139] J. Clarke, V. Srikumar, M. Sammons, and D. Roth, "An NLP Curator (or: How I learned to stop worrying and love NLP pipelines)," *Proc. LREC*, pp. 3276–3283, 2012. 57

[140] F. Coelho and C. Ribeiro, "Automatic illustration with cross-media retrieval in large-scale collections," *Proc. 9th International Workshop on Content-Based Multimedia Indexing*, pp. 25–30, 2011. DOI: 10.1109/cbmi.2011.5972515. 137, 138

[141] F. Coelho and C. Ribeiro, "Image abstraction in crossmedia retrieval for text illustration," in *Advances in Information Retrieval, Series, Image Abstraction in Crossmedia Retrieval for Text Illustration*, Springer, pp. 329–339, 2012. DOI: 10.1007/978-3-642-28997-2_28. 138

[142] M. Collins, "Head-driven statistical models for natural language parsing," *Computational Linguistics*, vol. 29, pp. 589–637, 2003. DOI: 10.1162/089120103322753356. 57

[143] D. Comaniciu, Mean Shift; http://www.caip.rutgers.edu/~{}comanici/SEGM/CODE/segm.tar.gz. 50

[144] C. Conati, "Probabilistic assessment of user's emotions in educational games," *Journal of Applied Artificial Intelligence, special issue on "Merging Cognition and Affect in HCI,"* vol. 16, 2002. DOI: 10.1080/08839510290030390. 33

[145] T. Cour, C. Jordan, E. Miltsakaki, and B. Taskar, "Movie/Script: alignment and parsing of video and text transcription," *Proc. European Conference on Computer Vision*, pp. 158–171, 2008. DOI: 10.1007/978-3-540-88693-8_12. 136

[146] T. Cour, B. Sapp, C. Jordan, and B. Taskar, "Learning from ambiguously labeled images," *Proc. Computer Vision and Pattern Recognition*, pp. 919–926, 2009. DOI: 10.1109/CVPR.2009.5206667. 24

[147] T. M. Cover and J. A. Thomas, *Elements of Information Theory*, John Wiley & sons, Inc, 1991. DOI: 10.1002/0471200611. 5

[148] I. J. Cox, M. L. Miller, T. P. Minka, T. V. Papathomas, and P. N. Yianilos, "The Bayesian image retrieval system, PicHunter: Theory, implementation and psychophysical experiments," *IEEE Transactions on Image Processing*, vol. 9, pp. 20–35, 2000. DOI: 10.1109/83.817596. 28, 29

[149] B. Coyne and R. Sproat, "WordsEye: an automatic text-to-scene conversion system," *Proc. Annual Conference on Computer Graphics*, pp. 487–496, 2001. DOI: 10.1145/383259.383316. 61, 137

[150] K. Crammer and Y. Singer, "On the algorithmic implementation of multiclass kernel-based vector machines," *Journal of Machine Learning Research*, vol. 2, pp. 265–292, 2001. 86

[151] G. Csurka, C. Dance, J. Willamowski, L. Fan, and C. Bray, "Visual categorization with bags of keypoints," *Proc. ECCV International Workshop on Statistical Learning in Computer Vision*, Prague, 2004. 51

[152] H. Cunningham, D. Maynard, and K. Bontcheva, *Text Processing with Gate*, Gateway Press, CA, 2011. 57

[153] H. Cunningham, D. Maynard, K. Bontcheva, and V. Tablan, "GATE: an architecture for development of robust HLT applications," *Proc. of the 40th Annual Meeting on Association for Computational Linguistics*, pp. 168–175, 2002. DOI: 10.3115/1073083.1073112. 57

[154] C. Cusano, G. Ciocca, and R. Schettini, "Image annotation using SVM," *Proc. Electronic Imaging 2004*, pp. 330–338, 2003. DOI: 10.1117/12.526746. 86

[155] L. Dahua, S. Fidler, K. Chen, and R. Urtasun, "Visual semantic search: retrieving videos via complex textual queries," *Proc. IEEE Conference on Computer Vision and Pattern Recognition*, pp. 2657–2664, 2014. DOI: 10.1109/cvpr.2014.340. 137, 138

[156] N. Dalal and B. Triggs, "Histograms of oriented gradients for human detection," *Proc. IEEE Computer Society Conference on Computer Vision and Pattern Recognition*, pp. 886–893, 2005. DOI: 10.1109/cvpr.2005.177. 48, 49

[157] E. S. Dan-Glauser and K. R. Scherer, The Geneva Affective Picture Database (GAPED): A 730 picture database for emotion induction; http://www.affective-sciences.org/researchmaterial. 38, 119

[158] E. S. Dan-Glauser and K. R. Scherer, "The Geneva Affective Picture Database (GAPED): a new 730 picture database focusing on valence and normative significance," *Behavior Research Methods*, vol. 43, pp. 468–477, 2011. DOI: 10.3758/s13428-011-0064-1. 38, 119

[159] P. Das, R. K. Srihari, and J. J. Corso, "Translating related words to videos and back through latent topics," *Proc. ACM International Conference on Web Search and Data Mining*, pp. 485–494, 2013. DOI: 10.1145/2433396.2433456. 133

[160] P. Das, C. Xu, R. Doell, and J. Corso, "A Thousand frames in just a few words: lingual description," *Proc. IEEE Conference on Computer Vision*, 2013. DOI: 10.1109/cvpr.2013.340. 42, 60, 133

[161] R. Datta, D. Joshi, J. Li, and J. Z. Wang, "Studying aesthetics in photographic images using a computational approach," *Proc. ECCV*, pp. 288–301, 2006. DOI: 10.1007/11744078_23. 121, 122

[162] R. Datta, J. Li, and J. Z. Wang, "Algorithmic inferencing of aesthetics and emotion in natural images: an exposition," *Proc. IEEE International Conference on Image Processing*, pp. 105–108, 2008. DOI: 10.1109/icip.2008.4711702. 31

[163] C. R. Dawson, J. Wright, A. Rebguns, M. V. Escarcega, D. Fried, and P. R. Cohen, "A generative probabilistic framework for learning spatial language," *Proc. IEEE 3rd Joint International Conference on Development and Learning and Epigenetic Robotics*, pp. 1–8, 2013. DOI: 10.1109/devlrn.2013.6652560. 123, 124

[164] T. de Campos, B. R. Babu, and M. Varma, "Character recognition in natural images," *Proc. International Conference on Computer Vision Theory and Applications*, 2009. DOI: 10.5220/0001770102730280. 57

[165] M.-C. De Marneffe, B. MacCartney, and C. D. Manning, "Generating typed dependency parses from phrase structure parses," *Proc. of LREC*, vol. 6, pp. 449–454, 2006. 57, 127

[166] L. Del Pero, P. Lee, J. Magahern, E. Hartley, K. Barnard, P. Wang, A. Kanaujia, and N. Haering, "Fusing object detection and region appearance for image-text alignment," *Proc. 19th ACM International Conference on Multimedia*, Scottsdale, Arizona, pp. 1113–1116, 2011. DOI: 10.1145/2072298.2071951. 24, 46, 53, 61, 106, 125

[167] D. Delgado, J. Magalhaes, and N. Correia, "Automated illustration of news stories," *Proc. IEEE 4th International Conference on Semantic Computing (ICSC)*, pp. 73–78, 2010. DOI: 10.1109/ICSC.2010.68. 138

[168] M. Dellagiacoma, P. Zontone, G. Boato, and L. Albertazzi, "Emotion based classification of natural images," *Proc. International Workshop on Detecting and Exploiting Cultural diversity on the Social Web*, pp. 17–22, 2011. DOI: 10.1145/2064448.2064470. 31, 120

[169] A. P. Dempster, N. M. Laird, and D. B. Rubin, "Maximum likelihood from incomplete data via the EM algorithm," *Journal of the Royal Statistical Society. Series B (Methodological)*, vol. 39, pp. 1–38, 1977. 26

[170] K. Demuynck, J. Roelens, D. Van Compernolle, and P. Wambacq, SPRAAK: an open source "Speech recognition and automatic annotation kit," *Proc. Annual Conference of the International Speech Communication Association*, pp. 495, 2008. DOI: 10.1007/978-3-642-30910-6_6. 56

[171] J. Deng, A. C. Berg, K. Li, and L. Fei-Fei, "What does classifying more than 10,000 image categories tell us?," *Proc. ECCV*, pp. 71–84, 2010. DOI: 10.1007/978-3-642-15555-0_6. 60

[172] J. Deng, W. Dong, R. Socher, K. L. L.-J. Li, and L. Fei-Fei, "ImageNet: A large-scale hierarchical image database," *Proc. Computer Vision and Pattern Recognition*, 2009. DOI: 10.1109/cvpr.2009.5206848. 36, 37, 64, 133

[173] J. Deng, J. Krause, A. C. Berg, and L. Fei-Fei, "Hedging your bets: optimizing accuracy-specificity trade-offs in large scale visual recognition," *Proc. IEEE Conference on Computer Vision and Pattern Recognition*, pp. 3450–3457, 2012. DOI: 10.1109/cvpr.2012.6248086. 133

[174] K. Deschacht and M.-f. Moens, "Text analysis for automatic image annotation," *Proc. Meeting of the Association for Computational Linguistics*, 2007. 60, 114

[175] K. Deschacht and M.-f. Moens, "Finding the best picture: cross-media retrieval of content," *Proc. European Colloquium on IR Research*, pp. 539–546, 2008. DOI: 10.1007/978-3-540-78646-7_53. 60, 114

[176] L. Diago, T. Kitaoka, I. Hagiwara, and T. Kambayashi, "Neuro-fuzzy quantification of personal perceptions of facial images based on a limited data set," *IEEE Transactions on Neural Networks*, vol. 22, pp. 2422–2434, 2011. DOI: 10.1109/tnn.2011.2176349. 120

[177] T. G. Dietterich, R. H. Lathrop, and T. Lozano-Perez, "Solving the multiple instance problem with axis-parallel rectangles," *Artificial Intelligence*, vol. 89, pp. 31–71, 1997. DOI: 10.1016/s0004-3702(96)00034-3. 64, 86

[178] S. Divvala, A. Farhadi, and C. Guestrin, "Learning everything about anything: webly-supervised visual concept learning," *Proc. IEEE Conference on Computer Vision and Pattern Recognition*, 2014. DOI: 10.1109/cvpr.2014.412. 129

[179] J. Donahue, L. A. Hendricks, S. Guadarrama, M. Rohrbach, S. Venugopalan, K. Saenko, and T. Darrell, "Long-term recurrent convolutional networks for visual recognition and description," *Proc. Computer Vision and Pattern Recognition*, 2015. DOI: 10.1109/cvpr.2015.7298878. 52, 134, 135

[180] Y. Dong, Z. Hu, K. Uchimura, and N. Murayama, "Driver inattention monitoring system for intelligent vehicles: A review," *IEEE Transactions on Intelligent Transportation Systems*, vol. 12, pp. 596–614, 2011. DOI: 10.1109/tits.2010.2092770. 33

[181] R. O. Duda, P. E. Hart, and D. G. Stork, *Pattern Classification*, 2nd ed, John Wiley & Sons, Inc., 2001. 51, 68

[182] P. Duygulu, K. Barnard, J. F. G. d. Freitas, and D. A. Forsyth, "Object recognition as machine translation: learning a lexicon for a fixed image vocabulary," *Proc. 7th European Conference on Computer Vision*, Copenhagen, Denmark, pp. IV-97–112, 2002. DOI: 10.1007/3-540-47979-1_7. 11, 40, 48, 51, 69, 77, 78, 79, 94, 108

[183] P. Duygulu and M. Bastan, "Multimedia translation for linking visual data to semantics in videos," *Machine Vision and Applications*, vol. 22, pp. 99–115, 2011. DOI: 10.1007/s00138-009-0217-8. 60

[184] P. Duygulu and A. Hauptmann, "What's news, what's not? associating news videos with words," *Proc. Image and Video Retrieval*, pp. 132–140, 2004. DOI: 10.1007/978-3-540-27814-6_19. 81

[185] P. Duygulu, D. Ng, N. Papernick, and H. Wactlar, "Linking visual and textual data on video," *Proc. Workshop on Multimedia Contents in Digital Libraries*, pp. 1–2, 2003. 81

[186] P. Duygulu and H. Wactlar, "Associating video frames with text," *Proc. Multimedia Information Retrieval Workshop, in Conjunction with ACM-SIGIR*, 2003. 81

[187] J.-P. Eakins, "Automatic image content retrieval—are we getting anywhere?," *Proc. 3rd International Conference on Electronic Library and Visual Information Research*, De Montfort University, Milton Keynes, pp. 123–135, 1996. 111

[188] J. P. Eakins, "Towards intelligent image retrieval," *Pattern Recognition*, vol. 35, pp. 3–14, 2002. DOI: 10.1016/s0031-3203(01)00038-3. 111

[189] J. Edwards, R. White, and D. Forsyth, "Words and pictures in the news," *Proc. HLT-NAACL Workshop on Learning Word Meaning from Non-Linguistic Data*, Edmonton, Alberta, pp. 6–13, 2003. DOI: 10.3115/1119212.1119214. 41, 112, 113, 114, 115

[190] P. Ekman, "Facial expression and emotion," *American Psychologist*, vol. 48, pp. 384, 1993. DOI: 10.1037//0003-066x.48.4.384. 32

[191] D. Elliott and F. Keller, "Image description using visual dependency representations," *Proc. Emperical Methods in Natural Language Processing*, pp. 1292–1302, 2013. 132

[192] P. Enser, "The evolution of visual information retrieval," *J. Inf. Sci.*, vol. 34, pp. 531–546, 2008. DOI: 10.1177/0165551508091013. 111

[193] P. G. B. Enser, "Query analysis in a visual information retrieval context," *Journal of Document and Text Management*, vol. 1, pp. 25–39, 1993. 28, 111

[194] B. Epshtein, E. Ofek, and Y. Wexler, "Detecting text in natural scenes with stroke width transform," *Proc. IEEE Conference on Computer Vision and Pattern Recognition*, pp. 2963–2970, 2010. DOI: 10.1109/cvpr.2010.5540041. 57

[195] K. Erk, "Vector space models of word meaning and phrase meaning: a survey," *Language and Linguistics Compass*, vol. 6, pp. 635–653, 2012. DOI: 10.1002/lnco.362. 61

[196] H. J. Escalante, Segmented and annotated IAPR TC-12 dataset; http://www.imagec lef.org/SIAPRdata. 41, 42

[197] H. J. Escalante, C. A. Hernandez, J. A. Gonzalez, A. Lopez-Lopez, M. Montes, E. F. Morales, L. E. Sucar, L. Villasenor, and M. Grubinger, "The segmented and annotated IAPR TC-12 benchmark," *Computer Vision and Image Understanding*, vol. 114, pp. 419–428, 2010. DOI: 10.1016/j.cviu.2009.03.008. 41, 42

[198] A. Esuli and F. Sebastiani, "SentiWordNet: a publicly available lexical resource for opinion mining," *Proc. LREC*, pp. 417–422, 2006. 36, 120

[199] A. Esuli, F. Sebastiani, and S. Baccianella, SentiWordNet; http://sentiwordnet.isti.cnr.it/. 36, 120

[200] M. Everingham, S. M. A. Eslami, L. Van Gool, C. I. Williams, J. Winn, and A. Zisserman, "The PASCAL visual object classes challenge: a retrospective," *International Journal of Computer Vision*, vol. 111, pp. 98–136, 2015. DOI: 10.1007/s11263-014-0733-5. 39

[201] M. Everingham, L. Van Gool, C. K. Williams, J. Winn, and A. Zisserman, "The PASCAL visual object classes (VOC) challenge," *International Journal of Computer Vision*, vol. 88, pp. 303–338, 2010. DOI: 10.1007/s11263-009-0275-4. 39, 99, 102, 109

[202] F. Eyben, M. Wollmer, T. Poitschke, B. Schuller, C. Blaschke, B. Farber, and N. Nguyen-Thien, "Emotion on the road—necessity, acceptance, and feasibility of affective computing in the car," *Advances in Human-Computer Interaction*, vol. 2010, 2010. DOI: 10.1155/2010/263593. 33

[203] A. Farhadi, M. Hejrati, A. Sadeghi, P. Young, C. Rashtchian, J. Hockenmaier, and D. Forsyth., Pascal Sentences Dataset; http://vision.cs.uiuc.edu/pascal-sentences/. 42

[204] A. Farhadi, M. Hejrati, M. A. Sadeghi, P. Young, C. Rashtchian, J. Hockenmaier, and D. Forsyth, "Every picture tells a story: generating sentences from images," *Proc. ECCV*, pp. 15–29, 2010. DOI: 10.1007/978-3-642-15561-1_2. 42, 61, 125, 131

[205] A. Fazly, A. Alishahi, and S. Stevenson, "A probabilistic computational model of cross-situational word learning," *Cognitive Science*, vol. 34, pp. 1017–1063, 2010. DOI: 10.1111/j.1551-6709.2010.01104.x. 78

[206] L. Fei-Fei, M. Andreetto, and M. A. Ranzato, 101 Object Categories; http://www.vision.caltech.edu/feifeili/101_ObjectCategories/. 64

[207] L. Fei-Fei, R. Fergus, and P. Perona, "Learning generative visual models from few training examples: an incremental Bayesian approach tested on 101 object categories," *Proc. Workshop on Generative-Model Based Vision*, Washington, DC, 2004. DOI: 10.1109/cvpr.2004.383. 37

[208] L. Fei-Fei, R. Fergus, and P. Perona, "One-shot learning of object categories," *IEEE Transactions on Pattern Analysis and Machine Intelligence*, vol. 28, pp. 594–611, 2006. DOI: 10.1109/tpami.2006.79. 37

[209] L. Fei-Fei and P. Perona, "A Bayesian hierarchical model for learning natural scene categories," *Proc. IEEE Conference on Computer Vision and Pattern Recognition*, 2005. DOI: 10.1109/cvpr.2005.16. 64

[210] C. Fellbaum, *WordNet: An Electronic Lexical Database*, MIT Press, 1998. 8

[211] P. Felzenszwalb, R. Girshick, D. McAllester, and D. Ramanan, "Object detection with discriminatively trained part-based models," *IEEE Pattern Analysis and Machine Intelligence (PAMI)*, 2009. DOI: 10.1109/tpami.2009.167. 106

[212] P. F. Felzenszwalb and D. P. Huttenlocher, "Efficient graph-based image segmentation," *International Journal of Computer Vision*, vol. 59, pp. 167–181, 2004. DOI: 10.1023/b:visi.0000022288.19776.77. 50

[213] S. L. Feng, R. Manmatha, and V. Lavrenko, "Multiple Bernoulli relevance models for image and video annotation," *Proc. IEEE Conference on Computer Vision and Pattern Recognition (CVPR)*, Washington, DC, pp. 1002–1009, 2004. DOI: 10.1109/cvpr.2004.1315274. 67, 107, 108, 109

[214] Y. Feng and M. Lapata, "Automatic image annotation using auxiliary text information," *Proc. Meeting of the Association for Computational Linguistics*, pp. 272–280, 2008. 107

[215] Y. Feng and M. Lapata, "How many words is a picture worth? Automatic caption generation for news images," *Proc. Annual Meeting of the Association for Computational Linguistics*, pp. 1239–1249, 2010. 132

[216] Y. Feng and M. Lapata, "Topic models for image annotation and text illustration," *Proc. Human Language Technologies: Conference of the North American Chapter of the Association for Computational Linguistics*, pp. 831–839, 2010. 137

[217] R. Fergus, H. Bernal, Y. Weiss, and A. Torralba, "Semantic label sharing for learning with many categories," *Proc. ECCV*, pp. 762–775, 2010. DOI: 10.1007/978-3-642-15549-9_55. 60

[218] R. Fergus, L. Fei-Fei, P. Perona, and A. Zisserman, "Learning object categories from Google's image search," *Proc. 10th IEEE International Conference on Computer Vision*, pp. 1816–1823, 2005. DOI: 10.1109/iccv.2005.142. 115

[219] R. Fergus and P. Perona, The Caltech Database; http://www.vision.caltech.edu/html-files/archive.html. 37

[220] V. Ferrari and A. Zisserman, "Learning visual attributes," *Proc. Advances in Neural Information Processing Systems (NIPS)*, 2007. 37, 116, 117

[221] D. Ferrucci and A. Lally, "UIMA: an architectural approach to unstructured information processing in the corporate research environment," *Natural Language Engineering*, vol. 10, pp. 327–348, 2004. DOI: 10.1017/s1351324904003523. 57

[222] S. Fidler, A. Sharma, and R. Urtasun, "A sentence is worth a thousand pixels," *Proc. IEEE Conference on Computer Vision and Pattern Recognition*, Portland, Oregon, pp. 1995–2002, 2013. DOI: 10.1109/CVPR.2013.260. 46, 53, 127

[223] M. Fink and P. Perona, "Mutual boosting for contextual inference," *Proc. Advances in Neural Information Processing Systems*, 2003. 100

[224] J. R. Finkel, T. Grenager, and C. D. Manning, "Incorporating non-local information into information extraction systems by Gibbs sampling," *Proc. Annual Meeting of the Association for Computational Linguistics (ACL)*, pp. 363–370, 2005. DOI: 10.3115/1219840.1219885. 57

[225] J. R. Finkel and C. D. Manning, "Hierarchical joint learning: improving joint parsing and named entity recognition with non-jointly labeled data," *Proc. Annual Meeting of the Association for Computational Linguistics (ACL)*, 2010. 57

[226] M. Fleischman and D. Roy, "Situated models of meaning for sports video retrieval," *Proc. North American Chapter of the Association for Computational Linguistics*, pp. 37–40, 2007. DOI: 10.3115/1614108.1614118. 10

[227] M. Fleischman and D. Roy, "Unsupervised content-based indexing of sports video," *Proc. of the International Workshop on Workshop on multimedia Information Retrieval*, Augsburg, Bavaria, Germany, pp. 87–94, 2007. DOI: 10.1145/1291233.1291347.

[228] M. Fleischman and D. Roy, "Grounded language modeling for automatic speech recognition of sports video," *Proc. Meeting of the Association for Computational Linguistics*, pp. 121–129, 2008. 10

[229] M. Flickner, H. Sawhney, W. Niblack, J. Ashley, Q. Huang, B. Dom, M. Gorkani, J. Hafner, D. Lee, D. Petkovic, D. Steele, and P. Yanker, "Query by image and video content: the QBIC system," *IEEE Computer*, vol. 28, pp. 22–32, 1995. DOI: 10.1109/2.410146. 29

[230] J. Foote, "An overview of audio information retrieval," *Multimedia Systems*, vol. 7, pp. 2–10, 1999. DOI: 10.1007/s005300050106. 56

[231] D. A. Forsyth, J. Malik, M. M. Fleck, H. Greenspan, T. Leung, S. Belongie, C. Carson, and C. Bregler, "Finding Pictures of Objects in Large Collections of Images," in *Object*

Representation in Computer Vision II, Series, Finding Pictures of Objects in Large Collections of Images, J. Ponce, A. Zisserman, and M. Hebert, Eds., Springer, 1996. DOI: 10.1007/3-540-61750-7_36. 63, 111

[232] D. A. Forsyth and J. Ponce, *Computer Vision—A Modern Approach*, 2nd ed, Upper Saddle River, New Jersey, Prentice Hall, 2013. 46, 47, 48

[233] W. A. Gale, K. W. Church, and D. Yarowsky, "One sense per discourse," *Proc. DARPA Workshop on Speech and Natural Language*, pp. 233–237, 1992. DOI: 10.3115/1075527.1075579. 58

[234] C. Galleguillos, A. Rabinovich, and S. Belongie, "Object categorization using co-occurrence, location and appearance," *Proc. Computer Vision and Pattern Recognition*, 2008. DOI: 10.1109/cvpr.2008.4587799. 94, 102

[235] H. Gao, J. Mao, J. Zhou, Z. Huang, L. Wang, and W. Xu, "Are you talking to a machine? Dataset and methods for multilingual image question," *Proc. Advances in Neural Information Processing Systems*, pp. 2287–2295, 2015. 52, 139

[236] T. Gevers, F. Aldershoff, and A. W. M. Smeulders, "Classification of images on internet by visual and textual information," *Proc. Internet Imaging, SPIE*, San Jose, 2000. 64

[237] W. R. Gilks, S. Richardson, and D. J. Spiegelhalter, *Markov Chain Monte Carlo in Practice*, Chapman and Hall, 1996. 77

[238] K. Gimpel, N. Schneider, B. O'Connor, D. Das, D. Mills, J. Eisenstein, M. Heilman, D. Yogatama, J. Flanigan, and N. A. Smith, "Part-of-speech tagging for twitter: annotation, features, and experiments," *Proc. Annual Meeting of the Association for Computational Linguistics: Human Language Technologies*, pp. 42–47, 2011. 57

[239] R. Girshick, J. Donahue, T. Darrell, and J. Malik, "Region-based convolutional networks for accurate object detection and semantic segmentation," *IEEE Transactions on Pattern Analysis and Machine Intelligence*, 2015 (accepted). DOI: 10.1109/tpami.2015.2437384. 51, 53

[240] S. Gobron, J. Ahn, G. Paltoglou, M. Thelwall, and D. Thalmann, "From sentence to emotion: a real-time three-dimensional graphics metaphor of emotions extracted from text," *The Visual Computer*, vol. 26, pp. 505–519, 2010. DOI: 10.1007/s00371-010-0446-x. 138

[241] Y. Goldberg and J. Orwant, "A dataset of syntactic n-grams over time from a very large corpus of english books," *Proc. Joint Conference on Lexical and Computational Semantics*, pp. 241–247, 2013. 133

[242] J. M. Gonfaus, X. Boix, J. Van de Weijer, A. D. Bagdanov, J. Serrat, and J. Gonzalez, "Harmony potentials for joint classification and segmentation," *Proc. Computer Vision and Pattern Recognition*, pp. 3280–3287, 2010. DOI: 10.1109/cvpr.2010.5540048. 106

[243] Y. Gong, L. Wang, M. Hodosh, J. Hockenmaier, and S. Lazebnik, "Improving image-sentence embeddings using large weakly annotated photo collections," *Proc. ECCV*, 2014. DOI: 10.1007/978-3-319-10593-2_35. 132

[244] A. Goodrum and A. Spink, "Image searching on the excite web search engine," *Information Processing and Management*, vol. 37, pp. 295–311, 2001. DOI: 10.1016/s0306-4573(00)00033-9. 28, 111

[245] R. Gopalan, R. Li, and R. Chellappa, "Domain adaptation for object recognition: an unsupervised approach," *Proc. ICCV*, pp. 999–1006, 2011. DOI: 10.1109/iccv.2011.6126344. 25

[246] P. Gorniak and D. Roy., "Situated language understanding as filtering perceived affordances," *Cognitive Science*, vol. 21, pp. 197–231, 2007. DOI: 10.1080/15326900701221199. 18

[247] S. Gould, J. Rodgers, D. Cohen, G. Elidan, and D. Koller, "Multi-class segmentation with relative location prior," *International Journal of Computer Vision*, vol. 80, pp. 300–316, 2008. DOI: 10.1007/s11263-008-0140-x. 100, 104

[248] K. Grauman and T. Darrel, "The pyramid match kernel: discriminative classification with sets of image features," *Proc. IEEE International Conference on Computer Vision*, 2005. DOI: 10.1109/iccv.2005.239. 64, 106

[249] P. J. Green, "Trans-dimensional Markov Chain Monte Carlo," in *Highly Structured Stochastic Systems, Series, Trans-dimensional Markov Chain Monte Carlo*, 2003. 77

[250] P. J. Green and A. Mira, "Delayed rejection in reversible jump metropolis-hastings," *Biometrika*, vol. 88, pp. 1035–1053, 2001. DOI: 10.1093/biomet/88.4.1035. 77

[251] G. Griffin, A. Holub, and P. Perona, "Caltech-256 Object Category Dataset," California Institute of Technology, 2007. 37

[252] J. J. Gross, "The emerging field of emotion regulation: an integrative review," *Review of General Psychology*, vol. 2, pp. 271, 1998. DOI: 10.1037/1089-2680.2.3.271. 32

[253] J. J. Gross and R. W. Levenson, "Emotion elicitation using films," *Cognition and Emotion*, vol. 9, pp. 87–108, 1995. DOI: 10.1080/02699939508408966. 32, 38

[254] M. Grubinger, ImageCLEF—IAPR TC-12 Benchmark; http://www.imageclef.org/photodata. 41

[255] M. Grubinger, C. P. D., M. Henning, and D. Thomas, "The IAPR benchmark: a new evaluation resource for visual information systems," *Proc. International Conference on Language Resources and Evaluation*, Genoa, Italy, 2006. 41

[256] S. Guadarrama, N. Krishnamoorthy, G. Malkarnenkar, S. Venugopalan, R. Mooney, T. Darrell, and K. Saenko, "Youtube2text: recognizing and describing arbitrary activities using semantic hierarchies and zero-shot recognition," *Proc. IEEE International Conference on Computer Vision*, pp. 2712–2719, 2013. DOI: 10.1109/iccv.2013.337. 125

[257] A. Guerin-Dugue and A. Oliva, "Classification of scene photographs from local orientations features," *Pattern Recognition Letters*, vol. 21, pp. 1135–1140, 2000. DOI: 10.1016/s0167-8655(00)00074-x. 64

[258] M. Guillaumin, T. Mensink, J. J. Verbeek, and C. Schmid, "TagProp: discriminative metric learning in nearest neighbor models for image auto-annotation," *Proc. International Conference on Computer Vision*, pp. 309–316, 2009. DOI: 10.1109/iccv.2009.5459266. 109, 110

[259] A. Gupta and L. S. Davis, "Beyond nouns: exploiting prepositions and comparative adjectives for learning visual classifiers," *Proc. ECCV*, 2008. DOI: 10.1007/978-3-540-88682-2_3. 13, 123

[260] A. Gupta and P. Mannem, "From image annotation to image description," *Proc. Neural Information Processing*, pp. 196–204, 2012. DOI: 10.1007/978-3-642-34500-5_24. 132

[261] A. Gupta, P. Srinivasan, J. Shi, and L. S. Davis, "Understanding videos, constructing plots learning a visually grounded storyline model from annotated videos," *Proc. Computer Vision and Pattern Recognition*, pp. 2012–2019, 2009. DOI: 10.1109/cvpr.2009.5206492. 125, 134

[262] S. Gupta, J. Kim, K. Grauman, and R. Mooney, "Watch, listen and learn: co-training on captioned images and videos," *Proc. Principles of Data Mining and Knowledge Discovery*, pp. 457–472, 2008. DOI: 10.1007/978-3-540-87479-9_48. 64

[263] A. Hanjalic and L.-Q. Xu, "Affective video content representation and modeling," *IEEE Transactions on Multimedia*, vol. 7, pp. 143–154, 2005. DOI: 10.1109/tmm.2004.840618. 56, 120

[264] R. M. Haralick, K. Shanmugam, and I. H. Dinstein, "Textural features for image classification," *IEEE Transactions on Systems, Man and Cybernetics*, vol. SMC-3, pp. 610–621, 1973. DOI: 10.1109/tsmc.1973.4309314. 64

[265] T. Hastie, R. Tibshirani, and J. Friedman, *The Elements of Statistical Learning; Data Mining, Inference, and Prediction*, New York, Springer-Verlag, 2001. 68

[266] C. Hauff and D. Trieschnigg, "Adding Emotions to Pictures," in *Advances in Information Retrieval Theory, Series, Adding Emotions to Pictures*, Springer, pp. 364–367, 2011. DOI: 10.1007/978-3-642-23318-0_40. 138

[267] A. G. Hauptmann and M. G. Christel, "Successful approaches in the TREC video retrieval evaluations," *Proc. ACM International Conference on Multimedia*, pp. 668–675, 2004. DOI: 10.1145/1027527.1027681. 56

[268] A. G. Hauptmann, M. G. Christel, and R. Yan, "Video retrieval based on semantic concepts," *Proc. of the IEEE*, vol. 96, pp. 602–622, 2008. DOI: 10.1109/jproc.2008.916355. 56

[269] A. G. Hauptmann, R. Yan, W.-h. Lin, M. G. Christel, and H. D. Wactlar, "Can high-level concepts fill the semantic gap in video retrieval? A case study with broadcast news," *IEEE Transactions on Multimedia*, vol. 9, pp. 958–966, 2007. DOI: 10.1109/tmm.2007.900150. 56

[270] J. Hays and A. A. Efros, "IM2GPS: Estimating geographic information from a single image," *Proc. Computer Vision and Pattern Recognition*, pp. 1–8, 2008. DOI: 10.1109/cvpr.2008.4587784. 28

[271] X. He and R. S. Zemel, "Latent topic random fields: learning using a taxonomy of labels," *Proc. IEEE Conference on Computer Vision and Pattern Recognition*, pp. 1–8, 2008. DOI: 10.1109/cvpr.2008.4587362. 99

[272] X. He, R. S. Zemel, and M. Carreira-Perpinan, "Multiscale conditional random fields for image labeling," *Proc. IEEE Computer Society Conference on Computer Vision and Pattern Recognition*, vol. 2, pp. II-695–702, 2004. DOI: 10.1109/cvpr.2004.1315232. 40, 41, 50, 99, 103, 104, 105

[273] X. He, R. S. Zemel, and D. Ray, "Learning and incorporating top-down cues in image segmentation," *Proc. ECCV*, pp. 338–351, 2006. DOI: 10.1007/11744023_27. 40, 103, 105

[274] J. L. Herlocker, J. A. Konstan, L. G. Terveen, and J. T. Riedl, "Evaluating collaborative filtering recommender systems," *ACM Transactions on Information Systems*, vol. 22, pp. 5–53, 2004. DOI: 10.1145/963770.963772. 122

[275] G. E. Hinton, S. Osindero, and Y.-W. Teh, "A fast learning algorithm for deep belief nets," *Neural Computation*, vol. 18, pp. 1527–1554, 2006. DOI: 10.1162/neco.2006.18.7.1527. 51

[276] A. Hiroike, Y. Musha, A. Sugimoto, and Y. Mori, "Visualization of information spaces to retrieve and browse image data," *Proc. Visual '99: Information and Information Systems*, pp. 155–162, 1999. DOI: 10.1007/3-540-48762-x_20. 29

[277] S. Hochreiter and J. Schmidhuber, "Long short-term memory," *Neural Computation*, vol. 9, pp. 1735–1780, 1997. DOI: 10.1162/neco.1997.9.8.1735. 135

[278] M. Hodosh and J. Hockenmaier, "Sentence-based image description with scalable, explicit models," *Proc. IEEE Conference on Computer Vision and Pattern Recognition Workshops*, pp. 294–300, 2013. DOI: 10.1109/cvprw.2013.51. 132

[279] M. Hodosh, P. Young, and J. Hockenmaier, "Framing image description as a ranking task: data, models and evaluation metrics," *Journal of Artificial Intelligence Research (JAIR)*, vol. 47, pp. 853–899, 2013. DOI: 10.1613/jair.3994. 61, 132

[280] T. Hofmann, "Learning and representing topic. A hierarchical mixture model for word occurrence in document databases," *Proc. Workshop on Learning from Text and the Web, CMU*, 1998. 89

[281] A. Hoogs and R. Collins, "Object boundary detection in images using a semantic ontology," *Proc. AAAI*, 2006. DOI: 10.1109/cvprw.2006.145. 60

[282] A. Hoogs, J. Rittscher, G. Stein, and J. Schmiederer, "Video content annotation using visual analysis and a large semantic knowledge base," *Proc. IEEE Computer Society Conference on Computer Vision and Pattern Recognition*, vol. 2, pp. II-327–334, 2003. DOI: 10.1109/cvpr.2003.1211487. 56, 59

[283] C.-J. Huang, C.-T. Li, and M.-K. Shan, "VizStory: visualization of digital narrative for fairy tales," *Proc. Technologies and Applications of Artificial Intelligence (TAAI)*, pp. 67–72, 2013. DOI: 10.1109/taai.2013.26. 138

[284] J. Huang and D. Mumford, "Image Statistics for the British Aerospace Segmented Database," Division of Applied Math, Brown University, 1999; http://www.dam.brown.edu/people/mumford/Papers/sowerbyHuang.pdf. 40

[285] L. Huang, T. Xia, J. Wan, Y. Zhang, and S. Lin, "Personalized portraits ranking," *Proc. ACM International Conference on Multimedia*, pp. 1277–1280, 2011. DOI: 10.1145/2072298.2071993. 122

[286] T. S. Huang, X. S. Xhou, M. Nakazato, Y. Wu, and I. Cohen, "Leaning in content-based image retrieval," *Proc. in the 2nd International Conference on Development and Learning*, 2002. 29

[287] D. Huggins-Daines, M. Kumar, A. Chan, A. W. Black, M. Ravishankar, and A. I. Rudnicky, "Pocketsphinx: A free, real-time continuous speech recognition system for hand-held devices," *Proc. IEEE International Conference on Acoustics, Speech and Signal Processing*, 2006. DOI: 10.1109/icassp.2006.1659988. 56

[288] M. J. Huiskes and M. S. Lew, "The MIR Flickr retrieval evaluation," *Proc. 1st ACM International Conference on Multimedia Information Retrieval*, Vancouver, British Columbia, Canada, pp. 39–43, 2008. DOI: 10.1145/1460096.1460104. 39

[289] M. J. Huiskes, B. Thomee, and M. S. Lew, "New trends and ideas in visual concept detection: the MIR Flickr retrieval evaluation initiative," *Proc. International Conference on Multimedia Information Retrieval*, pp. 527–536, 2010. DOI: 10.1145/1743384.1743475. 39

[290] R. J. Huster, S. Stevens, A. L. Gerlach, and F. Rist, "A spectralanalytic approach to emotional responses evoked through picture presentation," *International Journal of Psychophysiology*, vol. 72, pp. 212–216, 2009. DOI: 10.1016/j.ijpsycho.2008.12.009. 38

[291] M. Jamieson, Y. Eskin, A. Fazly, S. Stevenson, and S. Dickinson, "Discovering multi-part appearance models from captioned images," *Proc. ECCV*, pp. 183–196, 2010. DOI: 10.1007/978-3-642-15555-0_14. 116

[292] M. Jamieson, A. Fazly, S. Stevenson, S. Dickinson, and S. Wachsmuth, "Using language to learn structured appearance models for image annotation," *IEEE Transactions on Pattern Analysis and Machine Intelligence*, vol. 32, pp. 148–164, 2010. DOI: 10.1109/tpami.2008.283. 115, 116

[293] J. Jeon, V. Lavrenko, and R. Manmatha, "Automatic image annotation and retrieval using cross-media relevance models," *Proc. SIGIR*, 2003. DOI: 10.1145/860435.860459. 107, 108

[294] J. Jeon and R. Manmatha, "Using maximum entropy for automatic image annotation," *Proc. Conference on Image and Video Retrieval*, pp. 24–32, 2004. DOI: 10.1007/978-3-540-27814-6_7. 107, 108

[295] J.-W. Jeong and D.-H. Lee, "Automatic image annotation using affective vocabularies: attribute-based learning approach," *Journal of Information Science*, pp. 0165551513501267, 2014. DOI: 10.1177/0165551513501267. 121

[296] J. Jia, S. Wu, X. Wang, P. Hu, L. Cai, and J. Tang, "Can we understand Van Gogh's mood? Learning to infer affects from images in social networks," *Proc. ACM International Conference on Multimedia*, pp. 857–860, 2012. DOI: 10.1145/2393347.2396330. 120

[297] Y. Jia, E. Shelhamer, J. Donahue, S. Karayev, J. Long, R. Girshick, S. Guadarrama, and T. Darrell, "Caffe: convolutional architecture for fast feature embedding," *Proc. ACM International Conference on Multimedia*, pp. 675–678, 2014. DOI: 10.1145/2647868.2654889. 51, 135

[298] Y. Jiang, J. Liu, Z. Li, C. Xu, and H. Lu, "Chat with illustration: a chat system with visual aids," *Proc. 4th International Conference on Internet Multimedia Computing and Service*, pp. 96–99, 2012. DOI: 10.1145/2382336.2382364. 138

[299] Y.-G. Jiang, B. Xu, and X. Xue, "Predicting emotions in user-generated videos," *Proc. AAAI Conference on Artificial Intelligence*, 2014. 56, 120

[300] T. Jiayu and P. H. Lewis, "A study of quality issues for image auto-annotation with the corel dataset," *IEEE Transactions on Circuits and Systems for Video Technology*, vol. 17, pp. 384–389, 2007. DOI: 10.1109/tcsvt.2006.888941. 39

[301] L. Jie, B. Caputo, and V. Ferrari, "Who's doing what: joint modeling of names and verbs for simultaneous face and pose annotation," *Proc. Advances in Neural Information Processing Systems (NIPS)*, 2009. 114, 115

[302] Y. Jin, L. Khan, L. Wang, and M. Awad, "Image annotations by combining multiple evidence and WordNet," *Proc. ACM Multimedia*, 2005. DOI: 10.1145/1101149.1101305. 59

[303] M. I. Jordan, Z. Ghahramani, T. S. Jaakkola, and L. K. Saul, "An introduction to variational methods for graphical models," *Machine Learning*, vol. 37, pp. 183–233, 1999. DOI: 10.1007/978-94-011-5014-9_5. 77

[304] C. Jorgensen, *Image Retrieval: Theory and Research*: Scarecrow Press, 2003. 111

[305] D. Joshi, J. Z. Wang, and J. Li, "The story picturing engine: finding elite images to illustrate a story using mutual reinforcement," *Proc. 6th ACM SIGMM International Workshop on Multimedia Information Retrieval*, pp. 119–126, 2004. DOI: 10.1145/1026711.1026732. 137

[306] D. Joshi, J. Z. Wang, and J. Li, "The story picturing engine—a system for automatic text illustration," *ACM Transactions on Multimedia Computing, Communications, and Applications (TOMCCAP)*, vol. 2, pp. 68–89, 2006. DOI: 10.1145/1126004.1126008. 137

[307] B. Julesz, "Textons, the elements of texture perception, and their interactions," *Nature*, vol. 290, pp. 91–97, 1981. DOI: 10.1038/290091a0. 48

[308] K. Jung, K. In Kim, and A. K. Jain, "Text information extraction in images and video: a survey," *Pattern Recognition*, vol. 37, pp. 977–997, 2004. DOI: 10.1016/j.patcog.2003.10.012. 56

[309] H.-B. Kang, "Affective content detection using HMMs," *Proc. ACM International Conference on Multimedia*, pp. 259–262, 2003. DOI: 10.1145/957013.957066. 120

[310] H.-B. Kang, "Affective Contents Retrieval from Video with Relevance Feedback," in *Digital Libraries: Technology and Management of Indigenous Knowledge for Global Access, Series, Affective Contents Retrieval from Video with Relevance Feedback*, T. Sembok, H. Zaman, H. Chen, S. Urs, and S.-H. Myaeng, Eds., Springer Berlin Heidelberg, pp. 243–252, 2003. DOI: 10.1007/978-3-540-24594-0_23. 120

[311] Y. Karov and S. Edelman, "Similarity-based word sense disambiguation," *Computational Linguistics*, vol. 24, pp. 41–59, 1998. 58

[312] A. Karpathy and L. Fei-Fei, "Deep visual-semantic alignments for generating image descriptions," in *Computer Vision and Pattern Recognition*, 2015. DOI: 10.1109/cvpr.2015.7298932. 52, 53, 61, 135, 136

[313] A. Karpathy, A. Joulin, and F. F. F. Li, "Deep fragment embeddings for bidirectional image sentence mapping," *Proc. Advances in Neural Information Processing Systems*, pp. 1889–1897, 2014. 52, 136

[314] A. Karpathy, G. Toderici, S. Shetty, T. Leung, R. Sukthankar, and L. Fei-Fei, "Large-scale video classification with convolutional neural networks," *Proc. IEEE Conference on Computer Vision and Pattern Recognition (CVPR)*, 2014. DOI: 10.1109/cvpr.2014.223. 125

[315] Y. Ke and R. Sukthankar, "PCA-SIFT: a more distinctive representation for local image descriptors," *Proc. IEEE Computer Society Conference on Computer Vision and Pattern Recognition*, vol. 2 pp. II-506–513, 2004. DOI: 10.1109/cvpr.2004.1315206. 48

[316] K. Kesorn, S. Chimlek, S. Poslad, and P. Piamsa-nga, "Visual content representation using semantically similar visual words," *Expert Systems with Applications*, vol. 38, pp. 11472–11481, 2011. DOI: 10.1016/j.eswa.2011.03.021. 51

[317] A. Khosla, T. Zhou, T. Malisiewicz, A. A. Efros, and A. Torralba, "Undoing the damage of dataset bias," *Proc. ECCV*, pp. 158–171, 2012. DOI: 10.1007/978-3-642-33718-5_12. 25

[318] D.-H. Kim, C.-W. Chung, and K. Barnard, "Relevance feedback using adaptive clustering for image similarity retrieval," *Journal of Systems and Software*, vol. 78, pp. 9–23, 2005. DOI: 10.1016/j.jss.2005.02.005. 29

[319] G. Kim, S. Moon, and L. Sigal, "Ranking and retrieval of image sequences from multiple paragraph queries," *Proc. IEEE Conference on Computer Vision and Pattern Recognition*, pp. 1993–2001, 2015. DOI: 10.1109/cvpr.2015.7298810. 138

[320] R. Kindermann and J. L. Snell, *Markov Random Fields and their Applications*, vol. 1: American Mathematical Society Providence, RI, 1980. DOI: 10.1090/conm/001. 95

[321] R. Kiros, R. Salakhutdinov, and R. Zemel, "Multimodal neural language models," *Proc. 31st International Conference on Machine Learning*, pp. 595–603, 2014. 134, 135

[322] R. Kiros, R. Salakhutdinov, and R. S. Zemel, "Unifying visual-semantic embeddings with multimodal neural language models," in *arXiv preprint arXiv:1411.2539*, 2014. 135, 137

[323] R. Kiros, Y. Zhu, R. R. Salakhutdinov, R. Zemel, R. Urtasun, A. Torralba, and S. Fidler, "Skip-thought vectors," *Proc. Neural Information Processing Systems (NIPS)*, pp. 3276–3284, 2015. 61, 137

[324] J. J. Kivinen, E. B. Sudderth, and M. I. Jordan, "Learning multiscale representations of natural scenes using dirichlet processes," *Proc. International Conference on Computer Vision*, pp. 1–8, 2007. DOI: 10.1109/iccv.2007.4408870. 64

[325] D. Klein and C. D. Manning, "Fast exact inference with a factored model for natural language parsing," *Proc. Advances in Neural Information Processing Systems*, pp. 3–10, 2002. 57, 127

[326] P. Koehn, H. Hoang, A. Birch, C. Callison-Burch, M. Federico, N. Bertoldi, B. Cowan, W. Shen, C. Moran, R. Zens, C. Dyer, O. Bojar, A. Constantin, and E. Herbst, "Moses: open source toolkit for statistical machine translation," *Proc. Annual Meeting of the ACL on Interactive Poster and Demonstration Sessions*, Prague, Czech Republic, pp. 177–180, 2007. DOI: 10.3115/1557769.1557821. 56

[327] S. Koelstra, C. Muhl, M. Soleymani, J.-S. Lee, A. Yazdani, T. Ebrahimi, T. Pun, A. Nijholt, and I. Patras, "DEAP: a database for emotion analysis; using physiological signals," http://www.eecs.qmul.ac.uk/mmv/datasets/deap/. 32, 38

[328] S. Koelstra, C. Muhl, M. Soleymani, J.-S. Lee, A. Yazdani, T. Ebrahimi, T. Pun, A. Nijholt, and I. Patras, "DEAP: a database for emotion analysis; using physiological signals," *IEEE Transactions on Affective Computing*, vol. 3, pp. 18–31, 2012. DOI: 10.1109/t-affc.2011.15. 32, 38

[329] J. J. Koenderink, "The structure of images," *Biological Cybernetics*, vol. 50, pp. 363–370, 1984. DOI: 10.1007/bf00336961. 49

[330] A. Kojima, T. Tamura, and K. Fukunaga, "Natural language description of human activities from video images based on concept hierarchy of actions," *International Journal of Computer Vision*, vol. 50, pp. 171–184, 2002. 133

[331] D. Koller and N. Friedman, *Probabilistic Graphical Models*, MIT Press, 2009. 5, 18, 66, 76, 95

[332] O. Kolomiyets and M.-F. Moens, "Towards animated visualization of actors and actions in a learning environment," in *Methodologies and Intelligent Systems for Technology Enhanced Learning, Series, Towards Animated Visualization of Actors and Actions in a Learning Environment*, Springer, pp. 197–205, 2014. DOI: 10.1007/978-3-319-07698-0_25. 137, 138

[333] C. Kong, D. Lin, M. Bansal, R. Urtasun, and S. Fidler, "What are you talking about? Text-to-image coreference," *Proc. IEEE Conference on Computer Vision and Pattern Recognition*, pp. 3558–3565, 2014. DOI: 10.1109/cvpr.2014.455. 42, 126

[334] L. Kong, N. Schneider, S. Swayamdipta, A. Bhatia, C. Dyer, and N. A. Smith, "A dependency parser for tweets," *Proc. Empirical Methods in Natural Language Processing*, 2014. DOI: 10.3115/v1/D14-1108. 57

[335] N. Krishnamoorthy, G. Malkarnenkar, R. J. Mooney, K. Saenko, and S. Guadarrama, "Generating natural-language video descriptions using text-mined knowledge," *Proc. AAAI*, pp. 2, 2013. 61, 125, 133

[336] A. Krizhevsky, I. Sutskever, and G. E. Hinton, "Imagenet classification with deep convolutional neural networks," *Proc. Advances in Neural Information Processing Systems*, pp. 1097–1105, 2012. 51, 52

[337] B. Kulis, K. Saenko, and T. Darrell, "What you saw is not what you get: domain adaptation using asymmetric kernel transforms," *Proc. Computer Vision and Pattern Recognition*, pp. 1785–1792, 2011. DOI: 10.1109/cvpr.2011.5995702. 25

[338] G. Kulkarni, V. Premraj, S. Dhar, L. Siming, C. Yejin, A. C. Berg, and T. L. Berg, "Baby talk: understanding and generating simple image descriptions," *Proc. IEEE Conference on Computer Vision and Pattern Recognition (CVPR)*, pp. 1601–1608, 2011. DOI: 10.1109/cvpr.2011.5995466. 46, 132

[339] G. Kulkarni, V. Premraj, V. Ordonez, S. Dhar, S. Li, Y. Choi, A. C. Berg, and T. L. Berg, "Babytalk: understanding and generating simple image descriptions," *IEEE Transactions on Pattern Analysis and Machine Intelligence*, vol. 35, pp. 2891–2903, 2013. DOI: 10.1109/tpami.2012.162. 46, 132

[340] S. Kumar and M. Hebert, "Discriminative random fields: a discriminative framework for contextual interaction in classification," *Proc. 9th IEEE International Conference on Computer Vision*, pp. 1150–1157, 2003. DOI: 10.1109/iccv.2003.1238478. 95, 97

[341] S. Kumar and M. Hebert, "A hierarchical field framework for unified context-based classification," *Proc. 10th IEEE International Conference on Computer Vision*, vol. 2, pp. 1284–1291, 2005. DOI: 10.1109/iccv.2005.9.

[342] S. Kumar and M. Hebert, "Discriminative random fields," *International Journal of Computer Vision*, vol. 68, pp. 179–201, 2006. DOI: 10.1007/s11263-006-7007-9. 95, 97

[343] P. Kuznetsova, V. Ordonez, A. C. Berg, T. L. Berg, and Y. Choi, "Collective generation of natural image descriptions," *Proc. 50th Annual Meeting of the Association for Computational Linguistics: Long Papers*, vol. 1, pp. 359–368, 2012. 132

[344] P. Kuznetsova, V. Ordonez, T. L. Berg, and Y. Choi, "Treetalk: composition and compression of trees for image descriptions," *Transactions of the Association for Computational Linguistics*, vol. 2, pp. 351–362, 2014. 132

[345] L. Ladicky, P. Sturgess, K. Alahari, C. Russell, and P. H. Torr, "What, where and how many? combining object detectors and CRFs," *Proc. ECCV*, pp. 424–437, 2010. DOI: 10.1007/978-3-642-15561-1_31. 106

[346] J. Lafferty, A. McCallum, and F. C. Pereira, "Conditional random fields: probabilistic models for segmenting and labeling sequence data," *Proc. International Conference on Machine Learning*, pp. 282–289, 2001. 95, 97

[347] C. H. Lampert, H. Nickisch, and S. Harmeling, "Learning to detect unseen object classes by Between-class attribute transfer," *Proc. Computer Vision and Pattern Recognition*, pp. 951–958, 2009. DOI: 10.1109/cvpr.2009.5206594. 36, 37, 121

[348] C. H. Lampert, H. Nickisch, S. Harmeling, and J. Weidmann, Animals with Attributes; http://attributes.kyb.tuebingen.mpg.de/. 36, 37, 121

[349] P. J. Lang, M. M. Bradley, and B. N. Cuthbert, "International Affective Picture System (IAPS): Technical Manual and Affective Ratings," Gainesville, FL: The Center for Research in Psychophysiology, University of Florida, 1999, 32, 38, 119, 122

[350] P. J. Lang, M. K. Greenwald, M. M. Bradley, and A. O. Hamm, "Looking at pictures: affective, facial, visceral, and behavioral reactions," *Psychophysiology*, vol. 30, pp. 261–273, 1993. DOI: 10.1111/j.1469-8986.1993.tb03352.x. 32, 38

[351] S. Lazebnik, C. Schmid, and J. Ponce, "Beyond bags of features: spatial pyramid matching for recognizing natural scene categories," *Proc. Computer Vision and Pattern Recognition, Conference on IEEE Computer Society*, pp. 2169–2178, 2006. DOI: 10.1109/cvpr.2006.68. 64

[352] C. Leacock and M. Chodorow, "Combining Local Context and Wordnet Similarity for Word Sense Identification," in *WordNet: An Electronic Lexical Database*, *Series*, *Combining Local Context and Wordnet Similarity for Word Sense Identification*, C. Fellbaum, Ed., MIT Press, pp. 265–283, 1998. 58

[353] Y. LeCun, L. Bottou, Y. Bengio, and P. Haffner, "Gradient-based learning applied to document recognition," *Proc. of the IEEE*, vol. 86, pp. 2278–2324, 1998. DOI: 10.1109/5.726791. 51

[354] Y. LeCun, F. J. Huang, and L. Bottou, "Learning methods for generic object recognition with invariance to pose and lighting," *Proc. Computer Vision and Pattern Recognition*, pp. II-97–104, 2004. DOI: 10.1109/cvpr.2004.1315150.

[355] Y. LeCun, K. Kavukcuoglu, and C. Farabet, "Convolutional networks and applications in vision," *Proc. IEEE International Symposium on Circuits and Systems*, pp. 253–256, 2010. DOI: 10.1109/iscas.2010.5537907. 51

[356] A. Lee and T. Kawahara, "Recent development of Open-source speech recognition engine julius," *Proc. Annual Summit and Conference of the Asia-Pacific Signal and Information Processing Association*, pp. 131–137, 2009. 56

[357] A. Lee, T. Kawahara, and K. Shikano, "Julius—an open source real-time large vocabulary recognition engine," *Proc. EUROSPEECH*, 2001. 56

[358] H. Lee, A. Chang, Y. Peirsman, N. Chambers, M. Surdeanu, and D. Jurafsky, "Deterministic coreference resolution based on entity-centric, precision-ranked rules," *Computational Linguistics*, vol. 39, 2013. DOI: 10.1162/coli_a_00152. 57

[359] T. S. H. Lee, S. Fidler, A. Levinshtein, and S. Dickinson, "Learning categorical shape from captioned images," *Proc. Computer and Robot Vision*, pp. 228–235, 2012. DOI: 10.1109/crv.2012.37. 116

[360] Y. K. Lee and H. T. Ng, "An empirical evaluation of knowledge sources and learning algorithms for word sense disambiguation," *Proc. ACL-02 Conference on Empirical Methods in Natural Language Processing*, vol. 10, pp. 41–48, 2002. DOI: 10.3115/1118693.1118699. 58

[361] R. Levy and G. Andrew, "Tregex and tsurgeon: tools for querying and manipulating tree data structures," *Proc. 5th International Conference on Language Resources and Evaluation*, pp. 2231–2234, 2006. 123

[362] B. Li, W. Hu, W. Xiong, O. Wu, and W. Li, "Horror image recognition based on emotional attention," *Proc. ACCV*, pp. 594–605, 2011. DOI: 10.1007/978-3-642-19309-5_46. 119

[363] B. Li, W. Xiong, and W. Hu, "Web horror image recognition based on context-aware multi-instance learning," *Proc. IEEE 11th International Conference on Data Mining*, pp. 1158–1163, 2011. DOI: 10.1109/icdm.2011.155. 119

[364] B. Li, W. Xiong, W. Hu, and X. Ding, "Context-aware affective images classification based on bilayer sparse representation," *Proc. ACM International Conference on Multimedia*, pp. 721–724, 2012. DOI: 10.1145/2393347.2396296. 119

[365] J. Li and J. Z. Wang, "Automatic linguistic indexing of pictures by a statistical modeling approach," *IEEE Trans. on Pattern Analysis and Machine Intelligence*, vol. 25, 2003. DOI: 10.1109/tpami.2003.1227984. 64

[366] L. Li, M. Zhou, G. Sapiro, and L. Carin, "On the integration of topic modeling and dictionary learning," *Proc. 28th International Conference on Machine Learning*, pp. 625–632, 2011. 60, 107

[367] L.-J. Li and L. Fei-Fei, "What, where and who? classifying events by scene and object recognition," *Proc. 11th International Conference on Computer Vision*, pp. 1–8, 2007. DOI: 10.1109/iccv.2007.4408872. 92

[368] L.-J. Li and L. Fei-Fei, "OPTIMOL: automatic online picture collection via incremental model learning," *International Journal of Computer Vision*, vol. 88, pp. 147–168, 2010. DOI: 10.1109/cvpr.2007.383048. 115

[369] L.-J. Li, R. Socher, and L. Fei-Fei, "Towards total scene understanding: classification, annotation and segmentation in an automatic framework," *Proc. Computer Vision and Pattern Recognition*, 2009. DOI: 10.1109/cvpr.2009.5206718. 60, 92

[370] L.-J. Li, C. Wang, Y. Lim, D. M. Blei, and L. Fei-Fei, "Building and using a semantivisual image hierarchy," *Proc. IEEE Conference on Computer Vision and Pattern Recognition*, pp. 3336–3343, 2010. DOI: 10.1109/cvpr.2010.5540027. 60, 89

[371] S. Li, G. Kulkarni, T. L. Berg, A. C. Berg, and Y. Choi, "Composing simple image descriptions using web-scale n-grams," *Proc. Conference on Computational Natural Language Learning*, pp. 220–228, 2011. 132

[372] S. Li, Y.-J. Zhang, and H.-C. Tan, "Discovering latent semantic factors for emotional picture categorization," *Proc. IEEE International Conference on Image Processing*, pp. 1065–1068, 2010. DOI: 10.1109/icip.2010.5652558. 119

[373] T. Li, S. Yan, T. Mei, X.-S. Hua, and I.-S. Kweon, "Image decomposition with multilabel context: algorithms and applications," *IEEE Transactions on Image Processing*, vol. 20, pp. 2301–2314, 2011. DOI: 10.1109/tip.2010.2103081. 107

[374] Z. Li, Z. Shi, X. Liu, and Z. Shi, "Modeling continuous visual features for semantic image annotation and retrieval," *Pattern Recognition Letters*, vol. 32, pp. 516–523, 2011. DOI: 10.1016/j.patrec.2010.11.015. 107

[375] R. Lienhart, "Video OCR: a Survey and Practitioner's Guide," in *Video Mining, Series, Video OCR: a Survey and Practitioner's Guide*, Springer, pp. 155–183, 2003. DOI: 10.1007/978-1-4757-6928-9_6. 56

[376] D. Lin, "An information-theoretic definition of similarity," *Proc. International Conference on Machine Learning*, 1998. 132

[377] T.-Y. Lin, M. Maire, S. Belongie, J. Hays, P. Perona, D. Ramanan, P. Dollar, and C. L. Zitnick, "Microsoft COCO: Common Objects in Context," in *European Conference on Computer Vision*, vol. 8693, *Lecture Notes in Computer Science*, D. Fleet, T. Pajdla, B. Schiele, and T. Tuytelaars, Eds., Springer International Publishing, pp. 740–755, 2014. DOI: 10.1007/978-3-319-10602-1_48. 40, 42, 43

[378] Y. Lin, P. Meer, and D. J. Foran, "Multiple class segmentation using a unified framework over mean-shift patches," *Proc. IEEE Conference on Computer Vision and Pattern Recognition*, pp. 1–8, 2007. DOI: 10.1109/cvpr.2007.383229. 50

[379] T. Lindeberg, "Scale-space theory: a basic tool for analyzing structures at different scales," *Journal of Applied Statistics*, vol. 21, pp. 225–270, 1994. DOI: 10.1080/757582976. 49

[380] C. L. Lisetti and F. Nasoz, "Affective intelligent car interfaces with emotion recognition," *Proc. International Conference on Human Computer Interaction*, Las Vegas, NV, 2005. 33

[381] J. Liu, M. Li, Q. Liu, H. Lu, and S. Ma, "Image annotation via graph learning," *Pattern Recognition*, vol. 42, pp. 218–228, 2009. DOI: 10.1016/j.patcog.2008.04.012. 107

[382] N. Liu, E. Dellandrea, B. Tellez, and L. Chen, "Associating Textual Features with Visual Ones to Improve Affective Image Classification," in *Affective Computing and Intelligent Interaction*, Series, *Associating Textual Features with Visual Ones to Improve Affective Image Classification* Springer, pp. 195–204, 2011. DOI: 10.1007/978-3-642-24600-5_23. 119

[383] S. Liu, D. Xu, and S. Feng, "Emotion categorization using affective-pLSA model," *Optical Engineering*, vol. 49, pp. 127201–12, 2010. DOI: 10.1117/1.3518051. 119

[384] W.-H. Liu and C.-W. Su, "Automatic Peak Recognition for Mountain Images," in *Advanced Technologies, Embedded and Multimedia for Human-centric Computing*, Series, *Automatic Peak Recognition for Mountain Images*, Y.-M. Huang, H.-C. Chao, D.-J. Deng, and J. J. Park, Eds., Springer Netherlands, pp. 1115–1121, 2014. DOI: 10.1007/978-94-007-7262-5_127. 28

[385] P. Lovato, A. Perina, N. Sebe, O. Zandona, A. Montagnini, M. Bicego, and M. Cristani, "Tell me what you like and I'll tell you what you are: discriminating visual preferences on Flickr data," *Proc. ACCV*, pp. 45–56, 2013. DOI: 10.1007/978-3-642-37331-2_4. 122

[386] D. Lowe, SIFT Demo Program (Version 4); http://www.cs.ubc.ca/~lowe/keypoints/. 49

[387] D. G. Lowe, "Distinctive image features from scale-invariant keypoints," *International Journal of Computer Vision*, vol. 60, pp. 91–110, 2004. DOI: 10.1023/b:visi.0000029664.99615.94. 48, 49, 116

[388] D. Lu and Q. Weng, "A survey of image classification methods and techniques for improving classification performance," *International Journal of Remote Sensing*, vol. 28, pp. 823–870, 2007. DOI: 10.1080/01431160600746456. 64

[389] X. Lu, P. Suryanarayan, R. B. Adams Jr., J. Li, M. G. Newman, and J. Z. Wang, "On shape and the computability of emotions," *Proc. ACM International Conference on Multimedia*, pp. 229–238, 2012. DOI: 10.1145/2393347.2393384. 119

[390] J. Luo and M. Boutell, "Natural scene classification using over complete ICA," *Pattern Recognition*, vol. 38, pp. 1507–1519, 2005. DOI: 10.1016/j.patcog.2005.02.015. 64

[391] W. Luo, X. Wang, and X. Tang, "Content-based photo quality assessment," *Proc. IEEE International Conference on Computer Vision*, pp. 2206–2213, 2011. 121

[392] J. Machajdik and A. Hanbury, "Affective image classification using features inspired by psychology and art theory," *Proc. International Conference on Multimedia*, Firenze, Italy, pp. 83–92, 2010. DOI: 10.1145/1873951.1873965. 119, 120

[393] A. Makadia, V. Pavlovic, and S. Kumar, "A new baseline for image annotation," *Proc. ECCV*, 2008. DOI: 10.1007/978-3-540-88690-7_24. 109

[394] A. Makadia, V. Pavlovic, and S. Kumar, "Baselines for image annotation," *International Journal of Computer Vision*, vol. 90, pp. 88–105, 2010. DOI: 10.1007/s11263-010-0338-6. 109

[395] J. Malik, S. Belongie, T. Leung, and J. Shi, "Contour and texture analysis for image segmentation," *International Journal of Computer Vision*, 2001. DOI: 10.1007/978-1-4615-4413-5_9. 15, 48, 50, 98

[396] M. Malinowski and M. Fritz, "A multi-world approach to question answering about real-world scenes based on uncertain input," *Proc. Advances in Neural Information Processing Systems*, pp. 1682–1690, 2014. 43, 138

[397] M. Malinowski and M. Fritz, DAQUAR—Dataset for Question Answering on Real-world Images; https://www.d2.mpi-inf.mpg.de/visual-turing-challenge. 43

[398] M. Malinowski, M. Rohrbach, and M. Fritz, "Ask your neurons: a neural-based approach to answering questions about images," *Proc. ICCV*, 2015. 139

[399] C. D. Manning, M. Surdeanu, J. Bauer, J. Finkel, S. J. Bethard, and D. McClosky, "The Stanford CoreNLP natural language processing toolkit," *Proc. 52nd Annual Meeting of the Association for Computational Linguistics: System Demonstrations*, pp. 55–60, 2014. DOI: 10.3115/v1/p14-5010. 57

[400] J. Mao, W. Xu, Y. Yang, J. Wang, and A. Yuille, "Deep captioning with multimodal recurrent neural networks (m-RNN)," *Proc. ICLR*, 2015. 135

[401] L. Marchesotti, N. Murray, and F. Perronnin, "Discovering beautiful attributes for aesthetic image analysis," *International Journal of Computer Vision*, pp. 1–21, 2014. DOI: 10.1007/s11263-014-0789-2. 122

[402] L. Marchesotti, F. Perronnin, D. Larlus, and G. Csurka, "Assessing the aesthetic quality of photographs using generic image descriptors," *Proc. IEEE International Conference on Computer Vision*, pp. 1784–1791, 2011. DOI: 10.1109/iccv.2011.6126444. 121

[403] M. Markkula and E. Sormunen, "End-user searching challenges indexing practices in the digital newspaper photo archive," *Information Retrieval*, vol. 1, pp. 259–285, 2000. DOI: 10.1023/A:1009995816485. 28, 111

[404] M. Markkula, M. Tico, B. Sepponen, K. Nirkkonen, and E. Sormunen, "A test collection for the evaluation of content-based image retrieval algorithms-A user and task-based approach," *Information Retrieval*, vol. 4, pp. 275–293, 2001. DOI: 10.1023/A:1011954407169. 28, 111

[405] O. Maron and T. Lozano-Perez, "A framework for multiple-instance learning," *Proc. Neural Information Processing Systems*, 1998. 86, 87

[406] O. Maron and A. L. Ratan, "Multiple-instance learning for natural scene classification," *Proc. 15th International Conference on Machine Learning*, 1998. 86, 87

[407] D. Martin, C. Fowlkes, and J. Malik, " Learning to detect natural image boundaries using local brightness, color, and texture cues," *IEEE Trans. on Pattern Analysis and Machine Intelligence*, vol. 26, pp. 530–549, 2004. DOI: 10.1109/tpami.2004.1273918. 50

[408] D. Martin, C. Fowlkes, D. Tal, and J. Malik, "A database of human segmented natural images and its application to evaluating segmentation algorithms and measuring ecological statistics," *Proc. International Conference on Computer Vision*, pp. II-416–421, 2001. DOI: 10.1109/iccv.2001.937655. 40

[409] N. Mavridis and D. Roy, "Grounded situation models for robots: bridging language, perception, and action," *Proc. AAAI-05 Workshop on Modular Construction of Human like Intelligence*, 2005. 17

[410] N. Mavridis and D. Roy, "Grounded situation models for robots: where words and percepts meet," *Proc. IEEE/RSJ International Conference on Intelligent Robots and Systems*, 2006. DOI: 10.1109/iros.2006.282258. 17

[411] W. May, S. Fidler, A. Fazly, S. Dickinson, and S. Stevenson, "Unsupervised disambiguation of image captions," *Proc. First Joint Conference on Lexical and Computational Semantics*, Montreal, Canada, pp. 85–89, 2012. 126

[412] G. McLachlan and D. Peel, *Finite Mixture Models*, Wiley, 2004. DOI: 10.1002/0471721182. 26, 68

[413] A. Mehrabian, "Pleasure-arousal-dominance: a general framework for describing and measuring individual differences in temperament," *Current Psychology*, vol. 14, pp. 261–292, 1996. DOI: 10.1007/bf02686918. 32

[414] J.-B. Michel, Y. K. Shen, A. P. Aiden, A. Veres, M. K. Gray, J. P. Pickett, D. Hoiberg, D. Clancy, P. Norvig, J. Orwant, S. Pinker, M. A. Nowak, and E. L. Aiden, "Quantitative Analysis of Culture Using Millions of Digitized Books," *Science*, vol. 331, pp. 176–182, 2011. DOI: 10.1126/science.1199644. 129

[415] R. Mihalcea, "Using wikipedia for automatic word sense disambiguation," *Proc. HLT-NAACL*, pp. 196–203, 2007. 58

[416] R. Mihalcea and A. Csomai, " SenseLearner: word sense disambiguation for all words in unrestricted text," *Proc. 43nd Annual Meeting of the Association for Computational Linguistics*, Ann Arbor, MI, 2005. DOI: 10.3115/1225753.1225767. 58

[417] R. Mihalcea and D. Moldovan, "Word sense disambiguation based on semantic density," *Proc. COLING/ACL Workshop on Usage of WordNet in Natural Language Processing Systems*, Montreal, 1998. 58

[418] J. A. Mikels, B. L. Fredrickson, G. R. Larkin, C. M. Lindberg, S. J. Maglio, and P. A. Reuter-Lorenz, "Emotional category data on images from the International Affective Picture System," *Behavior Research Methods*, vol. 37, pp. 626–630, 2005. DOI: 10.3758/bf03192732. 32, 38, 119, 122

[419] K. Mikolajczyk and C. Schmid, "A performance evaluation of local descriptors," *IEEE Transactions on Pattern Analysis and Machine Intelligence*, vol. 27, pp. 1615–1630, 2005. DOI: 10.1109/tpami.2005.188. 48

[420] T. Mikolov, K. Chen, G. Corrado, and J. Dean, "Efficient estimation of word representations in vector space," *Proc. ICLR Workshop*, 2013. 61, 128

[421] T. Mikolov, I. Sutskever, K. Chen, G. S. Corrado, and J. Dean, "Distributed representations of words and phrases and their compositionality," *Proc. Advances in Neural Information Processing Systems*, pp. 3111–3119, 2013.

[422] T. Mikolov, W.-t. Yih, and G. Zweig, "Linguistic regularities in continuous space word representations," *Proc. HLT-NAACL*, pp. 746–751, 2013. 61

[423] A. K. Milicevic, A. Nanopoulos, and M. Ivanovic, "Social tagging in recommender systems: a survey of the state-of-the-art and possible extensions," *Artificial Intelligence Review*, vol. 33, pp. 187–209, 2010. DOI: 10.1007/s10462-009-9153-2. 122

[424] G. Miller, C. Leacock, T. Randee, and R. Bunker, "A Semantic Concordance," *Proc. 3rd DARPA Workshop on Human Language Technology*, Plainsboro, New Jersey, pp. 303–308, 1993. DOI: 10.3115/1075671.1075742. 58, 126

[425] G. A. Miller, "WordNet: a lexical database for english," *Communications of the ACM*, vol. 38, pp. 39–41, 1995. DOI: 10.1145/219717.219748. 8, 35

[426] G. A. Miller, R. Beckwith, C. Fellbaum, D. Gross, and K. J. Miller, "Introduction to WordNet: an on-line lexical database," *International Journal of Lexicography*, vol. 3, pp. 235–244, 1990. DOI: 10.1093/ijl/3.4.235. 8, 35

[427] G. A. Miller and W. G. Charles, "Contextual correlates of semantic similarity," *Language and Cognitive Processes*, vol. 6, pp. 1–28, 1991. DOI: 10.1080/01690969108406936. 61

[428] F. Monay and D. Gatica-Perez, "On image auto-annotation with latent space models," *Proc. ACM Int. Conf. on Multimedia (ACM MM)*, Berkeley, 2003. DOI: 10.1145/957013.957070. 107

[429] F. Monay and D. Gatica-Perez, "PLSA-based image auto-annotation: constraining the latent space," *Proc. ACM International Conference on Multimedia*, pp. 348–351, 2004. DOI: 10.1145/1027527.1027608. 107

[430] A. G. Money and H. Agius, "Analysing user physiological responses for affective video summarisation," *Displays*, vol. 30, pp. 59–70, 2009. DOI: 10.1016/j.displa.2008.12.003. 32

[431] L.-P. Morency, R. Mihalcea, and P. Doshi, "Towards multimodal sentiment analysis: harvesting opinions from the web," *Proc. International Conference on Multimodal Interfaces*, pp. 169–176, 2011. DOI: 10.1145/2070481.2070509. 56, 121

[432] Y. Mori, H. Takahashi, and R. Oka, "Image-to-word transformation based on dividing and vector quantizing images with words," *Proc. First International Workshop on Multimedia Intelligent Storage and Retrieval Management* (in Conjunction with ACM Multimedia Conference 1999), Orlando, Florida, 1999. 79

[433] R. Mottaghi, X. Chen, X. Liu, N.-G. Cho, S.-W. Lee, S. Fidler, R. Urtasun, and A. Yuille, "The role of context for object detection and semantic segmentation in the wild," *Proc. Computer Vision and Pattern Recognition*, pp. 891–898, 2014. DOI: 10.1109/cvpr.2014.119. 41

[434] H. Müller, S. Marchand-Maillet, and T. Pun, "The truth about corel—evaluation in image retrieval," *Proc. The Challenge of Image and Video Retrieval*, London, pp. 38–49, 2002. DOI: 10.1007/3-540-45479-9_5. 38, 39

[435] K. Murphy, *Machine Learning: A Probabilistic Perspective*, MIT Press, 2012. 66, 95, 97

[436] K. Murphy, A. Torralba, and W. Freeman, "Using the forest to see the trees: a graphical model relating features, objects and scenes," *Proc. Advances in Neural Information Processing Systems*, pp. 1499–1506, 2003. 100

[437] K. P. Murphy, Y. Weiss, and M. I. Jordan, "Loopy belief propagation for approximate inference: an empirical study," *Proc. UAI*, pp. 467–475, 1999. 99

[438] N. Murray, L. Marchesotti, and F. Perronnin, AVA: A Large-Scale Database for Aesthetic Visual Analysis; http://www.lucamarchesotti.com/ABS/papers/AVA/. 38

[439] N. Murray, L. Marchesotti, and F. Perronnin, "AVA: a large-scale database for aesthetic visual analysis," *Proc. Computer Vision and Pattern Recognition*, pp. 2408–2415, 2012. DOI: 10.1109/cvpr.2012.6247954. 38, 39, 121, 122

[440] V. Nair and G. E. Hinton, "Rectified linear units improve restricted boltzmann machines," *Proc. 27th International Conference on Machine Learning*, pp. 807–814, 2010. 52

[441] R. Navigli, "Word sense disambiguation: a survey," *ACM Computing Surveys (CSUR)*, vol. 41, pp. 10, 2009. DOI: 10.1145/1459352.1459355. 58

[442] R. Navigli and P. Velardi, "Structural semantic interconnections: a knowledge-based approach to word sense disambiguation," *IEEE Transactions on Pattern Analysis and Machine Intelligence*, vol. 27, pp. 1075–1086, 2005. DOI: 10.1109/tpami.2005.149. 58

[443] R. M. Neal, "Probabilistic Inference using Markov Chain Monte Carlo Methods," 1993. 77

[444] L. Neumann and J. Matas, "A method for text localization and recognition in real-world images," *Proc. Asian Converence on Computer Vision*, pp. 770–783, 2011. DOI: 10.1007/978-3-642-19318-7_60. 57

[445] J. Niu, X. Zhao, L. Zhu, and H. Li, "Affivir: an affect-based internet video recommendation system," *Neurocomputing*, vol. 120, pp. 422–433, 2013. DOI: 10.1016/j.neucom.2012.07.050. 56

[446] A. Odic, M. Tkalcic, J. F. Tasic, and A. Kosir, "Personality and social context: impact on emotion induction from movies," *Proc. UMAP Workshops*, 2013. 122

[447] A. Oliva and A. Torralba, "Modeling the shape of the scene: a holistic representation of the spatial envelope," *International Journal of Computer Vision*, vol. 42, pp. 145–175, 2001. DOI: 10.1023/A:1011139631724. 64

[448] V. Ordonez, J. Deng, Y. Choi, A. C. Berg, and T. L. Berg, "From large scale image categorization to entry-level categories," *Proc. IEEE International Conference on Computer Vision*, pp. 2768–2775, 2013. DOI: 10.1109/iccv.2013.344. 133

[449] V. Ordonez, G. Kulkarni, and T. L. Berg, SBU Captioned Photo Dataset; http://vision.cs.stonybrook.edu/~{}vicente/sbucaptions/. 42, 132, 133, 134

[450] V. Ordonez, G. Kulkarni, and T. L. Berg, "Im2text: describing images using 1 million captioned photographs," *Proc. Advances in Neural Information Processing Systems*, pp. 1143–1151, 2011. 42, 132

[451] S. Ornager, "The newspaper image database: empirical supported analysis of users' typology and word association clusters," *Proc. 18th Annual International ACM SIGIR Conference on Research and Development in Information Retrieval*, Seattle, Washington, pp. 212–218, 1995. DOI: 10.1145/215206.215362. 28, 111

[452] S. Ornager, "View a picture. Theoretical image analysis and empirical user studies on indexing and retrieval," *Swedish Library Research*, vol. 2, pp. 31–41, 1996.

[453] S. Ornager, "Image retrieval: theoretical analysis and empirical user studies on accessing information in images," *Proc. of the ASIS Annual Meeting*, pp. 202–211, 1997. 28, 111

[454] O. Owoputi, B. O'Connor, C. Dyer, K. Gimpel, N. Schneider, and N. A. Smith, "Improved part-of-speech tagging for online conversational text with word clusters," *Proc. HLT-NAACL*, pp. 380–390, 2013. 57

[455] E. F. Pace-Schott, E. Shepherd, R. M. Spencer, M. Marcello, M. Tucker, R. E. Propper, and R. Stickgold, "Napping promotes inter-session habituation to emotional stimuli," *Neurobiology of Learning and Memory*, vol. 95, pp. 24–36, 2011. DOI: 10.1016/j.nlm.2010.10.006. 33, 122

[456] S. Paek, C. L. Sable, V. Hatzivassiloglo, A. Jaimes, B. Shiffman, S. Chang, and K. McKeown, "Integration of visual and text based approaches for the content labeling and classification of photographs," *Proc. ACM SIGIR*, 1999. 64

[457] J.-Y. Pan, H.-J. Yang, P. Duygulu, and C. Faloutsos, "Automatic image captioning," *Proc. IEEE International Conference on Multimedia and Expo*, pp. 1987–1990, 2004. 107

[458] J.-Y. Pan, H.-J. Yang, C. Faloutsos, and P. Duygulu, "Automatic multimedia cross-modal correlation discovery," *Proc. of the 10th ACM SIGKDD international conference on Knowledge Discovery and Data Mining*, pp. 653–658, 2004. DOI: 10.1145/1014052.1014135. 107

[459] J.-Y. Pan, H.-J. Yang, C. Faloutsos, and P. Duygulu, "GCap: graph-based automatic image captioning," *Proc. IEEE Conference on Computer Vision and Pattern Recognition Workshop*, pp. 146–146, 2004. DOI: 10.1109/cvpr.2004.353. 107

[460] M. Pantic and L. J. M. Rothkrantz, "Toward an affect-sensitive multimodal human-computer interaction," *Proc. of the IEEE*, vol. 91, pp. 1370–1390, 2003. DOI: 10.1109/jproc.2003.817122. 33

[461] T. V. Papathomas, I. J. Cox, P. N. Yianilos, M. L. Miller, T. P. Minka, T. E. Conway, and J. Ghosn, "Psychophysical experiments of an image database retrieval system," *Journal of Electronic Imaging*, vol. 10, pp. 170–180, 2001. DOI: 10.1117/1.1333058. 28

[462] R. Parker, D. Graff, J. Kong, K. Chen, and K. Maeda, English Gigaword 5th ed.; https://catalog.ldc.upenn.edu/LDC2011T07. 128

[463] R. Pascanu, C. Gulcehre, K. Cho, and Y. Bengio, "How to construct deep recurrent neural networks," in *arXiv preprint arXiv:1312.6026*, 2013. 51

[464] T. Pedersen, S. Patwardhan, and J. Michelizzi, "WordNet similarity: measuring the relatedness of concepts," *Proc. Demonstration papers at HLT-NAACL*, pp. 38–41, 2004. DOI: 10.3115/1614025.1614037. 59

[465] J. Pennington, Richard Socher, and C. D. Manning, GloVe: Global Vectors for Word Representation; http://nlp.stanford.edu/projects/glove/. 61

[466] J. Pennington, R. Socher, and C. D. Manning, "Glove: global vectors for word representation," *Proc. Empirical Methods in Natural Language Processing*, 2014. DOI: 10.3115/v1/d14-1162. 61

[467] A. Pentland, R. W. Picard, and S. Sclaroff, "Photobook: content-based manipulation of image databases," *International Journal of Computer Vision*, vol. 18, pp. 233–254, 1996. DOI: 10.1007/bf00123143. 28

[468] P. Philippot, "Inducing and assessing differentiated emotion-feeling states in the laboratory," *Cognition and Emotion*, vol. 7, pp. 171–193, 1993. DOI: 10.1080/02699939308409183. 32, 38

[469] R. Picard, *Affective Computing*: MIT Press, 1997. DOI: 10.1037/e526112012-054. 33

[470] R. Plutchik, "A general psychoevolutionary theory of emotion," *Theories of Emotion*, vol. 1, 1980. DOI: 10.1016/b978-0-12-558701-3.50007-7. 32, 121

[471] L. Porzi, S. R. Bulo, P. Valigi, O. Lanz, and E. Ricci, "Learning contours for automatic annotations of mountains pictures on a smartphone," *Proc. International Conference on Distributed Smart Cameras*, pp. 13, 2014. DOI: 10.1145/2659021.2659046. 28

[472] D. Povey, A. Ghoshal, G. Boulianne, L. Burget, O. Glembek, N. Goel, M. Hannemann, P. Motlicek, Y. Qian, and P. Schwarz, "The Kaldi speech recognition toolkit," *Proc. IEEE Automatic Speech Recognition and Understanding Workshop*, 2011. 56

[473] H.-t. Pu, "An analysis of failed queries for web image retrieval," *Journal of Information Science*, vol. 34, pp. 275–289, 2008. DOI: 10.1177/0165551507084140. 28, 111

[474] J. Puzicha, T. Hofmann, and J. M. Buhmann, "Non-parametric similarity measures for unsupervised texture segmentation and image retrieval," *Proc. IEEE Computer Society Conference on Computer Vision and Pattern Recognition*, pp. 267–272, 1997. DOI: 10.1109/cvpr.1997.609331. 48

[475] P. Quelhas, F. Monay, J.-M. Odobez, D. Gatica-Perez, and T. Tuytelaars, "A thousand words in a scene," *IEEE Transactions on Pattern Analysis and Machine Intelligence*, vol. 29, pp. 1575–1589, 2007. DOI: 10.1109/tpami.2007.1155. 51, 64

[476] A. Rabinovich, A. Vedaldi, C. Galleguillos, E. Wiewiora, and S. Belongie, "Objects in context," *Proc. International Conference on Computer Vision*, 2007. DOI: 10.1109/ICCV.2007.4408986. 101, 102

[477] D. Ramanan, D. A. Forsyth, and K. Barnard, "Building models of animals from video," *IEEE Transactions on Pattern Analysis and Machine Intelligence*, vol. 28, pp. 1319–1334, 2006. DOI: 10.1109/tpami.2006.155. 19

[478] R. Ramanath, W. E. Snyder, Y. Yoo, and M. S. Drew, "Color image processing pipeline," *IEEE Signal Processing Magazine*, vol. 22, pp. 34–43, 2005. DOI: 10.1109/msp.2005.1407713. 47

[479] V. Ramanathan, A. Joulin, P. Liang, and L. Fei-Fei, "Linking people in videos with "their" names using coreference resolution," *Proc. European Computer on Computer Vision*, pp. 95–110, 2014. DOI: 10.1007/978-3-319-10590-1_7. 126

[480] C. Rashtchian, P. Young, M. Hodosh, and J. Hockenmaier, "Collecting image annotations using amazon's mechanical turk," *Proc. NAACL HLT 2010 Workshop on Creating Speech and Language Data with Amazon's Mechanical Turk*, Los Angeles, California, pp. 139–147, 2010. 42

[481] C. Rashtchian, P. Young, M. Hodosh, and J. Hockenmaier, Flikr 8k Image Caption Corpus; http://nlp.cs.illinois.edu/HockenmaierGroup/8k-pictures.html. 42

[482] D. Ren, P. Wang, H. Qiao, and S. Zheng, "A biologically inspired model of emotion eliciting from visual stimuli," *Neurocomputing*, vol. 121, pp. 328–336, 2013. DOI: 10.1016/j.neucom.2013.05.026. 119

[483] M. Ren, R. Kiros, and R. Zemel, "Exploring models and data for image question answering," *Proc. Advances in Neural Information Processing Systems*, pp. 2935–2943, 2015. 52, 139

[484] L. W. Renninger and J. Malik, "When is scene identification just texture recognition?," *Vision Research*, vol. 44, pp. 2301–2311, 2004. DOI: 10.1016/j.visres.2004.04.006. 64

[485] C. P. Robert and G. Casella, *Monte Carlo Statistical Methods*, New York, Springer-Verlag, 2005. DOI: 10.1007/978-1-4757-3071-5. 102

[486] A. Rohrbach, M. Rohrbach, N. Tandon, and B. Schiele, "A dataset for movie description," *Proc. IEEE Conference on Computer Vision and Pattern Recognition*, 2015. 43

[487] A. Rohrbach, M. Rohrbach, N. Tandon, and B. Schiele, MPII Movie Description Dataset; https://www.mpi-inf.mpg.de/departments/computer-vision-and-multimodal-computing/research/vision-and-language/mpii-movie-description-dataset/. 43, 137

[488] M. Rohrbach, M. Stark, G. Szarvas, I. Gurevych, and B. Schiele, "What helps where—and why? Semantic relatedness for knowledge transfer," *IEEE Conference on Computer Vision and Pattern Recognition*, pp. 910–917, 2010. DOI: 10.1109/cvpr.2010.5540121. 133

[489] C. Rother, V. Kolmogorov, and A. Blake, "GrabCut: Interactive foreground extraction using iterated graph cuts," *ACM Transactions on Graphics (TOG)*, vol. 23, pp. 309–314, 2004. DOI: 10.1145/1015706.1015720. 105

[490] D. Roy, "Semiotic schemas: a framework for grounding language in action and perception," *Artificial Intelligence*, vol. 167, pp. 170–205, 2005. DOI: 10.1016/j.artint.2005.04.007. 17

[491] D. Roy, K. Hsiao, and N. Mavridis, "Mental imagery for a conversational robot," *IEEE Transactions on Systems, Man, and Cybernetics, Part B*, vol. 34, pp. 1374–1383, 2004. DOI: 10.1109/tsmcb.2004.823327. 17

[492] O. Russakovsky, J. Deng, H. Su, J. Krause, S. Satheesh, S. Ma, Z. Huang, A. Karpathy, A. Khosla, M. Bernstein, A. C. Berg, and L. Fei-Fei, "ImageNet large scale visual recognition challenge," in *arXiv preprint arXiv:1409.0575*, 2014. DOI: 10.1007/s11263-015-0816-y. 36, 37, 52

[493] B. C. Russell, A. Torralba, K. P. Murphy, and W. T. Freeman, "LabelMe: a Database and Web-based Tool for Image Annotation," September, 2005, DOI: 10.1007/s11263-007-0090-8. 39, 41

[494] B. C. Russell, A. Torralba, K. P. Murphy, and W. T. Freeman, "LabelMe: a database and web-based tool for image annotation," *International Journal of Computer Vision*, 2008. DOI: 10.1007/s11263-007-0090-8. 36, 39, 41, 58, 60, 99

[495] J. A. Russell and A. Mehrabian, "Evidence for a three-factor theory of emotions," *Journal of research in Personality*, vol. 11, pp. 273–294, 1977. DOI: 10.1016/0092-6566(77)90037-x. 32

[496] K. Saenko and T. Darrell, "Unsupervised learning of visual sense models for polysemous words," *Proc. Advances in Neural Information Processing Systems*, pp. 1393–1400, 2008. 126

[497] K. Saenko and T. Darrell, "Filtering abstract senses from image search results," *Proc. Advances in Neural Information Processing Systems*, pp. 1589–1597, 2009. 37, 60, 126

[498] K. Saenko and T. Darrell, "Unsupervised learning of visual sense models for polysemous words," *Proc. Advances in Neural Information Processing Systems*, pp. 1393–1400, 2009. 37

[499] K. Saenko, B. Kulis, M. Fritz, and T. Darrell, "Adapting visual category models to new domains," *Proc. ECCV*, pp. 213–226, 2010. DOI: 10.1007/978-3-642-15561-1_16. 25

[500] S. Santini, "Mixed media search in image databases using text and visual similarity," *Proc. IEEE International Conference on Multimedia and Expo*, Tokyo, 2001. 28

[501] S. Santini, "A query paradigm to discover the relation between text and images," *Proc. SPIE Vol. 4315, Storage and Retrieval for Media Databases*, San Jose, 2001. DOI: 10.1117/12.410924. 28

[502] S. Santini, A. Gupta, and R. Jain, "Emergent semantics through interaction in image databases," *IEEE Transactions on Knowledge and Data Engineering*, vol. 13, pp. 337—351 2001. DOI: 10.1109/69.929893. 27

[503] S. Santini and R. Jain, "Beyond query by example," *Proc. ACM Multimedia*, Bristol, 1998. DOI: 10.1145/290747.290800.

[504] S. Santini and R. Jain, "Interfaces for emergent semantics in multimedia databases," *Proc. SPIE 3656 Storage and Retrieval for Image and Video Databases VII*, San Jose, U.S., 1999. DOI: 10.1117/12.333836.

[505] S. Santini and R. Jain, "User interfaces for emergent semantics in image databases," *Proc. 8th IFIP Working Conference on Database Semantics (DS-8)*, Rotorua, New Zealand, 1999. DOI: 10.1007/978-0-387-35561-0_9. 27

[506] A. Sartori, "Affective analysis of abstract paintings using statistical analysis and art theory," *Proc. International Conference on Multimodal Interaction*, pp. 384–388, 2014. DOI: 10.1145/2663204.2666289. 120

[507] T. Sato, T. Kanade, E. K. Hughes, M. A. Smith, and S. I. Satoh, "Video OCR: indexing digital news libraries by recognition of superimposed captions," *Multimedia Systems*, vol. 7, pp. 385–395, 1999. DOI: 10.1007/s005300050140. 56

[508] S. i. Satoh and T. Kanade, "Name-it: association of face and name in video," *Proc. Computer Vision and Pattern Recognition*, pp. 368–373, 1997. DOI: 10.1109/CVPR.1997.609351. 112

[509] B. Scholkopf and A. J. Smola, *Learning with Kernels*, MIT Press, 2002. 86

[510] M. Schuster and K. K. Paliwal, "Bidirectional recurrent neural networks," *IEEE Transactions on Signal Processing*, vol. 45, pp. 2673–2681, 1997. DOI: 10.1109/78.650093. 136

[511] A. Schwing, T. Hazan, M. Pollefeys, and R. Urtasun, "Distributed message passing for large scale graphical models," *Proc. IEEE Conference on Computer Vision and Pattern Recognition*, pp. 1833–1840, 2011. DOI: 10.1109/cvpr.2011.5995642. 106, 127

[512] N. Sebe, I. Cohen, T. Gevers, and T. S. Huang, "Emotion recognition based on joint visual and audio cues," *Proc. International Conference on Pattern Recognition*, pp. 1136–1139, 2006. DOI: 10.1109/icpr.2006.489. 56

[513] A. Senina, M. Rohrbach, W. Qiu, A. Friedrich, S. Amin, M. Andriluka, M. Pinkal, and B. Schiele, "Coherent multi-sentence video description with variable level of detail," in *arXiv preprint arXiv:1403.6173*, 2014. 133

[514] P. Sermanet, D. Eigen, X. Zhang, M. Mathieu, R. Fergus, and Y. LeCun, in *arXiv preprint arXiv:1312.6229*, 2013. 53

[515] N. Serrano, A. E. Savakis, and J. Luo, "Improved scene classification using efficient low-level features and semantic cues," *Pattern Recognition*, vol. 37, pp. 1773–1784, 2004. DOI: 10.1016/j.patcog.2004.03.003. 64

[516] L. Shapiro and G. C. Stockman, *Computer Vision*, Prentice Hall, 2001. 46

[517] J. Shi and J. Malik, "Normalized cuts and image segmentation," *Proc. IEEE Computer Society Conference on Computer Vision and Pattern Recognition*, pp. 731–737, 1997. DOI: 10.1109/34.868688. 98

[518] J. Shi and J. Malik, "Normalized cuts and image segmentation," *IEEE Transactions on Pattern Analysis and Machine Intelligence*, vol. 22, pp. 888–905, 2002. DOI: 10.1109/34.868688. 15, 50, 98

[519] J. Shotton, M. Johnson, and R. Cipolla, "Semantic texton forests for image categorization and segmentation," *Proc. Computer Vision and Pattern Recognition*, 2008. DOI: 10.1109/cvpr.2008.4587503. 101, 105, 106

[520] J. Shotton, J. Winn, C. Rother, and A. Criminisi, "Textonboost: joint appearance, shape and context modeling for multi-class object recognition and segmentation," *Proc. ECCV*, pp. 1–15, 2006. DOI: 10.1007/11744023_1. 41, 99, 102, 104, 105, 106

[521] J. Shotton, J. Winn, C. Rother, and A. Criminisi, "Textonboost for image understanding: multi-class object recognition and segmentation by jointly modeling texture, layout, and context," *International Journal of Computer Vision*, vol. 81, pp. 2–23, 2009. DOI: 10.1007/s11263-007-0109-1. 104, 105, 106

[522] S. Siersdorfer, E. Minack, F. Deng, and J. Hare, "Analyzing and predicting sentiment of images on the social web," *Proc. International conference on Multimedia*, pp. 715–718, 2010. DOI: 10.1145/1873951.1874060. 120

[523] C. Silberer, V. Ferrari, and M. Lapata, "Models of semantic representation with visual attributes," *Proc. Annual Meeting of the Association for Computational Linguistics*, pp. 572–582, 2013. 37

[524] N. Silberman, D. Hoiem, P. Kohli, and R. Fergus, "Indoor segmentation and support inference from RGBD images," *Proc. ECCV*, pp. 746–760, 2012. DOI: 10.1007/978-3-642-33715-4_54. 42, 43

[525] N. Silberman, D. Hoiem, P. Kohli, and R. Fergus, NYU Depth Dataset V2; http://cs.nyu.edu/~{}silberman/datasets/nyu_depth_v2.html. 42, 43

[526] K. Simonyan and A. Zisserman, "Two-stream convolutional networks for action recognition in videos," *Proc. Neural Information Processing Systems*, pp. 568–576, 2014. 125

[527] K. Simonyan and A. Zisserman, "Very deep convolutional networks for large-scale image recognition," *Proc. International Conference on Learning Representations*, 2014. 51

[528] J. M. Siskind, "A computational study of cross-situational techniques for learning word-to-meaning mappings," *Cognition*, vol. 61, pp. 39–91, 1996. DOI: 10.1016/s0010-0277(96)00728-7. 23, 93

[529] M. Slaney, "Semantic–audio retrieval," *Proc. IEEE International Conference on Acoustics, Speech and Signal Processing*, Orlando, Florida, 2002. 10

[530] A. W. M. Smeulders, M. Worring, S. Santini, A. Gupta, and R. Jain, "Content-based image retrieval at the end of the early years," *IEEE Transactions on Pattern Matching and Machine Intelligence*, vol. 22, pp. 1349–1379, 2000. DOI: 10.1109/34.895972. 28, 29, 30

[531] R. Socher and L. Fei-Fei, "Connecting modalities: semi-supervised segmentation and annotation of images using unaligned text corpora," *Proc. IEEE Conference on Computer Vision and Pattern Recognition*, pp. 966–973, 2010. DOI: 10.1109/cvpr.2010.5540112. 60

[532] R. Socher, A. Karpathy, Q. V. Le, C. D. Manning, and A. Y. Ng, "Grounded compositional semantics for finding and describing images with sentences," *Transactions of the Association for Computational Linguistics*, vol. 2, pp. 207–218, 2014. 132

[533] R. Socher, A. Perelygin, J. Y. Wu, J. Chuang, C. D. Manning, A. Y. Ng, and C. Potts, "Recursive deep models for semantic compositionality over a sentiment treebank," *Proc. Empirical Methods in Natural Language Processing*, pp. 1642, 2013. 57

[534] M. Soleymani, G. Chanel, J. J. Kierkels, and T. Pun, "Affective ranking of movie scenes using physiological signals and content analysis," *Proc. ACM Workshop on Multimedia Semantics*, pp. 32–39, 2008. DOI: 10.1145/1460676.1460684. 32

[535] M. Soleymani, M. Pantic, and T. Pun, "Multimodal emotion recognition in response to videos," *IEEE Transactions on Affective Computing*, vol. 3, pp. 211–223, 2012. DOI: 10.1109/t-affc.2011.37. 32

[536] E. B. Sudderth, A. Torralba, W. T. Freeman, and A. S. Willsky, "Learning hierarchical models of scenes, objects, and parts," *Proc. ICCV*, 2005. DOI: 10.1109/iccv.2005.137. 51, 99

[537] K. Sun, J. Yu, Y. Huang, and X. Hu, "An improved valence-arousal emotion space for video affective content representation and recognition," *Proc. IEEE International Conference on Multimedia and Expo*, pp. 566–569, 2009. DOI: 10.1109/icme.2009.5202559. 120

[538] S. Susstrunk, R. Buckley, and S. Swen, "Standard RGB color spaces," *Proc. Color and Imaging Conference*, pp. 127–134, 1999. 47

[539] I. Sutskever, O. Vinyals, and Q. V. Le, "Sequence to sequence learning with neural networks," *Proc. Advances in Neural Information Processing Systems*, pp. 3104–3112, 2014. 135

[540] C. Sutton and A. McCallum, "Piecewise training for undirected models," *Proc. Uncertainty in Artificial Intelligence*, 2005. 105

[541] C. Szegedy, A. Toshev, and D. Erhan, "Deep neural networks for object detection," *Proc. Advances in Neural Information Processing Systems*, pp. 2553–2561, 2013. 53

[542] R. Szeliski, *Computer Vision: Algorithms and Applications*, Springer Science and Business Media, 2010. DOI: 10.1007/978-1-84882-935-0. 46

[543] M. Szummer and R. W. Picard, "Indoor-outdoor image classification," *Proc. IEEE International Workshop on Content-based Access of Image and Video Databases*, Bombay, India, 1998. DOI: 10.1109/CAIVD.1998.646032. 64

[544] J. Takagi, Y. Ohishi, A. Kimura, M. Sugiyama, M. Yamada, and H. Kameoka, "Automatic audio tag classification via semi-supervised canonical density estimation," *Proc. IEEE International Conference on Acoustics, Speech and Signal Processing (ICASSP)*, pp. 2232–2235, 2011. DOI: 10.1109/icassp.2011.5946925. 10

[545] M. Tapaswi, M. Bauml, and R. Stiefelhagen, "Book2Movie: aligning video scenes with book chapters," *Proc. IEEE Conference on Computer Vision and Pattern Recognition*, pp. 1827–1835, 2015. DOI: 10.1109/cvpr.2015.7298792. 136

[546] M. Tapaswi, M. Bäuml, and R. Stiefelhagen, "Aligning plot synopses to videos for story-based retrieval," *International Journal of Multimedia Information Retrieval*, vol. 4, pp. 3–16, 2015. DOI: 10.1007/s13735-014-0065-9. 136

[547] B. Taskar, V. Chatalbashev, D. Koller, and C. Guestrin, "Learning structured prediction models: a large margin approach," *Proc. International conference on Machine learning*, pp. 896–903, 2005. DOI: 10.1145/1102351.1102464. 132

[548] R. M. A. Teixeira, T. Yamasaki, and K. Aizawa, "Determination of emotional content of video clips by low-level audiovisual features," *Multimedia Tools and Applications*, vol. 61, pp. 21–49, 2012. DOI: 10.1007/s11042-010-0702-0. 56, 120

[549] M. Thelwall, "Heart and soul: sentiment strength detection in the social web with SentiStrength," *Cyberemotions*, pp. 1–14, 2013. 120

[550] M. Thelwall, K. Buckley, and G. Paltoglou, "Sentiment in twitter events," *Journal of The American Society for Information Science and Technology*, vol. 62, pp. 406–418, 2011. DOI: 10.1002/asi.21462.

[551] M. Thelwall, K. Buckley, and G. Paltoglou, "Sentiment strength detection for the social web," *Journal of The American Society for Information Science and Technology*, vol. 63, pp. 163–173, 2012. DOI: 10.1002/asi.21662. 36

[552] M. Thelwall, K. Buckley, G. Paltoglou, D. Cai, and A. Kappas, "Sentiment strength detection in short informal text," *Journal of The American Society for Information Science and Technology*, vol. 61, pp. 2544–2558, 2010. DOI: 10.1002/asi.21416. 36, 120

[553] J. Thomason, S. Venugopalan, S. Guadarrama, K. Saenko, and R. Mooney, "Integrating language and vision to generate natural language descriptions of videos in the wild," *Proc. 25th International Conference on Computational Linguistics (COLING)*, 2014. 59, 125, 133

[554] W. B. Thompson, T. C. Henderson, T. L. Colvin, L. B. Dick, and C. M. Valiquette, "Vision-based localization," *Proc. DARPA Image Understanding Workshop*, pp. 491–498, 1993. 28

[555] M. Tkalcic, U. Burnik, and A. Kosir, "Using affective parameters in a content-based recommender system for images," *User Modeling and User-Adapted Interaction*, vol. 20, pp. 279–311, 2010. DOI: 10.1109/tmm.2012.2229970. 122

[556] M. Tkalcic, A. Odic, A. Kosir, and J. Tasic, "Affective labeling in a content-based recommender system for images," *IEEE Transactions on Multimedia*, vol. 15, pp. 391–400, 2013. DOI: 10.1109/tmm.2012.2229970. 33, 122

[557] A. Torralba and A. A. Efros, "Unbiased look at dataset bias," *Proc. Computer Vision and Pattern Recognition*, pp. 1521–1528, 2011. DOI: 10.1109/CVPR.2011.5995347. 25

[558] A. Torralba, K. P. Murphy, and W. T. Freeman, "Contextual models for object detection using boosted random fields," *Proc. Advances in Neural Information Processing Systems*, pp. 1401–1408, 2004. 100

[559] A. Torralba, K. P. Murphy, W. T. Freeman, and M. A. Rubin, "Context-based vision system for place and object recognition," *Proc. IEEE Intl. Conference on Computer Vision (ICCV)*, Nice, France, 2003. DOI: 10.1109/iccv.2003.1238354. 64

[560] A. B. Torralba, R. Fergus, and W. T. Freeman, "80 million tiny images: a large data set for nonparametric object and scene recognition," *IEEE Transactions on Pattern Analysis and Machine Intelligence*, vol. 30, pp. 1958–1970, 2008. DOI: 10.1109/tpami.2008.128. 60

[561] A.-M. Tousch, S. Herbin, and J.-Y. Audibert, "Semantic lattices for multiple annotation of images," *Proc. 1st ACM International Conference on Multimedia Information Retrieval*, Vancouver, British Columbia, Canada, pp. 342–349, 2008. DOI: 10.1145/1460096.1460152. 59

[562] K. Toutanova, D. Klein, C. D. Manning, and Y. Singer, "Feature-rich part-of-speech tagging with a cyclic dependency network," *Proc. Conference of the North American Chapter of the Association for Computational Linguistics on Human Language Technology*, vol. 1, pp. 173–180, 2003. DOI: 10.3115/1073445.1073478. 57, 127

[563] A. Tran, "Identifying Latent Attributes from Video Scenes Using Knowledge Acquired From Large Collections of Text Documents," Ph.D., Arizona, Computer Science, 2014. 128

[564] A. Tran, M. Surdeanu, and P. Cohen, "Extracting latent attributes from video scenes using text as background knowledge," *Proc. 3rd Joint Conference on Lexical and Computational Semantics (*SEM)*, 2014. DOI: 10.3115/v1/s14-1016. 61, 128

[565] J. Traupman and R. Wilensky, "Experiments in Improving Unsupervised Word Sense Disambiguation," Computer Science Division, University of California Berkeley, 2003, 58

[566] I. Tsochantaridis, T. Joachims, T. Hofmann, and Y. Altun, "Large margin methods for structured and interdependent output variables," *Journal of Machine Learning Research*, vol. 6, pp. 1453–1484, 2005. 86

[567] K. Tu, M. Meng, M. W. Lee, T. E. Choe, and S.-C. Zhu, "Joint video and text parsing for understanding events and answering queries," *IEEE MultiMedia*, vol. 21, pp. 42–70, 2014. DOI: 10.1109/MMUL.2014.29. 138

[568] M. Turk and A. Pentland, "Face recognition using eigenfaces," *Proc. IEEE Conference on Computer Vision and Pattern Recognition*, Maui, Hawaii, 1991. DOI: 10.1109/CVPR.1991.139758. 112

[569] D. Ustalov, "TagBag: Annotating a Foreign Language Lexical Resource with Pictures," in *Analysis of Images, Social Networks and Texts, Series, TagBag: Annotating a Foreign Language Lexical Resource with Pictures* Springer, pp. 361–369, 2015. DOI: 10.1007/978-3-319-26123-2_35. 137

[570] A. Vailaya, M. A. T. Figueiredo, A. K. Jain, and Z. Hong-Jiang, "Image classification for content-based indexing," *IEEE Transactions on Image Processing*, vol. 10, pp. 117–130, 2001. DOI: 10.1109/83.892448. 64

[571] A. Vailaya, A. Jain, and H. J. Zhang, "On image classification: city images vs. landscapes," *Pattern Recognition*, vol. 31, pp. 1921–1935, 1998. DOI: 10.1016/s0031-3203(98)00079-x. 64

[572] V. N. Vapnik, *The Nature of Statistical Learning Theory*, Springer, 1995. DOI: 10.1007/978-1-4757-2440-0. 86

[573] G. Varelas, E. Voutsakis, P. Raftopoulou, E. G. Petrakis, and E. E. Milios, "Semantic similarity methods in WordNet and their application to information retrieval on the web," *Proc. ACM International Workshop on Web Information and Data Management*, pp. 10–16, 2005. DOI: 10.1145/1097047.1097051. 59

[574] A. Vedaldi and B. Fulkerson, VLFeat: An Open and Portable Library of Computer Vision Algorithms; http://www.vlfeat.org/. 49

[575] A. Velivelli and T. S. Huang, "Automatic video annotation by mining speech transcripts," *Proc. Computer Vision and Pattern Recognition Workshop*, pp. 115, 2006. DOI: 10.1109/cvprw.2006.39. 107

[576] F. Vella, L. Chin-Hui, and S. Gaglio, "Boosting of maximal figure of merit classifiers for automatic image annotation," *Proc. IEEE International Conference on Image Processing (ICIP)*, pp. II-217–220, 2007. DOI: 10.1109/icip.2007.4379131. 107

[577] S. Venugopalan, M. Rohrbach, J. Donahue, R. Mooney, T. Darrell, and K. Saenko, "Sequence to sequence—video to text," *Proc. ICCV*, 2015. 52, 134, 135

[578] S. Venugopalan, H. Xu, J. Donahue, M. Rohrbach, R. Mooney, and K. Saenko, "Translating videos to natural language using deep recurrent neural networks," *Proc. HLT-NAACL*, pp. 1494–1504, 2015. DOI: 10.3115/v1/n15-1173. 52, 134, 135

[579] J. J. Verbeek, M. Guillaumin, T. Mensink, and C. Schmid, "Image annotation with TagProp on the MIRFLICKR set," *Proc. Multimedia Information Retrieval*, pp. 537–546, 2010. DOI: 10.1145/1743384.1743476. 109, 110

[580] J. J. Verbeek and B. Triggs, "Region classification with markov field aspect models," *Proc. Computer Vision and Pattern Recognition*, 2007. DOI: 10.1109/cvpr.2007.383098. 99

[581] O. Vinyals, A. Toshev, S. Bengio, and D. Erhan, "Show and tell: a neural image caption generator," *Proc. Computer Vision and Pattern Recognition*, 2015. DOI: 10.1109/cvpr.2015.7298935. 135

[582] F. Vivarelli and C. K. I. Williams, "Using Bayesian neural networks to classify segmented images," *Proc. IEE International Conference on Artificial Neural Networks*, 1997. DOI: 10.1049/cp:19970738. 40, 86

[583] J. Vogel and B. Schiele, "Semantic modeling of natural scenes for content-based image retrieval," *International Journal of Computer Vision*, vol. 72, pp. 133–157, 2007. DOI: 10.1007/s11263-006-8614-1. 64

[584] L. Von Ahn and L. Dabbish, "Labeling images with a computer game," *Proc. SIGCHI Conference on Human Factors in Computing Systems*, pp. 319–326, 2004. 39

[585] L. Von Ahn, R. Liu, and M. Blum, "Peekaboom: a game for locating objects in images," *Proc. SIGCHI Conference on Human Factors in Computing Systems*, pp. 55–64, 2006. DOI: 10.1145/1124772.1124782. 40

[586] S. Wachsmuth, S. Stevenson, and S. Dickinson, "Towards a framework for learning structured shape models from text-annotated images," *Proc. HLT-NAACL Workshop on Learning Word Meaning from Non-linguistic Data*, Edmonton, Alberta, pp. 22–29, 2003. DOI: 10.3115/1119212.1119216. 93, 99

[587] W. Walker, P. Lamere, P. Kwok, B. Raj, R. Singh, E. Gouvea, P. Wolf, and J. Woelfel, "Sphinx-4: A Flexible Open Source Framework for Speech Recognition," 2004. 56, 81

[588] C. Wang, D. Blei, and L. Fei-Fei, "Simultaneous image classification and annotation," *Proc. Computer Vision and Pattern Recognition*, 2009. DOI: 10.1109/cvpr.2009.5206800. 92

[589] F. Wang, D. Xu, W. Lu, and W. Wu, "Automatic Video Annotation and Retrieval Based on Bayesian Inference," in *Advances in Multimedia Modeling, Series, Automatic Video Annotation and Retrieval Based on Bayesian Inference*, T.-J. Cham, J. Cai, C. Dorai, D. Rajan, T.-S. Chua, and L.-T. Chia, Eds., Springer Berlin Heidelberg, pp. 279–288, 2006. DOI: 10.1007/978-3-540-69423-6_28. 107

[590] G. Wang, D. Hoiem, and D. Forsyth, "Building text features for object image classification," *Proc. IEEE Conference on Computer Vision and Pattern Recognition*, pp. 1367–1374, 2009. DOI: 10.1109/cvpr.2009.5206816. 109

[591] H. Wang, A. Kläser, C. Schmid, and C.-L. Liu, "Dense trajectories and motion boundary descriptors for action recognition," *International Journal of Computer Vision*, vol. 103, pp. 60–79, 2013. DOI: 10.1007/s11263-012-0594-8. 125

[592] H. L. Wang and L.-F. Cheong, "Affective understanding in film," *IEEE Transactions on Circuits and Systems for Video Technology*, vol. 16, pp. 689–704, 2006. DOI: 10.1109/tcsvt.2006.873781. 56, 120

[593] J. Wang, J. Yang, K. Yu, F. Lv, T. Huang, and Y. Gong, "Locality-constrained linear coding for image classification," *Proc. Computer Vision and Pattern Recognition*, pp. 3360–3367, 2010. DOI: 10.1109/cvpr.2010.5540018. 64

[594] K. Wang, B. Babenko, and S. Belongie, "End-to-end scene text recognition," *Proc. IEEE International Conference on Computer Vision*, pp. 1457–1464, 2011. DOI: 10.1109/ICCV.2011.6126402. 57

[595] K. Wang and S. Belongie, "Word spotting in the wild," *Proc. European Conference on Computer Vision*, 2010. DOI: 10.1007/978-3-642-15549-9_43. 57

[596] W. Wang and Q. He, "A survey on emotional semantic image retrieval," *Proc. IEEE International Conference on Image Processing*, pp. 117–120, 2008. DOI: 10.1109/icip.2008.4711705. 31

[597] X. Wang and E. Grimson, "Spatial latent Dirichlet allocation," *Proc. Advances in Neural Information Processing Systems*, pp. 1577–1584, 2007. 99

[598] X. J. Wang, Z. Lei, L. Ming, L. Yi, and M. Wei-Ying, "ARISTA—image search to annotation on billions of web photos," *Proc. Computer Vision and Pattern Recognition*, pp. 2987–2994, 2010. DOI: 10.1109/cvpr.2010.5540046. 109

[599] A. B. Warriner, V. Kuperman, and M. Brysbaert, "Norms of valence, arousal, and dominance for 13,915 english lemmas," *Behavior Research Methods*, vol. 45, pp. 1191–1207, 2013. DOI: 10.3758/s13428-012-0314-x. 32

[600] W. Wei-Ning, Y. Ying-Lin, and J. Sheng-Ming, "Image retrieval by emotional semantics: a study of emotional space and feature extraction," *Proc. IEEE International Conference on Systems, Man and Cybernetics*, pp. 3534–3539, 2006. DOI: 10.1109/icsmc.2006.384667. 120

[601] J. V. D. Weijer, C. Schmid, and J. J. Verbeek, "Learning color names from real-world images," *Proc. Computer Vision and Pattern Recognition*, 2007. DOI: 10.1109/CVPR.2007.383218. 116, 117, 118

[602] J. J. Weinman, E. Learned-Miller, and A. R. Hanson, "Scene text recognition using similarity and a lexicon with sparse belief propagation," *IEEE Transactions on Pattern Analysis and Machine Intelligence*, vol. 31, pp. 1733–1746, 2009. DOI: 10.1109/tpami.2009.38. 57

[603] S. Westman and P. Oittinen, "Image retrieval by end-users and intermediaries in a journalistic work context," *Proc. Information Interaction in Context*, pp. 102–110, 2006. DOI: 10.1145/1164820.1164843. 28, 111

[604] A. P. Witkin, "Scale-space filtering: a new approach to multi-scale description," *Proc. IEEE International Conference on Acoustics, Speech, and Signal Processing*, pp. 150–153, 1984. DOI: 10.1109/icassp.1984.1172729. 49

[605] C. Wolf and J.-M. Jolion, "Extraction and recognition of artificial text in multimedia documents," *Formal Pattern Analysis and Applications*, vol. 6, pp. 309–326, 2004. DOI: 10.1007/s10044-003-0197-7. 57

[606] M. E. J. Wood, N. W. Campbell, and B. T. Thomas, "Employing region features for searching an image database," *Proc. British Machine Vision Conference*, pp. 620–629, 1997. 111

[607] M. Worring, A. Smeulders, and S. Santini, "Interaction in content-based image retrieval: a state-of-the-art review," *Proc. International Conference on Visual Information Systems*, Lyon, France, 2000. DOI: 10.1007/3-540-40053-2_3. 27

[608] J. Wu and J. M. Rehg, "CENTRIST: a visual descriptor for scene categorization," *IEEE Transactions on Pattern Analysis and Machine Intelligence*, vol. 33, pp. 1489–1501, 2011. DOI: 10.1109/tpami.2010.224. 64

[609] O. Wu, W. Hu, and J. Gao, "Learning to predict the perceived visual quality of photos," *Proc. IEEE International Conference on Computer Vision*, pp. 225–232, 2011. DOI: 10.1109/iccv.2011.6126246. 33, 122

[610] D.-y. Xia, F. Wu, W.-h. Liu, and H.-w. Zhang, "Image interpretation: mining the visible and syntactic correlation of annotated words," *Journal of Zhejiang University SCIENCE A*, vol. 10, pp. 1759–1768, 2009. DOI: 10.1631/jzus.a0820856. 60

[611] J. Xiao, K. A. Ehinger, J. Hays, A. Torralba, and A. Oliva, "SUN database: exploring a large collection of scene categories," *International Journal of Computer Vision*, pp. 1–20, 2014. DOI: 10.1007/s11263-014-0748-y. 36, 37, 41, 121

[612] J. Xiao, J. Hays, K. A. Ehinger, A. Oliva, and A. Torralba, "Sun database: large-scale scene recognition from abbey to zoo," *Proc. IEEE Conference on Computer Vision and Pattern Recognition*, pp. 3485–3492, 2010. DOI: 10.1109/cvpr.2010.5539970. 36

[613] J. Xiao and L. Quan, "Multiple view semantic segmentation for street view images," *Proc. IEEE 12th International Conference on Computer Vision*, pp. 686–693, 2009. DOI: 10.1109/iccv.2009.5459249. 37, 41, 121

[614] C. Xu, P. Das, R. F. Doell, P. Rosebrough, and J. Corso, YouCook: An Annotated Data Set of Unconstrained Third-Person Cooking Videos; http://web.eecs.umich.edu/~{}jjcorso/r/youcook/. 42

[615] M. Xu, C. Xu, X. He, J. S. Jin, S. Luo, and Y. Rui, "Hierarchical affective content analysis in arousal and valence dimensions," *Signal Processing*, vol. 93, pp. 2140–2150, 2013. DOI: 10.1016/j.sigpro.2012.06.026. 120

[616] R. Xu, C. Xiong, W. Chen, and J. J. Corso, "Jointly modeling deep video and compositional text to bridge vision and language in a unified framework," *Proc. AAAI Conference on Artificial Intelligence*, 2015. 61, 133

[617] R. Xu, C. Xiong, W. Chen, and J. J. Corso, "Jointly modeling deep video and compositional text to bridge vision and language in a unified framework," *Proc. AAAI*, 2015. 52, 59, 133

[618] O. Yakhnenko and V. Honavar, "Annotating images and image objects using a hierarchical Dirichlet process model," *Proc. International Workshop on Multimedia Data Mining: Held in Conjunction with the ACM SIGKDD*, Las Vegas, Nevada, pp. 1–7, 2008. DOI: 10.1145/1509212.1509213. 91

[619] O. Yakhnenko and V. Honavar, "Multi-modal hierarchical Dirichlet process model for predicting image annotation and image-object label correspondence," *Proc. SIAM International Conference on Data Mining*, pp. 281–294, 2009. DOI: 10.1137/1.9781611972795.25. 91

[620] R. Yan and A. G. Hauptmann, "A review of text and image retrieval approaches for broadcast news video," *Information Retrieval*, vol. 10, pp. 445–484, 2007. DOI: 10.1007/s10791-007-9031-y. 56, 60

[621] K. Yanai and K. Barnard, "Image region entropy: a measure of 'Visualness' of web images associated with one concept," *Proc. ACM Multimedia*, Singapore, pp. 419–422, 2005. DOI: 10.1145/1101149.1101241. 37, 115, 116, 117, 118

[622] K. Yanai and K. Barnard, "Probabilistic web image gathering," *Proc. ACM Multimedia Workshop on Multimedia Information Retrieval (MIR)*, Singapore, 2005. DOI: 10.1145/1101826.1101838. 115

[623] K. Yanai, H. Kawakubo, and B. Qiu, "A visual analysis of the relationship between word concepts and geographical locations," *Proc. ACM International Conference on Image and Video Retrieval*, 2009. DOI: 10.1145/1646396.1646414. 28

[624] C. Yang, M. Dong, and F. Fotouhi, "Region based image annotation through multiple-instance learning," *Proc. 13th Annual ACM International Conference on Multimedia Singapore*, pp. 435–438, 2005. DOI: 10.1145/1101149.1101245. 87

[625] C. Yang and T. Lozano-Perez, "Image database retrieval with multiple-instance learning techniques," *Proc. 16th International Conference on Data Engineering*, pp. 233–243, 2000. DOI: 10.1109/icde.2000.839416. 64

[626] J. Yang, K. Yu, Y. Gong, and T. Huang, "Linear spatial pyramid matching using sparse coding for image classification," *Proc. IEEE Conference on Computer Vision and Pattern Recognition*, pp. 1794–1801, 2009. DOI: 10.1109/cvpr.2009.5206757. 64

[627] Y. Yang, C. L. Teo, H. Daume III, and Y. Aloimonos, "Corpus-guided sentence generation of natural images," *Proc. Empirical Methods in Natural Language Processing*, pp. 444–454, 2011. 132

[628] V. Yanulevskaya, J. Van Gemert, K. Roth, A.-K. Herbold, N. Sebe, and J.-M. Geusebroek, "Emotional valence categorization using holistic image features," *Proc. IEEE International Conference on Image Processing*, pp. 101–104, 2008. DOI: 10.1109/icip.2008.4711701. 119, 120

[629] B. Yao, Y. Xiong, and W. Tianfu, "Image parsing with stochastic grammar: the lotus hill dataset and inference scheme," *Proc. Computer Vision and Pattern Recognition Workshops*, pp. 8, 2009. DOI: 10.1109/cvprw.2009.5204331. 41

[630] B. Yao, X. Yang, and S.-C. Zhu, "Introduction to a Large-Scale General Purpose Ground Truth Database: Methodology, Annotation Tool and Benchmarks," in *Energy Minimization Methods in Computer Vision and Pattern Recognition, Series, Introduction to a Large-Scale General Purpose Ground Truth Database: Methodology, Annotation Tool and Benchmarks*, A. Yuille, S.-C. Zhu, D. Cremers, and Y. Wang, Eds., Springer Berlin Heidelberg, pp. 169–183, 2007. DOI: 10.1007/978-3-540-74198-5_14. 41

[631] B. Z. Yao, X. Yang, L. Lin, M. W. Lee, and S.-C. Zhu, "I2t: image parsing to text description," *Proc. of the IEEE*, vol. 98, pp. 1485–1508, 2010. DOI: 10.1109/jproc.2010.2050411. 132

[632] J. Yao, S. Fidler, and R. Urtasun, "Describing the scene as a whole: joint object detection, scene classification and semantic segmentation," *Proc. IEEE Conference on Computer Vision and Pattern Recognition*, pp. 702–709, 2012. DOI: 10.1109/cvpr.2012.6247739. 46, 53, 106, 127

[633] D. Yarowsky, "A method for disambiguating word senses in a large corpus," *Computers and the Humanities*, vol. 26, pp. 415–439, 1992. DOI: 10.1007/BF00136984. 58

[634] D. Yarowsky, "Unsupervised word sense disambiguation rivaling supervised methods," *Proc. 33rd Conference on Applied Natural Language Processing*, Cambridge, 1995. DOI: 10.3115/981658.981684. 58, 126

[635] C.-H. Yeh, Y.-C. Ho, B. A. Barsky, and M. Ouhyoung, "Personalized photograph ranking and selection system," *Proc. International Conference on Multimedia*, pp. 211–220, 2010. DOI: 10.1145/1873951.1873963. 122

[636] M.-C. Yeh and Y.-C. Cheng, "Relative features for photo quality assessment," *Proc. IEEE International Conference on Image Processing*, pp. 2861–2864, 2012. DOI: 10.1109/icip.2012.6467496. 121

[637] Q. You, J. Luo, H. Jin, and J. Yang, "Robust image sentiment analysis using progressively trained and domain transferred deep networks," *Proc. AAAI Conference on Artificial Intelligence*, 2015. 121

[638] P. Young, A. Lai, M. Hodosh, and J. Hockenmaier, Flikr 30k Image Caption Corpus; http://shannon.cs.illinois.edu/DenotationGraph/. 42

[639] S. Young, G. Evermann, M. Gales, T. Hain, D. Kershaw, X. Liu, G. Moore, J. Odell, D. Ollason, and D. Povey, *The HTK book*, Entropic Cambridge Research Laboratory Cambridge, 2009. 56

[640] C. Yu and D. H. Ballard, "A multimodal learning interface for grounding spoken language in sensory perceptions," *ACM Transactions on Applied Perception*, vol. 1, pp. 57–80, 2004. DOI: 10.1145/1008722.1008727. 78

[641] C. Yu, D. H. Ballard, and R. N. Aslin, "The role of embodied intention in early lexical acquisition," *Cognitive Science*, vol. 29, pp. 961–1005, 2005. DOI: 10.1207/s15516709cog0000_40. 78

[642] L. Yu, E. Park, A. C. Berg, and T. L. Berg, "Visual Madlibs: fill in the blank image generation and question answering," in *arXiv preprint arXiv:1506.00278*, 2015. 43

[643] L. Yu, E. Park, A. C. Berg, and T. L. Berg, Visual-Madlibs; http://tamaraberg.com/visualmadlibs/download.html. 43

[644] J. Yuan, S. Mcdonough, Q. You, and J. Luo, "Sentribute: image sentiment analysis from a mid-level perspective," *Proc. Second International Workshop on Issues of Sentiment Discovery and Opinion Mining*, pp. 10, 2013. DOI: 10.1145/2502069.2502079. 121

[645] K. Yun, Y. Peng, D. Samaras, G. J. Zelinsky, and T. L. Berg, "Studying relationships between human gaze, description, and computer vision," *Proc. IEEE Conference on Computer Vision and Pattern Recognition*, pp. 739–746, 2013. DOI: 10.1109/cvpr.2013.101. 36, 60, 133

[646] W. Zaremba, I. Sutskever, and O. Vinyals, "Recurrent neural network regularization," in *arXiv preprint arXiv:1409.2329*, 2014. 135

[647] Z. Zeng, M. Pantic, G. I. Roisman, and T. S. Huang, "A survey of affect recognition methods: audio, visual, and spontaneous expressions," *IEEE Transactions on Pattern Analysis and Machine Intelligence*, vol. 31, pp. 39–58, 2009. DOI: 10.1109/tpami.2008.52. 33, 56

[648] Q. Zhang and S. A. Goldman, "EM-DD: an improved multiple-instance learning technique," *Proc. Neural Information Processing Systems*, 2001. 86, 87

[649] Q. Zhang, S. A. Goldman, W. Yu, and J. E. Fritts, "Content-based image retrieval using multiple-instance learning," *Proc. 19th Int. Conf. Machine Learning*, 2001. 64, 86

[650] S. Zhang, Q. Huang, Q. Tian, S. Jiang, and W. Gao, "Personalized MTV affective analysis using user profile," in *Advances in Multimedia Information Processing-PCM, Series, Personalized MTV affective analysis using user profile* Springer, pp. 327–337, 2008. DOI: 10.1007/978-3-540-89796-5_34. 122

[651] W. Zhang and J. Kosecka, "Image based localization in urban environments," *Proc. 3rd International Symposium on 3D Data Processing, Visualization, and Transmission*, pp. 33–40, 2006. DOI: 10.1109/3dpvt.2006.80. 28

[652] S. Zhao, Y. Gao, X. Jiang, H. Yao, T.-S. Chua, and X. Sun, "Exploring principles-of-art features for image emotion recognition," *Proc. ACM International Conference on Multimedia*, pp. 47–56, 2014. DOI: 10.1145/2647868.2654930. 119, 120

[653] Y.-T. Zheng, M. Zhao, Y. Song, H. Adam, U. Buddemeier, A. Bissacco, F. Brucher, T.-S. Chua, and H. Neven, "Tour the world: building a web-scale landmark recognition engine," *Proc. Computer Vision and Pattern Recognition*, pp. 1085–1092, 2009. DOI: 10.1109/cvpr.2009.5206749. 28

[654] S.-C. Zhu, R. Zhang, and Z. Tu, "Integrating topdown/bottom-up for object recognition by data driven Markov chain Monte Carlo," *Proc. IEEE Computer Vision and Pattern Recognition*, 2000. DOI: 10.1109/cvpr.2000.855894. 77

[655] Y. Zhu, R. Kiros, R. Zemel, R. Salakhutdinov, R. Urtasun, A. Torralba, and S. Fidler, "Aligning books and movies: Towards story-like visual explanations by watching movies and reading books," *Proc. IEEE International Conference on Computer Vision*, pp. 19–27 2015. 61, 137

[656] C. L. Zitnick and D. Parikh, "Bringing semantics into focus using visual abstraction," *Proc. IEEE Conference on Computer Vision and Pattern Recognition*, pp. 3009–3016, 2013. DOI: 10.1109/cvpr.2013.387. 138

[657] C. L. Zitnick, D. Parikh, and L. Vanderwende, "Learning the visual interpretation of sentences," *Proc. IEEE International Conference on Computer Vision*, pp. 1681–1688, 2013. DOI: 10.1109/iccv.2013.211. 137, 138

Author's Biography

KOBUS BARNARD

Kobus Barnard is a professor of computer science at the University of Arizona. He also has appointments in the School of Information: Science, Technology, and Arts (SISTA), Statistics, Cognitive Science, Electrical and Computer Engineering (ECE), and the BIO5 Institute. He leads the Interdisciplinary Visual Intelligence Laboratory (IVILAB.org). Professor Barnard received his Ph.D. in computer science in 2000 from Simon Fraser University (SFU) in the area of computational color constancy, where his dissertation received the Governor General gold medal awarded across all disciplines. He then spent two years at the University of California at Berkeley as a postdoctoral researcher working on modeling the joint statistics of images and associated text, followed by moving to the University of Arizona. His current research addresses problems in interdisciplinary computational intelligence by developing top-down statistical models that are predictive, semantic, and explanatory. Application domains include computer vision, multimedia data, biological structure and processes, astronomy, and human social interaction. His work has been funded by multiple grants from NSF including a CAREER award, DARPA, ONR, ARBC (Arizona Biomedical Commission), and the University of Arizona BIO5 Institute.

Lightning Source UK Ltd.
Milton Keynes UK
UKOW07f1504080516

273744UK00002B/21/P